THE
SINGING SWAN

PUBLISHED ON THE
HENRY L. JOHNSON MEMORIAL FUND

ANNA SEWARD

BY ROMNEY (C. 1786)

Courtesy of the owner, Mr. John W. Hanes, of Rye, New York.

THE
SINGING SWAN

An Account of Anna Seward
and Her Acquaintance with Dr. Johnson,
Boswell, & Others of Their Time

By MARGARET ASHMUN

With a Preface by FREDERICK A. POTTLE
Professor of English in Yale University

New Haven
YALE UNIVERSITY PRESS
London · Humphrey Milford · Oxford University Press
MDCCCCXXXI

PREFACE

IT is not simply for convenience of nomenclature that we speak of the latter half of the eighteenth century as "The Age of Johnson." Johnson was not only the most arresting literary figure of the period; he dominated it personally. The Literary Club which he ruled contained, with surprisingly few exceptions, the men who give the age its peculiar glory. It is amazing that one small society should have included Johnson, Goldsmith, Reynolds, Garrick, Percy, Boswell, Malone, Steevens, Sheridan, Burke, Fox, Adam Smith, and Gibbon. When we add to this the fact that Johnson knew intimately most of the "female authors" of the day and regarded some of them as his *protégées,* his position as literary dictator appears something quite unparalleled in our annals.

Granting this, it is still possible to compile a considerable list of eighteenth-century authors whose connection with Johnson was tenuous or nonexistent. Sterne is such an author, and Beckford another—comets of the literary heaven following eccentric and solitary orbits. Churchill, Wilkes, and Lloyd were professed anti-Johnsonians. Smollett, though he lived beside Johnson in London for more than twenty years, was no member of his circle, and Macpherson, another expatriate Scot, was the Doctor's bitter enemy. Scotland had a distinguished group of writers who remained at home: Hume, Robertson, Kames, Monboddo, Home, Mackenzie, and Blair, only the last of whom joined Boswell in allegiance to the Great Cham. No one of that self-satisfied trio of university wits—Gray, Mason, and Walpole—seems ever to have spoken to Johnson. And finally there is the very interesting provincial group presented by Miss Ashmun in this book: Erasmus Darwin, Thomas Day, Richard Lovell Edgeworth, William Hayley, and Anna Seward.

At the present day no work by any of the five has the slightest currency unless it be Day's *Sandford and Merton,* and that, I fancy, has had few readers in this century. In the face of this eclipse, it is hard for us to realize how famous these people once were. Anna Seward received more acclaim than any other poetess of her day, probably more than any "female author" whatsoever, except Mrs. Macaulay and Fanny Burney. George Washington sent a special envoy to her with original papers to prove that her aspersions on him in her *Monody on Major André* were unfounded. Hayley's poems were more widely read than Johnson's, Goldsmith's, or Cowper's, and he had the distinction of declining the laureateship on the death of Thomas Warton. Wordsworth's famous essay on poetic diction is from beginning to end an anxious attack on the poetry of Erasmus Darwin, then much more popular than his own.

I do not mean to infer that our neglect of their writings is unjust. As writers they are all either a little mad or more than a little ridiculous. But as *persons* they are much more interesting to read about than Gray or Macpherson or half the members of the Literary Club. And Miss Seward undoubtedly furnishes the best focus for a study that shall contain them all. Besides the Lichfield group that revolved about Dr. Darwin, she was intimate with Hayley, and had the *entrée,* when she chose to avail herself of it, into Johnson's circle. It is in her writings that we find some of the most interesting (oh, that it were equally trustworthy!) information we possess concerning Darwin, Day, and Edgeworth. She also had connections, as few of the typical eighteenth-century authors had, with the new Romantic Age. She lived only fourteen years longer than Boswell, but those few years make startling differences in her literary outlook. When Boswell died in 1795, Wordsworth had published his "Poetical Sketches," but was still quite unknown. Miss Seward was the generous encourager of Henry Francis Cary; she lived to pronounce Southey the greatest epic poet since Milton; to say (in 1798!) that ignorance of Coleridge "would disgrace a poetic reader"; and to make Walter Scott her literary executor. I am glad that Miss Ashmun has allowed herself to be discursive and to insert biographical sketches of the many interesting men and women with whom her heroine associated. To most readers that will constitute the chief charm of her book.

If I have intimated that Miss Seward, apart from her literary connections, does not deserve a biography, I am sorry. I fancy that was my feeling before I read this book, but it is so no longer. One whose knowledge of the Swan of Lichfield is derived from a few passages of her worst poems and the contemptuous footnotes added by Boswell to the later editions of the *Life of Johnson,* is likely to see her as a typical *précieuse:* affected, plaintive, and ridiculous. Ridiculous she sometimes was when she took a pen in hand, but people in her presence never thought of applying that epithet to her. To those who knew her, Anna Seward was a tall, stout, handsome woman with the imperious bearing of Queen Elizabeth, but with a heart that was utterly enthusiastic and sentimental; a woman with a genius for inaccuracy but apparently no consciousness of malice; an outspoken lady who could not endure to have her own faults mentioned; a woman of courage who despised the great Dr. Johnson and withstood him to his face; finally, a woman who in youth declined offers of marriage but in middle age gave the passionate and unremitting devotion of her heart to a man she could not marry. It is typical of the genuine, though sometimes distorted, sense of fairness which ruled her actions, that when, in old age, she came to write an epitaph on this man who was the dearest to her of all human beings, she should have borrowed as a climax a line from Dr. Johnson.

Miss Ashmun's book will go far, I hope, toward making better known a remarkable personality which the world, to its own loss, has been willing to forget.

FREDERICK A. POTTLE.

Yale University,
  New Haven, Connecticut,
    October, 1930.

AUTHOR'S NOTE

IN offering to students of the eighteenth century a volume concerned with Anna Seward, the present writer
calls attention to the fact that no extended chronological
study of the life of the Swan of Lichfield has up to this
time been attempted. A notably pleasing book by Mr. E. V.
Lucas, entitled *A Swan and Her Friends,* gives an impres-
sionistic view of Miss Seward and her coterie, but makes
no pretensions to following a time sequence or marking the
consecutive events in the career of the provincial *précieuse.*

Miss Seward was an active-minded woman, who made
many contacts among the bookish groups of her day. Although her work has suffered almost complete effacement,
her personality survives by reason of the strong force
within itself. Her doings, her friendships, her correspondence, and her opinions are not without real significance to
those who are even slightly interested in the literary history
of the reign of George III.

The chief source of information regarding Miss Seward
must inevitably be the six volumes of her *Letters,* published
in 1811, two years after her death. In using the material
supplied by these letters, the biographer must proceed with
a degree of caution, since the emotional nature of the poetess
gave her a lofty contempt for mere accuracy, and for the
delving methods of scholastic study. Exact dates, impersonal facts, we must not too rigidly demand from an En-

thusiast, as Miss Seward discerningly labeled herself. In many matters, however, we can find our dates and facts elsewhere, and can put our own interpretation on the somewhat highly colored statements of the *Letters.*

In preparing the volume in hand, *The Singing Swan,* the author has been fortunate in obtaining needed assistance. Her thanks are due to the Right Rev. Leonard Jauncey White-Thomson, D.D., Lord Bishop of Ely; the Rev. H. Saunders Williams, present Rector of Eyam, in Derbyshire, Miss Seward's birthplace; Mayor W. A. Wood, Hon. Secretary of the Johnson Society, in Lichfield; the Rev. C. S. James of Birmingham (England); T. J. Burrowes, Esq., of Stradone, county Cavan, Ireland; Mrs. Stuart Shaw, formerly Mayor of Lichfield; Frederick A. Brabant, Esq., Solicitor, of Gray's Inn Square, London; Miss D. S. Curnow of Muswell Hill, London; Mr. Royal Cortissoz, noted art critic of New York; and Mr. Frank H. Chase, of the Reference Department of the Public Library of Boston. Gratitude belongs also to the staffs of the Public Library of New Haven, Connecticut; the Forbes Library of Northampton, Massachusetts; the Converse Library of Amherst, Massachusetts; and the Smith College Library of Northampton. Special thanks must be expressed for the help and encouragement of Professor Frederick A. Pottle of Yale University, who read the book in manuscript.

M. A.

Northampton, Massachusetts,
    October, 1930.

CONTENTS

ILLUSTRATIONS

ABBREVIATIONS
OF TITLES USED IN FOOTNOTES

LETTERS. *Letters of Anna Seward: Written Between the Years 1784 and 1807,* in six volumes. Printed by George Ramsey & Company, Edinburgh; for Archibald Constable & Company, Edinburgh; and Longman, Hurst, Rees, Orme, & Brown, William Miller, and John Murray, London, 1811.

POETICAL WORKS. *The Poetical Works of Anna Seward; With Extracts from Her Literary Correspondence,* edited by Walter Scott, Esq., in three volumes. Printed by James Ballantyne & Co., Edinburgh; for John Ballantyne & Co., Edinburgh; and Longman, Hurst, Rees, & Orme, London, 1810.

NICHOLS' ILLUSTRATIONS. *Illustrations of the Literary History of the Eighteenth Century, Consisting of Authentic Memoirs and Original Letters of Eminent Persons; and Intended as a Sequel to "The Literary Anecdotes,"* in eight volumes, 1817–1858. Volumes I–VI by John Nichols; Volumes VII–VIII by John Bowyer Nichols. Volumes I–IV, printed for the Author, by Nichols, Son, & Bentley, London; Volumes V–VIII, printed by and for J. B. Nichols & Son, London.

THE SINGING SWAN

CHAPTER I

1742–1765

LOVE, DEATH, AND A POETESS

ANNA SEWARD was born at the turn of England's literary history. The death of Pope[1] fol-
lowed closely upon her birth. The old era of
Queen Anne was passing; and the richness of the newer
age was to concentrate itself within the next seventy-five
years. George II was on the throne; but before Anna
Seward was out of her girlhood, the long reign of
George III was to begin. She lived through the period
upon which many of us look with envy—the time of
Johnson and his Boswell, of Joshua Reynolds and
George Romney, of the Blues, of Fanny Burney, of
David Garrick and Sarah Siddons, and of a hundred
others whose names give luster to the Picturesque Century of brocade and periwig, sedan chair, Chippendale
furniture, and early Wedgwood.

LIKE so many others who have figured in the world of
English letters, Anna Seward came out of a rectory. Her
father was the Rev. Thomas Seward, Rector of Eyam,[2]
in Derbyshire. He was the son of John Seward of Bad-

---

1. Pope died in 1744.   2. Pronounced ēēm.

sey, steward to Lord Windsor.[3] Thomas Seward was educated at Westminster and Cambridge, and was for several years private chaplain to the Duke of Grafton, and tutor to Lord Charles Fitzroy (the Duke's son), who died while on his travels, in 1739. Because of his connection with the ducal family, Mr. Seward saw much of polite society and traveled on the Continent. An entry in the Parish Register at Eyam shows that he was inducted April 28, 1740, and presented by Lord and Lady Burlington.[4]

He married Elizabeth Hunter, daughter of the Rev. Mr. John Hunter, Head Master of the Free School in Lichfield.

Of Hunter, who is remembered chiefly as the schoolmaster of Dr. Samuel Johnson, a curious story is told.[5] He was, it seems, a foundling, discovered in a field by some gentlemen of Solihull, Warwickshire, who had gone out with the not unusual British intention of shooting something. One of the group took the child, named him Hunter because of the manner of his advent into the world, and brought him up with advantages. It was sometimes said that Anna Seward was proud and snobbish; if so, the humble origin of her grandfather Hunter may have caused her some chagrin.

3. It is supposed that the Sewards were descended from Thomas Sheward of Tardebig (Lord Windsor's seat). They pronounced their name Sēē'ward.

4. This information is supplied by the Rev. H. S. Williams, the present Rector of Eyam, who has examined the church books.

5. Nichols' *Illustrations*, VI, 311. See also Appendix A of this book.

The Sewards, as we have seen, had no difficulty in tracing their ancestry. A Peter Lely portrait of the mother of Thomas Seward[6] adorned the walls of his dining room and gave authentic evidence of family consequence.

We may here insert a reference to an odd communication in the *Gentleman's Magazine* of 1782, regarding Mr. Seward's courtship of his wife. The writer of the letter, who signs himself *W.S.,* says that Miss Hunter, daughter of Mr. John Hunter, the schoolmaster, was much in company with Mr. Green, one of her father's assistants, who afterward became Bishop Green. Young Mr. Green, says the author of the letter, "very probably and naturally entertained a tenderness for her, for indeed she was a very sensible and amiable woman. . . . I have reason to think, too," he goes on, "that the lady had no dislike to him. . . . That there was some attachment between them is plain." Mr. Seward, who wanted the young lady for himself, pursued a bold course. He wrote a letter to Mr. Green (which the correspondent *W.S.* professed to have heard read aloud) in which he asked "to be informed from him how far that attachment had proceeded, and whether Miss Hunter and he were engaged to each other."

"Well," said Mr. Green to *W.S.,* after reading the letter, "I shall send them such an answer as I hope will please both parties." Evidently he relinquished all claim upon Miss Hunter. "His letter," adds *W.S.,* "I suppose

6. *Letters,* To Mr. Seward of Birmingham, VI, 322.

had the desired effect in producing the union that produced the excellent Miss Seward!"

In a note to her *Epistle to Nathaniel Lister, Esq.*
(1786), Miss Seward speaks of a rivalry between Dr.
Green and Dr. Newton (afterward Bishops of Lincoln
and Bristol) for the hand of Miss Hunter, who declined the attention of both in favor of Mr. Seward.

The Rev. Thomas Seward, who was thirty-two years
old, and Elizabeth Hunter, who was twenty-eight, were
married at Newton in the Thistle (Newton Regis),
Warwickshire, October 27, 1741.[7] Miss Hunter spent
much of her time with an uncle in Warwickshire,[8] and
this fact accounts for the place of the marriage. The
bondsmen were Charles Howard, of the Close of the
Cathedral Church in Lichfield, gentleman; and "John
Doe, gentleman." Charles Howard was the father of
Mary Howard, the first wife of Dr. Erasmus Darwin.

Mr. Seward took his wife to Eyam,[9] which was a
village picturesquely situated in the high hills, near the
Peak, celebrated by Sir Walter Scott in his novel,
Peveril of the Peak. Here their eldest daughter, Anne,
was born on December 12 (N.S.), 1742. A second
daughter, Sarah, was born in 1744, and other children

7. For information as to the place of the marriage, the present
writer is grateful to the Bishop of Ely and to the Rev. C. S. James of
Birmingham; and for the correct date of the marriage and the names
of the bondsmen (the marriage was by license) to Mr. James, who
has examined the transcript of Newton in the Thistle.

8. *Letters,* I, 38.

9. A description too long to quote, of Eyam and its surroundings,
is given in a letter written by Anna Seward in 1765. See Vol. I of
her *Poetical Works,* edited by Walter Scott, p. cliii.

followed: John, Jane, and Elizabeth, who died in infancy; and a son and a daughter "dead born."

A word may be said regarding the date of Anna Seward's birth. The date given in the *Dictionary of National Biography* and other reference books is 1747. Mr. Lucas says: "Miss Seward was born on 12th December, 1742, and baptised Anne on 24th December." He does not say what investigations impelled him to swerve from the generally accepted date; but anyone who attempts to reconcile it with facts[10] or even Miss Seward's unreliable data must soon find that it is wrong. At the present writer's request, the Rector of Eyam, the Rev. H. S. Williams, kindly consented to search the church books for the record of baptism of Anne Seward, which he discovered to be dated December 28, 1742. In one of her early letters, Miss Seward says that her birthday was December 12. We may therefore fix the date of her birth as December 12, 1742.

In this connection, it may be interesting to note that a Bible which once belonged to Elizabeth Seward, wife of the Rev. Thomas Seward, is now in the possession of the Right Rev. Leonard Jauncey White-Thomson,[11] D.D., Lord Bishop of Ely, who is related to the cousins of Anna Seward, the Henry and Thomas White so often mentioned in her *Letters*. The Rev. Henry White was sacrist of the cathedral at Lichfield, a man of learn-

10. Miss Seward says that she was eight years younger than John Saville. He died in 1803, aged sixty-eight (see his obituary in the *Gentleman's Magazine*). Miss Seward's obituary in the *Gentleman's Magazine* for April, 1809, says that she died at the age of sixty-six.

11. Son of the late Sir Robert White-Thomson.

ing and culture, and a collector of rare books. Thomas White, his brother, was named as residuary legatee in the will of Anna Seward. The Bible in question was printed in 1736, and has "Eliz^th Seward" written in ink on the title-page, and bears the bookplate of T. H. White (probably the Thomas White mentioned above). The family record entered in the Bible shows, among other dates, those of the birth of all the Rev. Thomas Seward's children, and of the death of Elizabeth Seward and of Thomas Seward. The date of the birth of Anne is given as December 1 (O.S.), 1744,[12] and the date of her baptism is given as December 28, 1744. Her sponsors were "her Uncle Norton, her Aunt Martin and Mrs. Jackson of Burton." The names of the sponsors may be correct, but the date of birth and date of baptism are undoubtedly wrong, since the church register at Eyam must be given precedence in the point of accuracy. The Bishop of Ely writes: "It appears . . . that the years' dates of the marriage,[13] of Anne's birthday, of Sarah's birthday, and John's, also perhaps Jane's, have all been altered, I suggest by the writer of the interpolation on the opposite page—T. H. White, whose book plate is on page 3." He adds that he considers the evidence of the Bible "discredited" by the alterations.

Here is a case in which the family Bible, so often a source of authentic information, comes under a sus-

12. The information in this paragraph is taken from letters to the present writer from his Lordship, the Bishop of Ely.

13. The date of the marriage of Thomas Seward and Elizabeth Hunter is given as October 27, 1742.

picion of unreliability. In fact, it is proved wrong by the registers in two parish churches, those of Eyam and Newton in the Thistle. We therefore must adhere to the dates given above: the date of the marriage of Thomas Seward as October 27, 1741; and the birth of Anne Seward as December 12, 1742.

When Anna was seven years old, the Sewards removed from the picturesque country of Derbyshire to Lichfield, in Staffordshire, seat of a cathedral and home of a cultivated circle of clerical people. Mr. Seward became Prebendary of Salisbury and Canon Residentiary of Lichfield, and took a permanent place in the church group. His home became a center of agreeable entertainment, with a background of dignity and social importance which made its hospitality a privilege to be sought.

In his *Memoirs,* written in 1808, Richard Lovell Edgeworth says:[14] "The bishop's palace at Lichfield, where Mr. Seward a canon of the cathedral, resided, was the resort of every person in that neighborhood, who had any taste for letters. Every stranger, who came well recommended to Lichfield, brought letters to the palace. His popularity in the literary world was well deserved, for Mr. Seward was a man of learning and taste; he was fond of conversation, in which he bore a considerable part, good-natured, and indulgent to the little foibles of others; he scarcely seemed to notice any animadversions that were made upon his own. . . . Mrs. Seward was a handsome woman, of agreeable manners.

14. *Memoirs of Richard Lovell Edgeworth, Esq.,* I, 106.

She was generous, possessed of good sense, and capable of strong affection."

Perceiving that his daughter Anna (called Nancy) had a lively and retentive mind, Mr. Seward introduced her in earliest youth (at the age of three, to be exact) to Milton, Shakespeare, and the later English writers, particularly those of the time of Queen Anne. This acquaintance with literature was to be widened by her own constant reading, so that she became in time a notably well-educated woman, with a prodigious fund of apt quotation, in an age when women were contented with the household arts and the ability to write a fairly accurate letter.

When she was nine years old,[15] little Nancy was able to recite verbatim the first three books of *Paradise Lost,* and that, too, with the precision and inflection of understanding. When she was ten or twelve, she began composing verse of a semi-religious character. Her father was amused with her efforts, and did not discourage her until he began to see in her a rival for the family laurels.

When Anna was in her thirteenth year, the Sewards took up their abode in the Bishop's Palace, in the Cathedral Close. This stately building had been erected in 1687; but though designed for a Bishop, it had always been let to slightly less exalted tenants. It was as noble a house as any Canon of the church need wish to occupy. Here the father and mother spent their remaining days, and their daughter lived on after them till her death in 1809.

15. *Gentleman's Magazine,* LXXIX (April, 1809), 378.

The two girls, Anna and Sarah, led a happy, and, it seems, a remarkably free out-of-door life. It was shortly after the removal to the Palace that Anna took on that plumpness of body which mortified her to her latest days, but which Sir Walter Scott chivalrously termed "a majestic presence." Nancy was sent to the country for a month's visit with an ultra-refined lady, to whom the idea of a girl's playing or romping out of doors was anathema. Nancy spent four weeks in unbearable dulness, varied only by the advent of food, and still more food, chiefly in the form of thick chocolate, creams, syllabubs, cakes, and other sugary titbits. She ate for mere ennui's sake, growing stouter and stouter, and more and more bored. When at last she was set free from her hateful imprisonment, she was an unseemly sight, fat, puffy, and unwieldy. Her scandalized parents consoled themselves with the thought that a rigid diet would restore her slenderness, but, though she regained a more shapely form, she never returned to the sylphlike thinness of her earlier years. That she was humiliated by this near-obesity, knowing herself otherwise of unusual beauty, is shown by her deprecating references to her "portly self."

When she was nearly fourteen, an event took place which was to prove of supreme importance to her as girl and woman. A child of five, the daughter of Edward Sneyd of Lichfield, came to live in the Seward household. Mr. Sneyd had lost his wife, who had left him with a family of eight children. The Sewards, having ample means and kindly hearts, took the little

Honora into their home to be a foster sister to their own two daughters. Anna, between eight and nine years older than the small newcomer, formed a passionate attachment for the child, and constituted herself tutor, guardian, and mentor to the unusually lovely little creature. It was well that this new interest came to provide expression for a too-romantic temperament. The native impulses of the girl were being purposely repressed. Mr. and Mrs. Seward had taken alarm at her studious bent, and her pleasant gift of poetizing, and had become terrified lest their Nancy should turn out to be a learned lady and a celibate rhymester. The overeducated woman, particularly if she showed a tendency to scribble, was viewed askance in provincial circles. She was a hybrid being, who ought to be suppressed in the self-willed stage, lest she lack a husband, and remain to the end of the chapter a literary spinster.

Dr. Darwin, local physician, and a new arrival in Lichfield, seems to have been at least partially responsible for Mr. Seward's dictum that no more verses were to be allowed. For twenty-five years he was a neighbor of the Seward family, and his name is closely associated with theirs in both a personal and a literary way.

Erasmus Darwin was born in 1731. As a boy he showed poetical talent; but, after his graduation at Cambridge in 1754, he turned from literature to medicine, which he studied at Edinburgh. After a short sojourn at Nottingham, he chose Lichfield as a promising district for a country practice, and settled there in 1756. He did not at first attract either friends or patients, since he was large and corpulent, with stooped shoulders and heavy limbs, had suffered from the common affliction of smallpox, and possessed an irritating tendency to stammer. However, he soon had the good fortune to assist in restoring the health (or, as it was thought, saving the life) of a young Mr. Inge, a valued member of the Staffordshire gentry. The report of his success was the means of establishing Dr. Darwin in practice, without a local rival.

At the time with which we are now concerned, he had only recently come to Lichfield and had not achieved the great fame which he won in later years. In 1757 Darwin married Miss Mary Howard, a girl of eighteen. Richard Lovell Edgeworth says[16] that Nancy Seward was jealous of Mrs. Darwin, and that she had hoped to marry the Doctor herself. This statement seems somewhat far-fetched, in view of the fact that Nancy was only fifteen years old at the time of the Doctor's marriage. Since Edgeworth was writing of his first visit to Lichfield, which took place in 1766, he cannot refer to Dr. Darwin's second marriage, which occurred in 1781; so we shall dismiss the rivalry between Nancy Seward and Mary Howard as a figment of Edgeworthian fancy.

Erasmus Darwin interested himself in the attractive and brilliant daughter of Canon Seward, and encouraged her to show him her smoothly flowing verses. As time went on he read these compositions with growing perplexity. They seemed too good for a girl of fifteen or

16. *Memoirs of Richard Lovell Edgeworth, Esq.*, I, 166.

sixteen to write. Mr. Seward was a versifying man; and the Doctor began to suspect[17] that Nancy was merely parading (in innocence or guile) the purloined lyrics of her father. To decide the question he set her a task in which she was to write certain verses, on a stated subject, while her father was away in Derbyshire. The girl nonchalantly composed the required stanzas, to the Doctor's entire satisfaction. They are given below, on the authority of the *European Magazine*. Darwin pretended to scoff at Nancy's exaggerated love for *Paradise Lost;* and so, when he set her the task, she seized the opportunity to defend her passion. Dr. Darwin wrote the first stanza, and told her to finish the poem:

> To mark how fair the primrose blows,
>   How soft the feather'd muses sing,
> My wand'ring step had pressed the dews,
>   My soul enraptur'd hail'd the Spring.
>
> But in an evil hour I stray'd
>   Since from a yew-tree's cleaving side,
> Issued a pale disdainful maid;
>   No good to me she did betide!
>
> A squalid, sickly tastless dame,
>   Of false incongruous pride the child;
> She lights her innovating flame
>   And scornful sports her fancies wild;
>
> Caprice her name; disdain, said she,
>   To sail along the common tide,
> But launch upon a wider sea,
>   While I thy tow'ring bark shall guide.

17. *European Magazine,* Vol. I, for April, 1782, p. 288.

Alas! what notice canst thou claim,
　Condemning what has no one's laud?
Be thine a nicer, subtler flame,
　To blame what all the world applaud.

She ceas'd; but still my ears retain'd
　The deep vibration of her lays;
And in her magic fetters chain'd,
　She guides my censure and my praise.

Hence he, who on seraphic wings
　Soar'd high above the starry spheres,
And heav'n-inspir'd enraptured sings
　Seraphic strains to mortal ears.

Impell'd by her vain whims I tried
　To veil his bright meridian rays;
And fain I would, ah! strange the pride!
　From Milton's temples snatch the bays.

The Doctor, being convinced that Nancy's talent was all her own, encouraged the young girl to go on writing, while he advised and corrected. It is likely that his well-meant meddling was the reverse of beneficial; for to his influence may be traced a good deal of that ornateness which disfigured the maturer writings of Miss Seward, and made them too often an object of ridicule instead of discriminating praise. Moreover, the Doctor, with more enthusiasm than tact, bluntly told the Rev. Mr. Seward that his daughter's verses were better than any that he could show. This was too much for Mr. Seward's *amour propre,* which seems to have been well developed. He gave commands and all verses, if not all smiles, stopped together.

Nancy Seward was put to the harmless tasks of

needlework, in which she soon excelled. The finished specimens of her art were much extolled at bazaars and other sales for charity. Letter cases, embroidered ruffles, netted bags, and beaded purses consoled her for that which was denied. Her eager mind, exuberant spirit, and untiring industry made her an adept in all that she undertook. The matching of rhymes was a pastime forbidden by high clerical authority. A fragment of an early letter may be quoted here:

It is true that I have written verses, but it is not true that I have written them often. A propensity of that sort appeared early in my infancy. At first my father encouraged it, but my mother threw cold water on the rising fires; and even my father ceased to smile encouragement upon those attempts after my 16th year, in which Dr. Darwin unluckily told him that his daughter's verses were better than his; a piece of arch injustice to my father's muse, which disgusted him with mine.[18]

Anna herself admits that there was jealousy behind the commands issued by the Rev. Mr. Seward. It would never do to have a chit of a girl supersede her father as family poet. He had published some anonymous verses in Dodsley's *Collection,* and (with Mr. Simpson) an edition of Beaumont and Fletcher. Anna was always loyal. She never tired of calling attention to his somewhat undistinguished achievements, and she readily forgave the sinister motive in his repression of her talents. Apparently she did not even resent the tyranny which forced her to exchange the pen for the needle and the shuttle.

18. *Poetical Works,* Introduction, I, lxviii, dated February, 1763.

The child Honora was an ever satisfying diversion, with her awakening mind, her precocious prattle, and her sweet responsiveness to love. Life was full enough. There was incessant visiting among relatives and friends. There were parties and tea drinkings and *soirées,* with plenty of dancing and feasting. At home there was good talk, from an unstemmed stream of callers. Sir Brooke Boothby, Dr. Erasmus Darwin, the surgeon and the banker, the various church officials, and other eminent Lichfieldians vied with visitors from the great world, who were drawn unerringly to the Canon's *salon.* It must not be forgotten that there was ever the sound of music in the absent Bishop's halls, for young John Saville, one of the vicars choral of the Cathedral, was a near neighbor, and he made the Sewards' house his second home.

The little city[19] did not seem restricted or monotonous to the avid gaze of growing Nancy. There was never a dearth of amusement. Then, too, people went up to London and came down again, bringing tales of fashionable doings and of the opera and the drama; and there was the King's eclipse to hear about; and a young King's succession, and a royal marriage, and a coronation. Sometimes the great Dr. Johnson himself, just in from the metropolis, came rolling and shuffling down the street, putting on the airs of a Shah, when there were still a goodly number of old residents to recall his early history and to refuse to be browbeaten or

19. The population of Lichfield was 4,000 in 1781 (*Harwood's History of Lichfield*).

impressed. Nancy knew a good deal about Dr. Johnson. Her mother was in a distant way related to the Lexicographer (only she did not call him that; she called him "Sam Johnson," with a little scornful twang). The relationship was nothing to boast about. Mrs. Seward's stepmother was a sister of Henry Porter, whose widow (poor Tetty, dead since 1752) Johnson had married. Nancy had associated since her childhood with Lucy Porter, the great Shah's stepdaughter; she had heard his letters read (privately marveling at their commonplace quality); and she had seen him (no very enticing sight), and heard him declaim in Lichfield drawing rooms and her father's library.

After all, the coming or going of that familiar figure was of secondary import. More significant were her own well-chaperoned trips into Derbyshire, to Eyam or Derby, her sojournings at the watering places, Buxton and Matlock. There were gowns to be planned and bought and made; and laces and fans and slippers and headdresses and mantles to be chosen. There were interminable letters to be written (outlets for the bubbling ardor of youth) to the new acquaintances who came into being at each of the journeyings and tarryings. And always there was little Honora to be dressed, and decked, displayed, and teased, and caressed, and adored to the point of idolatry.

It must not be supposed that sister Sarah was a negligible part of the Seward household. She seems to have been less forceful than Anna, but girlishly pretty and alluring. Anna loved her with all the strength of a nature almost too ardent in its affections. The two girls occupied a suite of three rooms on the second floor of the Palace, sharing the same chintz-hung bed, the same hearth, the same dressing table; living as nearly as possible the life of two-in-one, without emulation or strife. They had their incipient love affairs, the wonderings and titillatings of misses who expect as a matter of course to become madams. With beauty, breeding, good family, sufficient money, and social position, why should either of the sisters anticipate less than early and happy marriage? No shadow yet had fallen on that high-spirited pair, destined, in their parents' hopes, to change speedily into chastened brides.

The Sewards, *pater* and *mater,* began to look about, in the furtive manner of prudent parents, for eligible young men, not averse to becoming bridegrooms. A Mr. Sneyd, of Belmont, showed a disposition to seek Miss Sarah in marriage. She was, Anna Seward tells us, in a letter of 1788, "his first love." "But his family were desirous that he should marry to higher rank, and ampler fortune; and succeeded in persuading him to stifle the fast-growing tenderness. Vanity, I think," she continues, "more than passion, gave his hand to a proud Beauty, who alienated him from his former friends. Our family were of that number." After his second marriage, the breach was healed; but the gentle Sarah had then no need of mortal reparations.

Anna was having a tentative affair of her own; though all we know of it is gathered from a few lines in letters written thirty years later. A young man named Vyse,[20] who was afterward to attain to the dignity of a Canon's place in the Lichfield Cathedral, had singled her out from the bevy of girls who fluttered across the Close. There were sighs, glances, notes, pressings of the hand, but no confessions. ". . . From infancy, we were intimate neighbors, and had each other's first unspoken, though, as it proved, transient love," wrote Miss Seward to William Hayley, in 1793.[21] So tenuous and undefined a *tendresse* must be left to the imagination. Dr. Vyse, as the youth in time became, was a quite unsentimentalized object on Miss Seward's horizon in the years which were then to come. He ignored her poetic performances, out of sheer desire to vex her, we infer; breaking his silence on the subject only to adjure her with "angry earnestness" to refrain from translating the classics when she knew no Latin or Greek. Thus the first sweetheart, either too cautious or too cool to speak, becomes merely the querulous caviler of middle age.

It has been remarked that Mrs. Seward was, in somewhat intricate fashion, connected with the Porters of Birmingham, and that Lucy Porter was long a friend of the Seward family. These relationships resulted, through what process we do not know, in negotiations for a marriage between Sarah Seward and Joseph Porter, son of Henry Porter, and, of course, stepson to Dr. Johnson. The story of this brief engagement is told by

20. William Vyse, elder brother of General Vyse. See p. 28.
21. *Letters,* III, 235.

Anna Seward in letters dated 1764, to be found in the
Literary Correspondence edited by Sir Walter Scott, in
his Introduction to the three volumes of her *Poetical
Works*.

Joseph Porter, who had passed his first youth, had
prospered in trade with Italy, and is spoken of as "a
merchant from Leghorn." Whatever suggestions had
been made regarding the marriage must have been by
letter; for they were well understood when Mr. Porter
arrived unexpectedly from Italy. There were no cables
in those days to herald the approach of a bridegroom.
Lucy Porter sent word that she was bringing brother
Joseph to a card party and tea which Mrs. Seward was
giving. Some inkling of the situation had got abroad.
"Nothing can be secret if my father is to know it,"
writes Anna resignedly.

The guests are all agog to see the long-absent brother
and happy man. Sarah, young and shy, is flustered and
frightened. She droops and sighs as she adjusts her light
hat and "ribbands." She and Anna go down to the
drawing-room. Everybody arrives, except the "most interesting." A loud rap sounds at the door. Sarah grows
crimson. In rustles Lucy Porter, her fair but faded
prettiness set off by her gown of blue-and-white tissue,
trimmed with Brussels lace. Mr. Porter follows, the
cynosure of "twenty pairs of curious eyes."

He is a thin, pale personage, somewhat below middle
height, with too much of a stoop in his shoulders, and
a more withered aspect than his forty years would ne-
cessitate; clad in "a black velvet coat and waistcoat,

richly embroidered, wearing a bag wig in crimp buckles, powdered as white as the new-shorn fleece." He has features not irregular, and very fine teeth, and he looks "extremely clean"! Yet Anna thinks him vulgar, and notes that he might pass for a quack doctor. "He has not the air of a gentleman, nor tone, nor voice."

He devotes himself, oddly enough, to Nancy and her *beaux yeux.* She is not averse to being thought able, if not willing, to cut her sister out. Sarah sulks and shows signs of jealousy. The minds of the guests are anywhere but on their cards. Nods and whispers give a hint of their surmises. "I saw," says Nancy, "in the half-suppressed, but significant smiles of our guests, that they thought the elder sister likely to bear away the Hymeneal wreath from the milder brow of the appointed fair one."[22] The party breaks up at nine. Mr. Porter and his sister have a supper engagement with the Whites, their cousins, also cousins of the Seward girls. "The instant the brother and sister were decamped," Anna goes on, "everybody spoke at once, and all in jocose invective upon your poor friend's[23] mischievous eyes, as they called them." Nancy loudly disclaims any interest in the "Italian prince." However, reports of his "imaginary" preference for the elder sister are, the next day, rapidly circulated through the little city. The "prince" makes no motion to confirm or deny. He merely sends a message of inquiry for the health of the Seward household.

22. *Poetical Works,* Introduction, I, cxviii.
23. Anna's.

On the third day he calls again, this time in a more sober coat, and walks out with the young ladies, to inspect the new house which Lucy Porter is building with a part of a fortune which she has inherited.[24] During the excursion Porter proposes marriage to Sarah, and is accepted. The tension is relieved. Gaiety ensues.

The bridegroom goes home with the three girls (little Honora, who is now about twelve, has taken her part in the affair) and spends the day with the Sewards. He tells strange tales of Italian intrigue, one of which, at least, Nancy is to remember and tell, many years later.[25] The plan is made that Anna is to go to Italy with the married pair, and stay two years. The girls are wild with excitement at the prospect. The shortcomings of the bridegroom, and his dangerous nearness to vulgarity, are, for the moment, forgotten. The glitter of his money lights what otherwise might be gloom.

The bridegroom is impatient to claim his bride and be off. Preparations for the wedding go forward. Even now, feeling some misgivings, the parents are inclined to wish the contract broken. Nancy, in spite of her elation, remarks sadly that her sister is entering "a cage! a golden one, 'tis true, but still a cage." Sarah, who has grown captious and fretful, is "warmly and solemnly adjured" to recede from her agreement if she finds it irksome. She has become obstinate, and refuses to change her plan.

24. She received £10,000 from her brother, a captain in the navy.
25. *Letters*, I, 170.

Then a subtle illness seizes the little bride-elect. "Her
spirits have been too much hurried for a constitution
so delicate," cries Anna. Sarah fails to rally, in spite of
Dr. Darwin's blisters and bleedings. She pines, pales,
grows languid, takes to her bed. The indications, as we
now see them, point to a strong inner repugnance for
her middle-aged lover. Mr. Porter himself shows little
real emotion. "His sensations seem more like vexation
than grief." Every remedy is tried. A "clergyman in
Worcestershire" is sent for, because he has been known
to administer James's Powders with success. He agrees
with Dr. Darwin that there is no hope, but recommends "musk medicines," instead of the famous powders. Sarah grows better, grows worse again, lingers a
little, and presently is gone. Six of her young comrades,
robed in white, bear the pall while she is carried to
the tomb.

The bridegroom recovers, Nancy thinks, too easily
from his loss. Mrs. Seward, Anna, and Honora go away
for a change of scene. Porter joins them at Eyam and
returns with them to Lichfield. He intimates a willingness to transpose his affections from the dead Sarah to
the living and bewitching Anna. But she has had
enough of middle-aged silk merchants.[26] She flouts him,
as his sister Lucy is reported to have flouted his stepfather, when he wooed her with rhymes instead of
guineas.

Sarah Seward was dead, and Anna, her dreams of

26. Very little is known of the further history of Porter, except
that he died in 1783.

Italy renounced, came back, after a season of visits, to the rooms which she and her sister had shared in the blithe mood of hopeful youth. She thought at first that she could never enter those rooms again.[27] But the arguments of her mother, and the sweet persuasions of Honora prevailed. She shared her rooms with little Honora as she had shared them with Sarah, and consoled her grief with the tender care and instruction which she gave to the ardent and understanding child.

Life was not now the gay thing that it had been before the coming of Joseph Porter of Leghorn. Nancy Seward, not much over twenty, was beginning to find that the world takes more than it can give. She was enduring the first of its buffetings, of which there were many to come. She faced them with courage, though with lamentations: all but the last, under which she bent and broke—but in 1764 that was forty years away.

She went back to her reading. She wrote a little verse, because she could not keep her sorrows out of measured lines. People called, and kept on calling. There were more tea parties, and there were more laughing groups of friends with their gay brocades and velvets and powdered locks and sportive talk. There was more music, too; for John Saville still came and went, lifting up his voice in most entrancing sweetness. Anna took lessons on the harpsichord, and labored hard to make herself proficient. She wanted to play her part in the little concerts which John Saville was always planning; and she wanted to understand what there

27. *Poetical Works*, I, cxlii.

was about music that lifted him into a realm of heavenly happiness, too far beyond those who knew only the solid earth.

In October Anna Seward took her first and long-anticipated journey to London. She was to stay a month, with some people named L—— [Levett, probably], whom she had known since childhood. Mrs. L——; so Anna's early letters say,[28] was the *fiancée* of David Garrick, when he went to make his fortune in London. "The soul of everything that was gay and agreeable in Lichfield," Miss L—— (as she was then; she later married her cousin of the same name) had many lovers, who were attracted by her wit and charm. Her people, who had money, rejected the proposals of young Garrick. She was willing to wait for him. "But unreasonably mortified pride, and the charms of the fair Violetta, obliterated the remembrance of those graces, once so passionately adored." One of Nancy Seward's juvenile poems pays tribute to those graces.[29]

There is no record of the joys of that visit to London, but in spite of mourning, they must have been many. The eager mind of the young woman from the provinces would have been alert for every opportunity to see and hear and understand the good things of the metropolis. Music, pictures, plays, and social diversions must have filled the days with pleasures and the nights

28. *Poetical Works,* I, cxlvii.
29. *Ibid.,* p. 13: "Portrait of Miss Levett" (written when Anna Seward was eighteen).

ANNA SEWARD, AGED 19
BY KETTLE, 1762
Courtesy of the National Portrait Gallery, London.

with dreams. With an enlarged outlook upon the world, Miss Seward would go back to Lichfield, treasuring the memories of that month in "Great Babylon," as of course she called it, and looking forward to the next sojourn within its gates.

About this time a love affair was developing in which the heart of Miss Nancy seems to have been truly, if temporarily, involved. In 1762 she had met a young Mr. T—— [Taylor?], destined for a military career. He was notable for a "dignified seriousness, an air of refined attachment," pensive because of an unfortunate devotion to a Miss Chadwick, afterward Lady Middleton. Making a confidante of the sympathetic Miss Seward, he found himself transferring his affections to her, from the object of his hopeless regard. "The regiment then removing," says a reminiscent letter of 1796, "we separated with tender, but not visibly impassioned regret. Two years after, in the winter of 1764, we met accidentally in London, renewed our friendship, which soon became mutual and acknowledged love."[30]

At this point we may go back to a letter which is contained in Miss Seward's early correspondence, edited by Walter Scott:

O Emma! I am sick of many griefs—my hopes for Mr. T——'s happiness and my own are vanished as a dream. His guardians, somewhat incredibly, declare that the expences of his education, the purchase of his commissions, and the port at which he has lived since he went into the army, have reduced his original fortune to little more than half what it was. He is not yet twenty-four, has not been an officer more than four years—has never gamed, nor had

30. *Letters,* IV, 176.

libertine expences—and what is become of what ought to have been the savings of so long a minority? But there is no redress.

By the officiousness of mistaken friends, I have endured needless vexation, and an added weight of grief. Their information caused my father to question me upon the subject—to be angry at the correspondence which I acknowledged—to write an ill-judged letter to Mr. T——, and violently to insist on the dissolution of an engagement which we had mutually agreed to renounce, of our own accord, if the guardian-éclaircissement proved what it does prove.[31]

There was a "storm," she says, in the "little domestic atmosphere" of the Seward abode; and she, being guilty of loving an impoverished young man, was "obliged to 'abide the hourly shot of angry eyes'"— evidently the Canon's.[32] Mr. T——'s delicacy was "wounded to no sort of purpose." The whole affair was a lamentable one, of the sort best calculated to grieve the affections and hurt the pride of sensitive young people. The Rev. Thomas Seward was perhaps no more of a tyrant than most fathers of the period, nor than most British fathers have been since; yet he appears in an unenviable light during this episode. His willingness to see his daughter Sarah sacrificed in a loveless marriage with a moneyed man, and his refusal to give his daughter Anna where the amount of money which he had anticipated was lacking, show him conventional and mercenary, if no worse.

If the last "Evander and Emilia"[33] poem was not written on this occasion, it accurately describes the *impasse* which existed between Nancy Seward and Mr. T——. The first stanza is here given:

31. *Poetical Works*, I, clxxxiii. This letter is dated March 27, 1765.
32. No pun intended.   33. *Poetical Works*, I, 62.

'Tis o'er!—the bright star like a meteor fire,
An instant shone, then vanish'd from our sight!
Fierce, in unbaffled rule, paternal ire
Quenches its beams in everlasting night.
With guardian care a dying mother[34] strove
To shield from penury resistless love;
But that kind care a father's proud disdain
Meets with derision's smile, and sternly proves it vain.

The letter of 1796 says: "My father on discovering, disapproved and dissolved it [the engagement]. I believed that so placid a lover would not suffer severely from the disappointment, nor once imagined that his attachment would be proof against time. This conviction extinguished that part of my own regard which was more tender than esteem and left my heart vacant to receive another impression more distinct and enthusiastic than I had ever before experienced. Its vivacity induced me to think that I had till then mistaken friendship for love." Thus easily did Miss Anna, after the first throes of disappointment and humiliation, renounce her love for the man who afterward became Colonel T——, and who figured in the strange sequel to this affair, disclosed in letters of later years.[35] All was not over yet. "Four years after parental authority had dissolved my engagements to Colonel T—— we again accidentally met in London. Imagine my feelings," exclaimed the mature Miss Seward, "when he declared his unceasing affection, and told me that he had returned to England, with the hope that an acquisition to his fortune would induce my father to consent to our

34. This probably refers to the source of the young man's fortune.
35. *Letters*, IV, 272–273, 359–361.

union! Conceive the shame of which I became susceptible, on finding myself so much surpassed in constancy!" This letter was, oddly enough, written to the
wife of this same Colonel T——, its surprising frankness designed to quell some impulses of jealousy on the
part of the married lady. "I could not on the instant,"
it continues, "explain my sentiments; but I wrote to
him, the next day, confessing the change in my heart
respecting himself; but I forget whether pride did, or
did not, withhold the circumstance which had produced
it, and the acknowledgment that I had been, in my
turn, forsaken."

Pride, after so many years, had so far lost its power
that it permitted Miss Seward to relate the details of
the other romance which had meant so much more to
her than her fleeting love for Colonel T——. "This happened the ensuing year, 1765," she wrote. "The in-
spirer [of love] was the present General, then Cornet
V—— [Vyse], a native of Lichfield, but absent six years
to receive a military education in France and Dublin. . . . At that period, he returned with the united
graces of early youth,[36] the dignity of manhood, and
with politeness which had the first polish. He was tall,
and, in my eyes, extremely lovely. If my susceptibility
of these attractions was fickleness to Mr. T——, Mr.
V——'s inconstancy to me avenged it at full."

After paying court to her for three months, during
which he was "assiduously attentive," Vyse suddenly
changed his manner, until he was treating her with

36. Richard Vyse was born in 1746.

"cool civility, bordering on neglect." The shock was painful. "I felt, during a short time, tortured and wretched in the extreme," she confessed to Mrs. T——, in this letter written thirty years afterward; "but I had pride, high spirits, intellectual resources, and fancied myself not born to be the victim of contemned affection. I had proposals of marriage from several, whom my father wished me to approve." But marriage without love, now that she had discovered the meaning of the word, offered no charms to the high-minded girl. She resolved to put aside all thoughts of love and marriage, and give herself up to social and intellectual pursuits. How far she succeeded we shall discover on a later page.[37] She had suffered not a little, and was to suffer more as events unfolded in a period still remote.

It may be pertinent to relate the later history of Cornet Vyse. He married one of the "most intimate friends" of Anna Seward, on whose bosom the deserted girl "had shed those mingled tears of indignation and lacerated tenderness, which he had caused to flow." Mrs. Vyse died in childbirth the year after her marriage. Anna Seward, who had generously remained friendly to her, in spite of seeming treachery, wrote a monody on her death. The poem is entitled "Monody on Mrs. Richard Vyse, addressed to her husband, since General Vyse." What the poem lacks in merit is atoned for by the forgiving charity of the author, who had not faltered in friendship for either the man or his wife, when both had humiliated her. No one who studies the life

37. See page 178.

and writings of Anna Seward can fail to remark the
fact that she was singularly free from jealousy, either of
the professional or the personal sort.

Vyse married a second time, and became again a
widower. His progress in military rank was steady. He
was a cornet when Anna Seward fell in love with him
in 1765. By 1771 he had become a captain. In 1781 he
was a colonel. In 1784 he received command of the first
dragoon guards. He became a major general in 1794,
lieutenant general in 1801. In 1806, he was returned to
Parliament for Beverley. He rose to the rank of general
in 1812. For some years he was Comptroller of the
Household of the Duke of Cumberland. He died in
1825, sixteen years after Anna Seward had left the
disappointments of this world behind her.

Back in 1765 and 1766 she had taught herself to forget him. Before many years, she was pouring the treasures of her affections into the hands of another.

CHAPTER II

1765-1773

THE MATCHLESS HONORA

IN 1766 a startlingly handsome and dashing young man entered, with enviable ease, into the social life of Lichfield. He had come to call on Dr. Erasmus Darwin, on a matter of coach construction, and had sent a note in advance stating the probable time of his arrival.

Dr. Darwin had made many experiments in chemistry, physics, and mechanics. One of his hobbies was the construction of coaches and chaises, which were the universal conveyances of the period. His own long rides through the country (for his practice had extended as his skill and fame increased) were rendered less tiresome than they otherwise would have been, by reason of the improvements which he had thought out for the vehicles in which he traveled. He invented a carriage with a high seat, from which he was several times thrown. Mrs. SchimmelPenninck thus describes the Doctor's equipage as she saw it when she was a child at Barr, in Staffordshire:

It was in the latter part of the morning that a carriage drove up to our door, of that description then called a "Sulky," because calculated to hold one person only. The carriage was worn, and bespattered with mud. Lashed on the place appropriated to the boot in ordinary carriages, was a large pail for the purpose of watering the horses, together with some hay and oats beside it. In the top of

the carriage was a sky-light, with an awning that could at pleasure
be drawn over; this was for the purpose of giving light to the
Doctor, who wrote most of his works on scraps of paper with a pencil
as he travelled.

The front of the carriage within was occupied by a receptacle
for writing-paper and pencils, likewise for a knife, fork, and spoon;
on one side was a large pile of books reaching from the floor to
nearly the front window of the carriage; on the other a hamper containing fruit and sweetmeats, cream, and sugar, great parts of which,
however, were demolished during the time the carriage traversed the
forty miles which separated Derby[1] from Barr.[2]

It was the initial stages, at least, of the ingenuity here
displayed, which drew the handsome young stranger
to Lichfield after he had dispatched a noncommittal
letter requesting an interview with the Doctor. When
he presented himself at the house of Dr. Darwin, Mrs.
Darwin explained that, though the Doctor expected
him, he was away at the moment. She invited him to
stay to tea, and he made himself agreeable, talking of
books and other general topics. The Doctor still delay-
ing, after darkness came on, the stranger was asked to
stay for supper. When the meal was nearly finished, a
loud rapping and uproar announced the arrival of the
Doctor. Some men who were with him carried in a
man, apparently dead. The Doctor had found him lying
in a ditch. Candles were brought. The seemingly dead
man was found to be merely intoxicated. To the con-
sternation of all, he turned out to be Mrs. Darwin's
brother! For the first time in his life, so the caller was
assured, the young man had taken a drop too much.

1. Dr. Darwin removed to Derby in 1781.
2. *Life of Mary Anne SchimmelPenninck,* edited by her relation,
Christiana C. Hankin, I, 151.

After the miscreant had been put to bed, the Doctor and his guest sat down to discuss the construction of coaches. The Doctor very soon discovered that the stranger had received a classical education.

"Why! I thought," said the Doctor, "that you were only a coachmaker!"

"That was the reason," the younger man replied, "that you looked surprised at finding me at supper with Mrs. Darwin."

The strange young gentleman was Richard Lovell Edgeworth, of Edgeworthstown, Ireland—Oxonian and dilettante, though owning to a passion for invention and mechanics.

Prospective heir to Irish estates, he was, for the time being, a gentleman of leisure. On the next evening after his arrival, the Doctor and Mrs. Darwin gave a dinner party for him, to which they invited Nancy Seward and her particular group of friends. Little did Edgeworth and Miss Anna foresee how their wills and wishes were to clash in times to come. Edgeworth, writing his *Memoirs,* many years later, paid tribute to the beauty of Anna Seward,[3] at the same time hinting that she was ready to become enamored of his prospects and attractions; and that she was chagrined at finding him already married. Inasmuch as the fact that he was not a free man was revealed to her on the first evening of their meeting, it seems scarcely likely that her hopes had risen high; and we may attribute Edgeworth's intimations to the vanity with which most men delude

3. *Memoirs of Richard Lovell Edgeworth, Esq.,* I, 72–73.

themselves. He returned, however, with fervor, the glances from her beautiful eyes ("More beautiful eyes I never saw in any human countenance," wrote Robert Southey, forty years later); and made her a compliment on her thick, rich auburn hair. Upon the pages of his memoirs there stands a vivid little picture of the gay young things at the Doctor's dinner table, animated by their own good spirits rather than their host's good wines (for the Doctor was well-nigh a teetotaler), flinging the light jest about, and capping bright retort with repartee.

No jealousy nor hatred dimmed the luster of those hours. Perhaps, if they had been less memorable hours, young Mr. Edgeworth would not have wandered back to Lichfield four or five years later, and marred forever the peace of Anna Seward. He was living at this time at Hare Hatch, in Berkshire, where he had a wife who had been a Miss Elars,[4] and one child, at least, of the amazing troop who were to call him father.[5] After a few days, he flitted out of the Lichfield scene, and returned to his neglected wife, leaving behind him the proverbial host of friends, by whom he was not soon to be forgotten.

Of the next year or two, there is not much to be recorded, except that in 1768, Anna Seward met with an accident[6] in which her knee was injured, so that she

4. Or Elers.
5. The number of Edgeworth's children is variously reported as from eighteen to twenty-two.
6. *Letters.* See Letter to Mrs. Adey, June 5, 1794.

ever afterward walked with a noticeable limp. In the year immediately following her recovery, she seems to have gone about with freedom, and to have delighted in long walks and the strenuous exercise prescribed for her tendency to *embonpoint*. As time went on, her increasing lameness made her walk "with pain and difficulty," and was the cause of a number of falls which restrained her naturally active inclination. At the time which we are now considering, she was able to get about with much the same ease as the unscathed.

THE Sewards were in the habit of making summer visits to the watering places in Derbyshire (Miss Seward retained to the last a firm faith in "waters" as a source of healing); and it was during one of these excursions to Buxton, in 1769, that they formed an acquaintance,[7] which, like that with Edgeworth, was to show momentous consequences in the course of time. They met a smooth-faced, well-favored lad, who was recovering his spirits and readjusting his plans after the loss of a good father. This young man was John André, eighteen-year-old son of a Genevese family not long settled in England. The exact manner in which he met the Sewards is not clear, but the progress of his friendship with the two young women was rapid. He and Anna Seward and Honora Sneyd were soon involved in a triangular romance. John André staked the most on its *dénouement*. He had frankly fallen in love with the youthful ward of the Sewards. Honora herself, frail in

7. *Letters*, III, 260.

health, and too young to know her own mind, accepted the lad's adoration with puzzled serenity, leaving the management of affairs to her mentor. The position of proxy was quite to the taste of the poetic Anna, who dearly loved a romance.

It is hard to visualize the particular charms of the fascinating women of the past, and so we must take Miss Honora's allurements largely on faith. So extravagant are the praises with which she has been characterized, both in body and mind, that one wonders whether to discount them, or merely to conclude that she must have been a phenomenally beautiful and spirited girl and woman.

Most of what we know on the subject of Major André's love for Honora Sneyd is to be found in the *Monody* which Anna Seward wrote at the time of his death, and the notes which she subjoined to the poem in published form. These include three letters written by John André in 1769, when he was back in London, after the summer episode was over. From these sources[8] we gather that "Cher Jean," as he was called among his friends, accompanied the girls and their chaperon to Lichfield, and spent some days with them before returning to London. He speaks in one letter of the first sight of the Cathedral spires, which Honora pointed out, and of the studious gaiety of the trio gathered around the fire in Anna's blue boudoir. A few of his wistful phrases follow:

8. See also Winthrop Sargent, *The Life and Career of Major John André*.

It is seven o'clock—you and Honora, with two or three more select friends, are probably encircling your dressing-room fire-place. What would I not give to enlarge that circle! The idea of a clean hearth and a snug circle round it, formed by a few sincere friends, transports me. . . . Since I can not be there in reality, pray imagine me with you; admit me to your conversations; . . . think how I wish for the blessing of enjoying them! and be persuaded that I take part in all your pleasures, in the dear hope, that ere it be very long, your blazing hearth will burn again for me. Pray keep me a place: . . . let the poker, tongs, or shovel represent me;—But you have Dutch tiles, which are infinitely better;—So let Moses, or Aaron, or Balaam's ass be my representative.

André complains of his unhappy lot in being immured in a countinghouse, when his heart is in Lichfield, and his ambitions are ranging the earth. He takes fantastic vows to make himself a hero in the world, that he may win fame and riches for Honora.

These letters, which are remarkable for so young a man, Miss Seward treasured for many years. They are too long to quote entire, but they show an ambitious young man, deeply enamored, stirred to restlessness in his present situation, and eagerly hoping for some good fortune which may make him eligible as a suitor for the hand of Honora Sneyd.

But letters are only letters; and everyday incidents absorb the mind. Anna and Honora cannot dwell continually on a dejected lad in a countinghouse. Some anxiety is felt and expressed for the health of Honora, who is delicate, and who wavers toward the dreaded "decline," so fatal to the young women of her day. Dr. Darwin is called in, looks wise, recommends a nourishing diet, pats the patient's hand, and departs. Long afterward Anna wrote regarding this illness of Honora:

"She was . . . rescued, but O for what a fate, after two smiling years had fled away!" Routs and tea parties follow one another, as heretofore. An impatient boy in a London office wins only a half-hearted remembrance. Out of sight, he is not completely out of mind, but there are other people to demand and receive attention.

In fact, when the slow winter had been passed, the spring of 1770 brought to Lichfield two newcomers well worthy of notice, not to say of gossip and conjecture. One of these, Mr. Richard Lovell Edgeworth, had previously been a flattered guest in the *salons* of the Close. He had now come into his patrimony, and was an absentee landlord, fleeing the dulness of Edgeworthstown in darkest Ireland. His host and companion was Thomas Day,[9] another Oxonian, foot-loose and well endowed.

Despite their personal occupations (and Day, at least, was engaged upon an enterprise before which most men would quail), the two friends were soon in the thick of the social life of Lichfield. "All of the city and its vicinity," says Miss Seward, "who comprehended and tasted those powers of mind which take the *higher* range of intellect were delighted to mingle in such associations." To her credit it must be said that wherever two or three or a hundred were gathered together for the exercise of the higher powers of the intellect, she was always in the midst of them. Her active mind and cultivated tastes brought her instant recognition in any

9. For an account of Day, see Blackman, *Memoirs of Thomas Day.* See also, J. Keir's small book on *Thomas Day.*

group; and the assurance which conscious merit gave, usually focused upon her the limelight of any such assemblage. This assurance has been called by the hard names of egotism and self-esteem. Possibly there was reason for such comment; but Anna Seward had the personal charm which could win her way in any company, and elicit the adulation of others. While it drew envy and malice as well, the Miss Seward of this time and later had reason to esteem herself more highly than a mere modern survey of her literary works would justify. Times enough since her day, seductive women have been observed queening it in literary groups, when an unprejudiced analysis of their actual performance would show even less claim than Anna Seward's to any sort of supremacy.

In the year 1770 Miss Seward had recovered from the shock of her sister's death, and from whatever grief was attached to her own affairs of the heart. Her zest was keen for social enjoyment and the stimulus of the fine arts. She had read widely, and, moreover, carefully; she could quote with rare facility from the British poets (she had no foreign language); she made music herself in a modest way, and appreciated the best with almost painful intensity; she was well informed on topics of general worth, such as politics and religious preferment; she could converse brilliantly with anyone— except perhaps that old Dictator, Samuel Johnson—were he never so learned and renowned. Though she had published little or nothing, she was known to be a poet, and she could be coaxed into reciting her own verses,

with a fiery vivacity which made them seem better than
they were. So melodious was her voice, and so acute
her perception of *nuances* that she was in constant demand for reading aloud and for declaiming choice bits
of literature in the semipublicity of the best Lichfield
drawing-rooms.

Mr. Edgeworth and Mr. Day fitted neatly into this society, in which Miss Seward was a reigning personage.
They loved books and they loved discussion, and the
pro and *con* of aesthetic and ethical questions. Differing
from each other as the hill differs from the valley, they
were nevertheless agreeable companions and stimulating
opponents in debate. That they valued the social opportunities held out to them, is proved by their quick
grasp of all that was offered. That there was a superlative pleasure in their intimacy with the Cathedral
group was attested by the way in which they looked at
Honora Sneyd.

Honora had now reached her eighteenth year. According to all reports, she was, as we have noted, a most
entrancing creature, of the pure eighteenth-century type,
with more intellect than was deemed actually necessary
for feminine perfection. Both Edgeworth and Day
found her fully as charming as her foster sister by
whom she was usually overpowered.[10]

Edgeworth had a wife and a rapidly increasing family
(his daughter Maria, who was to outshine her father,
was now three years old); hence he must be mute, however fierce his passion. Day, in spite of his experiments

10. *Memoirs of Richard Lovell Edgeworth, Esq.,* I, 107.

tending toward matrimony, could with more reason aspire to winning Honora's heart.

Of Day a volume might be (and has been) written. Nobody ever mentions him without affixing to his name the adjectives "odd," "peculiar," or "eccentric." In her *Notes on the Life of Dr. Darwin,* Anna Seward gives a full account of him, which has furnished the basis for most of the stories of his life.

By the death of his father, Thomas Day was left in the care of his mother in 1749, when he was only a year old. His father had had "a place in the customs," and left ample provision for his family. The mother soon married for the second time. Thomas was sent to the Charter House School, and in his sixteenth year was entered at Corpus Christi College, in Oxford. His stepfather, one Phillips, is described as a carping, disagreeable churl, who made the young man's life miserable by interference and tyranny. "It was Mr. Day's first act, on coming of age, and into possession of his estate," says Miss Seward, "to augment his mother's jointure to four hundred [pounds], and to settle it upon Mr. Phillips during his life. This bounty, to a man who had needlessly mortified and embittered so many years of his own infancy and youth, evinced a very elevated spirit." Truly it did.

Though Day still possessed a sufficient income to enable him to live in leisure (he had £1,200 *per annum*), he employed his means and his mind "more in the service of others than in the pursuit of pleasure for himself." He was nothing if not generous, and his alert humaneness extended not only to the poor in any region where he happened to be, but to animals as well—then even less regarded than in the present age. When he appeared in Lichfield in the summer of 1770, Day was about twenty-three years of age. He had made the acquaintance of Edgeworth at Hare Hatch, and was, like him, attracted to Lichfield by the repute of Dr. Darwin in the field of physical science. He was in many ways the exact opposite of Edgeworth. He was tall and awkward, though not lacking in dignity. He wore simple and unostentatious clothes, and did not powder his hair. He was, says Miss Seward, "less graceful, less amusing, less brilliant" than Mr. Edgeworth, but "more highly imaginative, more classical, and a deeper reasoner." "Strict integrity, energetic friendship, open-handed bounty, sedulous and diffusive charity greatly over balanced, on the side of virtue, the tincture of misanthropic gloom and proud contempt of common-life society that marked the peculiar character [of Mr. Day]."

Before his advent in Lichfield, he had engaged in a curious experiment, which is the chief reason for dubbing him one of the oddities of the earth. His feelings had been wounded by some frivolous girl; and in a fit of pique he had resolved to train up a wife after his own taste, so that she might in all ways be suited to his choice. He went about this task in a systematic and businesslike manner.

He had a friend somewhat older than himself, named Bicknel (or Bicknell), a lawyer with a good practice, a

man of (at that time) unblemished reputation. With
Bicknel's help, Day procured affidavits of his moral
rectitude; and then the two repaired to Shrewsbury,
where, from a foundling hospital, they selected an attractive girl, twelve years of age. From the Foundling
Hospital in London they selected another. One, Mr.
Day named Sabrina; the other he called Lucretia. The
conditions on which they were handed over to him
were these: Mr. Day must within a year give one over
to the protection of some chaste tradeswoman, paying
one hundred pounds to bind the girl as an apprentice.
Upon her marriage, or in the event of her beginning
business for herself, he was to transfer to her the sum
of four hundred pounds more, a very considerable sum
in those days. The other girl, whom he was to retain
under his own charge, was to be bred up as his future
wife. He solemnly swore to treat her with the utmost
respect, and give her unexceptionable care and culture.
In case he ultimately decided not to marry her, he
promised to pay for her lodging with some good family,
and endow her with £500 as a marriage portion. Upon
the signing of these agreements, he immediately removed his *protegées* from the foundling asylums and
took them with him to France.

Thus did the trusting youth, not much out of his
teens, undertake one of the most hazardous of adven-
tures, the upbringing of two young damsels, both un-
restrained in temper, and each, as it presently appeared,
violently jealous of the other. Poor Mr. Day! His life
became one tempestuous attempt to reconcile the pas-

sions of the two wicked little jades, who "quarreled and fought incessantly," pestering him with whims and japes, unreasonable demands, and outrageous hand-to-hand combats. To crown all, they came down with smallpox, and "chained him to their bedside by crying and screaming, if they were left a moment with any person who could not speak to them in English. . . . He was obliged to sit up with them many nights; to perform for them the lowest offices of assistance." Thus Miss Seward.

When they recovered, he was relieved to note that their beauty had not suffered diminution. He took them on a trip which necessitated crossing the Rhône River in a boat. The boat overturned, and he saved the girls at great peril to himself, not without regretting, perhaps, that his conscience would not let them drown. In eight months he came back with them to England. Sabrina, the auburn-haired, had proved herself the less objectionable. He therefore apprenticed Lucretia to a milliner. She behaved with propriety, and eventually married "a respectable linen-draper" in London. Sabrina lived for a time in the house of Mr. Bicknel's mother, in a country village, while Day looked after his neglected business affairs. In the notable summer of 1770, he leased a house in Lichfield, which Edgeworth later took over for his wife and family. Here Mr. Day established himself with the fair Sabrina, then thirteen years old, and resumed the task of making her a model of feminine deportment. It is said that he dropped hot sealing wax on her arms to inure her to pain, and fired blank cartridges at her petticoats to train her in self-control.[11] These tales seem improbable, considering the humane spirit which Day exhibited in other circumstances.

Sabrina showed no disposition to study, nor to apply herself to the investigation of the sciences; but maintained a lamentable indifference to the serious side of life. In other words, she remained provokingly young and feminine. In vain did the philosophic Mr. Day point out to her the importance of being earnest, and the moral advantage of directing her mental powers to the problems of the universe. Sabrina refused to be interested in problems. Adhering to a fixed principle, Mr. Day scorned the unworthy incentives of prizes or luxuries or privileges. He relied on argument alone, and the motive of pleasing a mentor who was to the girl an inscrutable mystery, since she knew nothing of his object or intentions.

For many months, while he kept her at Lichfield, Mr. Day strove to bend the twig in the way in which he opined it should lean. It was a perverse and obstinate twig, straying in the direction toward which no tree should be inclined. The hours given up to the education of his ward did not consume every hour of the

11. Miss de Luc, daughter of a Swiss gentleman who was reader to Queen Charlotte, told these stories to Mary Anne SchimmelPenninck, *née* Galton, in 1784 or thereabouts. Miss de Luc boarded with the family that harbored Sabrina Sidney, the *protegée* of Mr. Day, before her marriage to Mr. Bicknel. At this time, Mrs. SchimmelPenninck's parents, the Galtons, lived at The Five Ways, near Birmingham. See the *Life of Mary Anne SchimmelPenninck*, I, 12.

twenty-four, and Mr. Day was able to devote a suitable amount of time to society. So pleasing were he and his more sprightly companion, Mr. Edgeworth, that they were soon involved in most of the social events of Miss Seward's and Dr. Darwin's set.

Now Mr. Day, being admitted into the best society of Lichfield, had met, not once, but many times, the alluring Miss Honora Sneyd, then living with the Sewards. It is not unlikely that his acquaintance with Miss Sneyd had some relation to his dissatisfaction with Sabrina. Although he had repeatedly declared his hatred of social life and his contempt for society women, Mr. Day was lost in admiration for Miss Sneyd, overlooking the fact that she was a butterfly of leisure. It must, however, be said in her favor that she lacked nothing of intellect or liberal culture, having absorbed this latter element without pain in the Seward household.

Day stayed on in Lichfield during the year 1770, occupied with his unlucky experiment, but happy in his friendship with the family of Canon Seward. There is little to record of a specific nature at this time, in the life of Anna Seward, except that her friend Mrs. Darwin died in spite of the ministrations of her learned consort.

Mrs. Darwin was a refined and delicate woman, warmly liked by her husband's friends and willing to promote the hospitality which he enjoyed showing alike to neighbors and to strangers. But she was not strong, and, as Miss Seward says, "the frequency of her maternal situation" resulted in a permanent loss of health. For thirteen years Dr. Darwin assuaged her sufferings, and retained her devoted affection. In her last days, she said to "two female friends" (Miss Seward presumably being one), "Married to any other man, I do not suppose I should have lived a third part of those years which I have passed with Dr. Darwin; he has prolonged my days and he has blessed them." She died "passionately regretted," as Miss Seward wrote, "by the selected few whom she honored with her personal and confidential friendship."

At Christmas time Edgeworth was back again for a fortnight's visit with Day. In his own words: "In the year 1770, I spent some time at Christmas with my friend Mr. Day, at Stow-Hill. We went every day to Lichfield, and most days to the palace, where the agreeable conversation of the whole family, and in particular the sprightliness and literary talents of Miss Seward, engaged us to pass many agreeable hours."[12]

Another and younger admirer of Honora was in Lichfield, too: John André, released for a space from his countinghouse, and privileged to pass the holiday season with the friends whom he most loved. "Whilst I was upon this visit," says Edgeworth, "Mr. André, afterwards Major André, who lost his life so unfortunately in America, came to Lichfield. . . . The first time I saw Major André at the palace, I did not perceive from his manner, or from that of the young lady [Honora Sneyd] that any attachment subsisted between

12. *Memoirs of Richard Lovell Edgeworth, Esq.*, I, 107.

them. On the contrary, from the great attention which Miss Seward paid to him, and from the constant admiration which Mr. André bestowed on her, I thought that, though there was a considerable disproportion in their ages,[13] there might exist some courtship between them. Miss Seward, however, undeceived me. I never met Mr. André again."

Slowly the webs of fate were being woven. Among this little band of revelers, with their charades, and their dancing, and their music (for there was always John Saville), strange complications were being knotted, and destinies were being interlaced.

Anna Seward, watching her beloved Honora with the jealous eyes of long possession, felt a coldness at her heart when she beheld the motives, but ill concealed, in the souls of the three men. Honora was her darling (sister, husband, and child combined), and it was torture to think of what her loss might mean. To one only could she bear the thought of relinquishing Honora, and that was the one palpably designed for such a tender maid. To whom should she belong, but to "Cher Jean," the young knight, ambitious, high-minded, and passionately in love?

Honora's emotions seem to have been of the quiescent sort, and it is difficult to say how much she cared for John André. Her relatives, however, were decided in their opposition. The young man was poor and portionless. It was clear that Honora, with all her charms, could do better than to fix her choice upon a man whose

13. Anna Seward was twenty-eight at this time.

worldly prospects were so entirely hypothetical. She
herself was obedient to authority, and apparently made
no struggle to win the approval of her father for the
youthful London clerk. Miss Seward in her "Monody
on Major André" thus analyzes the situation:

> Oh, when such pairs their kindred spirit find,
> When sense and virtue deck each spotless mind,
> Hard is the doom that shall the union break,
> And fate's dark billow rises o'er the wreck.
> Now Prudence, in her cold and thrifty care,
> Frowned on the maid and bade the youth despair;
> For power parental sternly saw, and strove
> To tear the lily bands of plighted love;
> Nor strove in vain;—but while the fair-one's sighs
> Disperse like April-storms in sunny skies,
> The firmer lover, with unswerving truth,
> To his first passion consecrates his youth.

The Christmas season, with all its brisk succession of
festivities, saw the dramatic rise and fall of hopes and
the succession of yearnings and anxieties. Presently, the
principals in the drama drew apart, and life went on as
usual in the sober precincts of the Cathedral Close.

In 1771 Mr. Sneyd, who had now reëstablished his
home (he was three times married), recalled his daughter Honora from the Seward protection. Perhaps he
feared the influence of Anna when the choice of a bridegroom must be made. Perhaps he was merely concerned
about Honora's health, which was precarious. At any
rate she was, willingly or not, ensconced under her
father's roof, after fourteen years in the Seward household. This altered circumstance, though it did not involve actual parting, was full of pain for Anna Seward,

who had clutched and held the young girl's love, and would not let it go. These are her own words on the subject of Honora's departure: "The charms of [Honora's] society, when her advancing youth gave equality to our connection, made Lichfield an Edenic scene to me, from the year 1766 to 1771. Her father then recalled her to his own family, after having been fourteen years resident in ours. The domestic separation proved very grievous; but still she was in the same town; we were often together, and her heart was unchanged."[14]

Discouraged, but not hopeless, John André had returned to his work in London, and continued to make progress, not only with his figures, but with his reading, writing, and drawing. In March, 1771, he suddenly left his dreary countinghouse, and secured a commission in the army. Such a step may have indicated despair of the happy outcome of his suit, or simply the hope of winning in some quick fashion the wealth and glory which he coveted for Honora's sake. He had begun the course which was to lead to a most harrowing tragedy when, involved with a traitor, he was to suffer ignominious death.

John André thus disposed of, Mr. Day (in 1771) began to cherish hopes of his own success in wooing. He was not without rivals. It appears that there were several. Lord Warwick, then Lord Greville, is mentioned[15] as an admirer of Miss Sneyd, but he seems to have made

14. *Letters*, IV, 217.
15. *Ibid.*, p. 95.

no advances toward marriage. Colonel Barry of Worcester, who in later years succeeded Major André as Adjutant General to the Armies in America, told Anna Seward about 1785 that Honora Sneyd was the only woman he ever loved, "that he never beheld a being in whom the blended charms of mind and person, could approach the lustre of those which glowed in the air, the look, the smile, the glance, and the eloquence of Honora Sneyd."[16]

Richard Lovell Edgeworth, who was himself (though married) in love with Miss Sneyd, gives this account[17] of the acts and attitudes of his friend Day: "During the early part of the year, 1771, Mr. Day's intentions with regard to Sabrina began to change, for his mind turned towards Miss Honora Sneyd. He learned from her friend [Miss Seward], that this lady had no engagement or attachment that could prevent his success, if he could convince her, that the views of life, and the plan of happiness in marriage, which he laid down, could be made compatible with those, which she had determined to pursue. Few courtships ever began between such young people with so little appearance of romance; both however were perfectly sincere and in earnest, and for many months they were asked together to every party at Lichfield, and were allowed, by a kind of tacit consent, to converse with each other, to have every reasonable opportunity of becoming acquainted with each other's tempers, tastes, and dispositions."

16. *Ibid.,* I, 390.
17. *Memoirs of Richard Lovell Edgeworth, Esq.,* I, 110.

Perfect amity continued between Day and Edgeworth, and perfect frankness as to the sentiments of
both. Day pointed out to Edgeworth "the folly and
meanness of indulging a hopeless passion for any
woman, let her merit be what it might; declaring, at
the same time, that he never would marry so as to
divide himself from his chosen friend." Edgeworth assured Mr. Day that no obstacles would be put in the
way of his winning Miss Sneyd if he could do so.

Day wrote Honora an appallingly long letter, asking
her to marry him, expounding his idea of the life they
should lead together, and insisting that it would be wise
for them to retire from the world. He requested Edgeworth to deliver this letter. Edgeworth says, "I delivered
it with real satisfaction to Honora." She told him to
come the next day for an answer. "Mr. Day experienced
extreme anxiety during the interval." In the morning
Miss Sneyd's answer was handed to Mr. Day. Edgeworth left him alone to peruse it. "When I returned,"
says Edgeworth, "I found him actually in a fever." Miss
Sneyd had, after due deliberation, rejected his philosophic hand. She could not, she said, "admit the unqualified control of a husband over all her actions; she
did not feel that seclusion from society was indispen-
sably necessary to preserve female virtue, or to secure
domestic happiness." Day was ill for some days after
the shock of his rejection. He was confined to his bed,
and Dr. Darwin bled and blistered him according to
medical custom. His self-esteem, the rallyings of the
gruff Doctor, and the friendly consolations of Edge-

worth, assisted him to regain some degree of his usual poise. Half in pique and half in resignation, he turned his attention to Honora's sister Elizabeth, who had now come to live with her father, after spending a number of years with her relatives, Mr. and Mrs. Henry Powys of Shrewsbury. Elizabeth Sneyd was thought by some people to be even handsomer than Honora. "Her eyes," Edgeworth says, "were uncommonly beautiful and expressive. . . . She had more of what is called the manners of a person of fashion, had more wit, more vivacity, and certainly more humour than her sister. She had, however, less personal grace."

Elizabeth did not immediately reject the advances of Mr. Day. She gave him hope. He packed off the tormented Sabrina to a boarding school; and since she soon drops out of the story, we may as well follow her career to the end. She stayed in school three years, becoming "elegant and amiable." After leaving school, she boarded for some years near Birmingham, subsisting on the fifty pounds which her guardian allowed her annually. Often the guest of Dr. Darwin and other Lichfield people, she was liked and approved wherever she went. In her twenty-sixth year, she was won in marriage by—whom do you suppose? Why, the very Mr. Bicknel who had been the accomplice (shall we say?) of Mr. Day in lifting her from the scanty comforts and graces of the orphanage, and giving her the means of bettering herself in life. She married Mr. Bicknel, we repeat, with the somewhat ungracious consent of her guardian, from whom she received the £500 promised

in the document which released her from the orphanage. Though she married Mr. Bicknel "for prudential
reasons," she seems to have been reasonably happy. She
gave him two sons. When the eldest was about five
years old, the father died suddenly, leaving the widow
with limited means. Some disclosures, we may say
parenthetically, of his early irregularities were made
after his death; whereupon Miss Seward, lapsing a
little from her rôle of perfect lady, cried out, "Lord!
what a pale maidenish looking animal for a volup-
tuary!—so reserved as were his manners!—and his
countenance!—a very tablet upon which the ten com-
mandments seemed written!"[18] Her suggestions in a
letter to George Hardinge, an eminent jurist, resulted
in his collecting the sum of £800 from Bicknel's fellow
lawyers, which sum was turned over to the widow. Mr.
Day allowed her £30 a year, which seems a slender
stipend enough. Miss Seward thought it so, and criticized Day severely for his parsimony.[19]

In the winter of 1788–89, "sweet" Mrs. Bicknel was in
Lichfield, visiting Mr. Saville's daughter, Mrs. Smith,
and was described by Miss Seward as "more graceful,
more attractive, and more eloquent than ever, though
less beautiful." In later life, she was housekeeper and
assistant to Dr. Charles Burney, in his academy at
Greenwich, where she took her place as a gentlewoman
and not as a servant. Thus Sabrina Sidney vanishes
from the scene, esteemed and provided for in a manner
which few lone orphans can expect. Though she failed

18. *Letters*, II, 250.   19. *Ibid.*, p. 195.

to win the honor of becoming the wife of Thomas Day, she did not do so badly in the world as might have been prophesied of one who so lightly resigned the privilege.

Once her shadow struck across the Lichfield lady's path.

After the publication of her *Life of Dr. Darwin,* in 1804, Miss Seward was much annoyed at receiving an "abusive" letter from the son of Sabrina, Mrs. Bicknel. He showed extreme resentment at the freedom with which Miss Seward had discussed his mother's affairs. "His foolish pride," says the poetess in a letter to Dr. Whalley[20] (January 22, 1805), "is stung by the publicity of circumstances concerning his mother's singular story, which cast no shade of reflection upon her in any respect, viz. her being originally a foundling child, and having been left in straitened circumstances, and a subscription having been raised for her. Surely she appears in a very amiable light from my representation, and for that glowing testimony to her merit, this is my reward. Every circumstance, except that subscription, I know to be exactly, and without a shadow of exaggeration, given in the memoirs. Mr. George Hardinge (now Judge Hardinge) informed me by letter of that subscription and its amount. If he was inaccurate, the fault is not mine. The abusive letter states no particular complaint, but avers that all the anecdotes of the author's mother are falsehoods, and that as such he

20. *Journals and Correspondence of Thomas Sedgewick Whalley, D.D., of Mendip Lodge, Somerset,* ed. Rev. Hill Wickham, M.A., 1863, II, 263.

shall publicly brand them. If he does, I must publicly defend my own truth, by calling upon several credible witnesses who are yet living, and who knew all the circumstances I have stated to be true. Mrs. Bicknel well knows that they are all unvarnished facts. If she has sanctioned this dark, malicious, and lying scroll, the virtues which I believed she possessed, and with which my memoirs have invested her, could not have been genuine. This ungrateful accusation has hurt me more then it ought."

AFTER lingering for a while at Lichfield, in the house which had served for him and Mr. Day, Edgeworth left his wife and children with the Elars family at Black-Bourton, and went to France, where he stayed for two years. This voluntary exile does him credit, since his now firmly settled love for Honora Sneyd was both hopeless and forbidden. He says in his *Memoirs* that he had definitely fallen in love with Honora during the Christmas holidays of 1770. "I had long suffered much," he writes, "from the want of that cheerfulness in a wife, without which marriage could not be agreeable to a man of such a temper as mine. I had borne this evil, I believe, with patience; but my not being happy at home exposed me to the danger of being too happy elsewhere."[21] "I knew," he adds on another page, "that there is but one certain method of escaping such dangers—*flight.*"

Being a man of honor, as his withdrawal from the

21. *Memoirs of Richard Lovell Edgeworth, Esq.*, I, 123.

scene in Lichfield shows, Edgeworth doubtless desired to control his thoughts as well as his actions, and make the best of his bad bargain. We are left to conjecture what may have been the feelings of the unloved wife. She came over to France, and stayed for some months at Lyons, where Edgeworth was engaged in some engineering work. Mr. Day was with the Edgeworths at Lyons, and interested himself in the education of the young son of the family, applying his favorite theories, culled from the works of Rousseau.

Elizabeth Sneyd had not been so summary as her sister in her dismissal of Day's affections. She intimated that she *might* learn to love her suitor if he would soften the ruggedness of his appearance and demeanor, and adapt himself to the usages of society. Acquiescent to her demands, he went to France, where he essayed to master the mysteries of dancing, fencing, elegant dress, and the deportment of the parlor and the ballroom. He applied himself vigorously to his scheme for improvement. He put himself into the hands of experts, who took his money, inflicted tortures upon him, and left him much as he was before, in reality, though changed in outward semblance. He returned to England in the autumn of 1772, accompanied by Mrs. Edgeworth and her sister. Day was in fine feather. He was richly dressed, and caused amazement among his acquaintances by making prodigious bows, twirling a sword, and footing it in the minuet and the cotillion.

Alas! the fickle Elizabeth only giggled behind her fan. Her friends remarked openly that Mr. Day had merely made himself ridiculous by aping the fashionable world. Elizabeth, in short, rejected him after all his hard endeavors to transform himself for her approval. It seemed as if the ill-starred Mr. Day were doomed to remain a bachelor.

Anna Seward, a spectator of the comedy, and, we may be sure, a critic and commentator as well as an observer, had not changed her place or manner of living, as Honora and Day and Edgeworth and André had done. She had stayed sedately at home, or had taken short journeys to provincial towns to visit friends and relatives; she had probably gone up to London for a sojourn or two—how many we do not know, but enough to put her in touch with what was going on in the musical, dramatic, and literary world. For the most part her days had been uneventful; yet they were satisfying, with their round of parties, their spaces of reading and writing, and their hours of exquisite music made by John Saville.

It seemed as if things might go on indefinitely as they were. Then, early in 1773, news came, presaging other changes. Mrs. Richard Lovell Edgeworth had died after the birth of a child, and the discontented husband was free again. He hurried back to England, and was met at Woodstock by his faithful friend Day. "The first words he said to me," wrote Edgeworth in his *Memoirs,* "were, 'have you heard anything of Honora Sneyd?'"

Edgeworth had held heroically to his resolve "never to keep up the slightest intercourse with her, by letter, message, or inquiry." He asked eager questions and re-

ceived encouraging answers. Miss Sneyd was still un-
engaged, and apparently uninvolved in any affair of
the heart. Edgeworth went at once to Lichfield, and to
Dr. Darwin's house. The Doctor's sister, who kept his
house, invited Edgeworth to go to a tea party at Mr.
Sneyd's, whither she herself was bound. Edgeworth
went, and met again his adored Honora, who appeared
to him more lovely than when he had seen her last. No
doubt she knew what the cheerful widower would do;
probably, in secret, she knew what she would say.
Sewards and Sneyds and Darwins and Savilles, who
had watched the little dramas being played within the
Bishop's Palace, would have been more than human if
they had not been moved to speculate and prophesy.
They had not long to wait. Edgeworth lost no time in
pretended mourning. He brooked no hypocritical delay. On July 17, 1773, five months after the death of
his wife, he was married to Honora Sneyd in the Ladies'
Choir of the Cathedral. Honora may have given a
thought to her recently dead predecessor; but if she did,
she kept her meditation to herself. Women can be
strangely callous.

Mr. Seward performed the ceremony. "The good old
man," says Edgeworth, "shed tears of joy, while he
pronounced the nuptial benediction." "Mrs. Seward
showed every possible mark of tenderness and affection." Edgeworth adds airily that though Anna Seward
was dissatisfied about a bridesmaid, he believed she was
really glad to see Honora united to a man "suited to her
taste and disposition." This statement glosses over a

disagreeable situation. Anna Seward states distinctly
that Honora was forever alienated from her foster sister,
from or before the time of her wedding. Anna Seward
had fastened her affections on the child Honora with
passionate attachment. She had trained up the little girl
with devoted care, had instructed her in the arts of
needlework and music, and had inculcated in her a
taste for good reading. She had made her a constant and
intimate companion, and had given her the benefit of
her own social prestige. In more than sisterly fashion,
she had centered her hopes and ambitions upon the
growing Honora. That she should have felt the pangs
of separation upon the marriage of the younger girl is
not unnatural. But her poems and letters reveal a degree of grief and misery which is accounted for only
by a sense of total estrangement and loss.

The indications are that jealousy between Miss
Seward and Edgeworth harassed Honora so painfully
that she was in the end compelled to choose between
friend and husband. One of Miss Seward's sonnets,
written as early as April, 1773, shows signs of the break.
A half-dozen sonnets written in July (the month of the
marriage) are gloomy with forebodings. One of these
begins:

> Ingratitude, how deadly is thy smart
> Proceeding from the form we fondly love!

Other passages written during the same month are of
the same nature:

> Chilled by unkind Honora's altered eye,
> Why droops my heart with fruitless woe,
> Thankless for so much good?

And:

> Affection is repaid by causeless hate!
> A plighted love is changed to cold disdain!
> But turn, my heart, to blessings which remain;
> And let this truth the wise resolve create:
> *The heart estranged no anguish can regain.*

During this year (1773) Anna Seward undoubtedly passed through a period of peculiar anguish, which ever after left its mark. It is not easy to analyze her emotions. Did she perhaps desire to marry Edgeworth herself? She was thirty years old—better suited[22] to him in age and experience than Honora. Was she jealous of the easy success of her foster sister? Would she have snatched away, if she could have done so, the mature yet youthful bridegroom, so providentially released from his ten years' bondage?

From the study of her letters and poems, the inference must be that her desire for marriage with Edgeworth, if it existed, was well suppressed. She believed, or professed to believe, that her suffering was caused only by the loss of her heart's darling; by the separation, both material and spiritual, which must ensue; and by her conviction that Edgeworth would make his wife supremely miserable. She fought the marriage with all the force she dared to use, and estranged herself forever from the bride. She never ceased, to her last

22. Edgeworth was born in 1744.

day, to deplore it as the ruin of Honora's life, and her own tragic and irreplaceable bereavement.

Years after, still mourning for her lost angel, she wrote of this year and its successors: "The established habits of my life were broken, and the native gaiety of my spirit eternally eclipsed, however time might restore constitutional cheerfulness. . . . No sprightly parties did I promote, or when I could help it, join, through the years 1773–4–5–6." In that summer of 1773 Anna Seward went down into the dark valley of grief, and never fully recovered from what she suffered there. Whether jealousy mingled with her sorrow, it is not possible to say; but there were surely resentment and self-pity, and the sharp sting of benefits forgot.

Honora Sneyd was, after all, no real sister; and even if she had been, giving her up to a promising marriage need cause no such ecstasies of pain. But the mere losing of Honora was not all. There was the added pang of counsels neglected, of love discarded, seemingly without regret, of ingratitude flaunted after years of unswerving devotion. Then there were the actual or fancied comments of the lookers-on, some of them maliciously pleased to see the Queen brought low, or gratified to see a foolish passion baffled. There was shame at being so poor a judge of human nature as to believe a love eternal, which could so easily be killed. There may have been (but this is not likely) the secret torment of disappointed hopes at seeing so eligible a bridegroom captured by a younger woman. Many emotions must surely have contributed to the furious hatred which

Anna Seward ever after expressed for Edgeworth, and the mingled fondness and spite with which she viewed the future fortunes of Honora.

In 1791 she was startled by seeing Edgeworth and his wife glide past in a phaeton close to her chaise, in the environs of the city of Worcester. If she had started earlier, she would have met them at the Hop Pole Inn. "I have had a great escape," she wrote, "for I know not how I should have stood the shock of being addressed by him."[23] She characterized him at this time as "the specious, the false, the cruel, the murderous Edgeworth, who cankered first and then crushed to earth, the finest of human flowers." These words are a direct refutation of Edgeworth's genial remarks to the effect that he and Miss Seward had always, in spite of trifling disagreements, remained on the most friendly terms.

23. *Journals and Correspondence of Thomas Sedgewick Whalley, D.D., of Mendip Lodge, Somerset,* ed. Rev. Hill Wickham, II, 56.

CHAPTER III

1773–1780

BEAUTY THAT PERISHES

IN writing of a person's life, it is easy to pass over a
period of seven years with a few paragraphs, but
the living of seven years on the part of an emotional
and sensitive woman is another matter. The space of
time from 1773 to 1780 was a definitely outlined era in
Anna Seward's career. It was begun in suffering and in
double measure of misery it was concluded.

The old busy life of the provincial town was taken up
again, but without the ardor of the days when Honora
shared the minutest happening and the smallest pleasure. The hour unvaryingly devoted to the harpsichord
was not remitted; neither was the endless turning over
of books. Whether John Saville was Anna's teacher of
music is uncertain. He probably was; and he was
assuredly her companion in the reading and discussing
of books in the garden overlooking the Stow, or around
the hearth in the blue boudoir.

Poems Nancy wrote and amended and laid away.
They were somber poems, with a touch of bitterness
here and there. She accepted the usual round of visits
and parties, when they could not be avoided. Very likely
she grew to delight in them again, if memories were
not too poignantly aroused. She saw something of the
distinguished visitors to Lichfield, among them Dr.

Johnson and his voluble friend Boswell.[1] She made journeys to London and to less diverting towns. She interested herself in politics. In the war with America, her sympathies were with the Colonies, and she never ceased to cast reproaches on an insensate ministry who drove them to the fury of rebellion.

Lichfield was the same, and yet with Honora gone, it was different. Dr. Darwin still flourished, though his sister had now taken the place of the lost wife in his household. He had "three fine boys, talented and obedient," says Miss Seward. They grew up to cause him both comfort and grief. During his married years, the Doctor had been laboring hard at his immense practice, which took him to all the adjoining regions; and had diverted himself with scientific experiments and theories, with occasional poetic attempts, and with the highly congenial social life of which we have spoken.

In 1771 he had begun his *Zoönomia,* a scientific prose work, which was added to and corrected for many years, and not published till 1794. Miss Seward describes the *Zoönomia* as "an exhaustless repository of interesting facts, of curious experiments in natural productions, and in medical effects; a vast and complicated scheme of disquisition, incalculably important to the health and comforts of mankind, so far as they relate to objects merely terrestrial; throwing novel, useful, and beautiful light on the secrets of physiology, botanical, chemical, and aerological." Whether this repository would now be considered "incalculably important" is doubtful; but

1. She met Boswell at her own home in 1776.

like so many records of the investigations of the period, it helped to form the foundations of modern physical science. Conceivably it was the starting point and inspiration of the work of the Doctor's celebrated grandson, Charles R. Darwin, in his scientific researches. It is to be noted that Miss Seward in her characterization of the *Zoönomia* is careful to insert the words, "so far as they relate to objects merely terrestrial." This is her deprecation of the great Doctor's irreligious attitude toward man and the universe. In this connection one of the Doctor's commentators aptly says of him "he dwelt so long on second causes that he seemed to forget that there is a *first.*"

Though begun fairly early in the Doctor's professional career, the *Zoönomia* had to wait for publication till after the more frivolous and consequently more popular *Botanic Garden* had made its appearance. Miss Seward gives a detailed account of the genesis of this long poetical rigmarole which brought its author enviable amounts of praise and hard practical cash.

About the year 1777, she tells us, Dr. Darwin purchased "a little wild umbrageous valley," a mile from Lichfield. This little dell was wet and swampy from springs, which encouraged a multitude of aquatic plants. The Doctor took steps to improve this sequestered place, widening the lake, and guiding the brook into curved channels. He planted many botanical specimens, partly for their beauty and partly for their use in making experiments in embryonic development and pollination. He would not permit Miss Seward to

see this delightful nook until he had put it into the best
possible order, and beautified it with his most cunning
art.

At last the day came on which she was to have her
first glimpse of the little Eden. Then the Doctor, who
was to accompany her in this long-desired visit, was
called away. Anna, alone in the cool, silent, flowery
plantation, was moved to poetic expression. She took
pencil and paper (which she usually had at hand) and
wrote:

> O, come not here, ye Proud, whose breasts infold
> Th'insatiate wish of glory or of gold;
> O come not ye, whose branded foreheads wear
> Th'eternal frown of envy or of care.

The poem extended itself to something like seventy
lines, a panegyric in which the charms of the Doctor's
botanic garden were amply praised. Dr. Darwin approved the poem, as its author had approved his garden. "I shall send it to the periodical publications," said
he; "but it ought to form the exordium of a great
work." He outlined then and there this visionary great
work, which was to propound, in magnificent detail,
the complete Linnaean system. Miss Seward blushingly
remarked that the projected poem was "not strictly
proper for a female pen." The Doctor, having no such
modest scruples, responded that he would write it,
except for the fear that being known as a poet would
injure his reputation as a doctor.

Someone (probably Mr. Stevens of Repton) sent Miss
Seward's poem to the *Gentleman's Magazine,* where it

was printed in 1783 though in changed form. Dr. Darwin had altered the ending, putting in eight lines of his own. Shortly after this episode of the garden and the verses, he began his "great work," *The Botanic Garden,* which was to bring him glory enough. He used Miss Seward's lines as an exordium to the first part of his enormously long poem; though this first part was not published till some years after the second part had appeared and won the extravagant applause which now seems so inexplicable. The Doctor did not acknowledge this high-handed borrowing of the lady's verses. His oversight seems disingenuous, to say the least. The rights of women to recognition for their personal achievements were somewhat misty to the gentlemen of the period.

Now we find the Doctor hard at work (in the intervals of professional cares), writing away at his somewhat appalling compositions, the *Zoönomia,* and *The Botanic Garden.* The latter was to consist of two parts: one scientific—*The Economy of Vegetation;* the other imaginative and amatory—*The Loves of the Plants.* To the jogging of his horses, perhaps, he measured the rhythm of his verse; since the greater part of the long poems was composed within his chaise.

HAVING accounted for the Doctor and indicated the strictly literary nature of his association with Miss Seward, we may take time here to follow the fortunes of Mr. Day, whose solid friendship for Richard Lovell Edgeworth had not been shaken by the sight of that gay gentleman carrying off the prize of prizes, Miss Honora Sneyd, and immuring her in his Irish fastnesses.

It is a pleasure to know that Mr. Day did not go unrewarded; though he had to wait, like Jacob, for seven years. He went to London, and mingling there with the sort of people whom he professed to despise (the devotees of fashion and frivolity), he met Miss Esther Milnes of Yorkshire, whose virtues had been reported to him by Dr. Small. She gave plain evidence of regarding him with favor. Sighing, he succumbed to her allurements. These consisted of good looks, a trained mind, and a fortune of twenty-three thousand pounds. He asked her if she would renounce the world for him, and live in real retirement, giving up her energies and her riches to benevolence. She would. The cautious Mr. Day, however, with a modern spirit truly surprising, insisted that her fortune be kept in her own name, and that she consider herself free to leave him whenever she tired of the simple life. They were married in 1778, and went to live at Stapleford Abbots, in Essex. Later they removed to Anningsley, in Surrey. It was said that Day required his wife to cut herself off from her numerous relatives in the North of England, and keep herself from all entangling alliances in the way of family claims and connections. Wise Mr. Day! How many men might wish for his courage! We can well believe the assertion that his marriage was supremely happy. He never had reason to regret the renunciation of either of his wards; and he was never heard to murmur in the midst of conjugal altercations, "If I had only married Sabrina!" Briefly, there were no altercations.

Although he had no children on whom to try experiments in education, his wife showed herself so amenable to all his theories, and so willing to accede to his demands, that his highest aspirations were fulfilled. They lived without luxuries, denying themselves servants and even a carriage. They gave away a large share of their income, and did all in their power to relieve suffering wherever it came to their knowledge. With his farm, his books, his benevolences, and his writing, Mr. Day led a busy life. He wrote vehemently against the slave trade, which he abhorred. He published a number of pamphlets on subjects arising from the war with America. He argued in print for annual parliaments and equal representation. He gave forth advanced opinions on education. He made himself famous with his book, *Sandford and Merton,* which was brought out in parts between the years 1783 and 1789.

These dates anticipate, of course, the period which we are now considering, which is that extending between 1773 and 1780.

We may now go back to Anna Seward, who had little or no association with Mr. Day, and watched his career from afar.

LIFE was beginning to be somewhat flat when a new zest was given to it by a chance encounter with Lady Miller.[2] This lady was the hostess at the famous Bath-

2. See Ruth A. Hesselgrave, *Lady Miller and the Batheaston Literary Circle* (New Haven: Yale University Press).

Easton poetical contests, then much discussed in the literary circles of England. For some years, she had conducted, with marked social success, the poetry society which lured the bookish and the frivolous alike, since exclusiveness gave a high value to admission. If we may trust the article in the *European Magazine* for April, 1782, it was in 1778 that Anna Seward met Lady Miller. The hostess of the Bath-Easton villa, perceiving the charm, and hearing of the poetical gifts, of the Lichfield woman, urged her to send in some verses for the competitions. The first poem which Miss Seward sent was the *Invocation of the Comic Muse,* which immediately won a prize—a myrtle wreath. It is vaguely reminiscent of Milton's *L'Allegro,* which, as a baby, Anna Seward was taught to lisp:

> On this mirth-devoted day,
> From these festal bowers away,
> In your sable vestments flee,
> Train of sad Melpomene!
> Ye, who midnight horrors dart
> Through the palpitating heart;
> Fear, that flies its shadowy cause,
> With hurried step and startled pause;
> Straw-crowned Phrenzy's glaring gaze,
> Chanting shrill her changing lays:
> Nor let dim-eyed Grief appear,
> Weaving mournful garlands here,
> Cypress-buds, and fading flowers,
> Wet with cold November's showers;
> Nor with the damp, wan brow, and streaming wound,
> Let stern, self-pierc'd Despair her hollow groans resound.

. . . .

Nor let this Delphic Vase[3] alone
Thy all-enlivening influence own;
Exert then still thy magic power
To whiten every passing hour
For him, whose taste decided shines
In the fair Priestess of these shrines;
For her who guides the devious feet
Of Genius to this fair retreat,
Her verdant prize extending there;—
Ah still for them, the generous pair,
Collect thou each idea bright
From Fancy's shrine of missive light;
From Health, from Love, from Virtue's ray,
To gild through life their varied day,
Illume the night, and bless the rising morn,
And with the beams of bliss the golden sun adorn.

It appears that this somewhat incoherent rhapsody
was *sent* to Bath-Easton, when the author was absent.
How many times she was actually present at the contests is only to be surmised. She seems to have met there
a number of people with whom she formed a permanent friendship. She must have found the atmosphere
at Lady Miller's villa consolingly congenial. She was in
the full bloom of her extraordinary beauty, and conscious of unusual powers. All her love affairs had come
to nothing. She was beginning to think that she might
never marry. She was too much of a lady, too much
hampered by her sense of social values, to burst boldly
forth and seek a free channel for her talents as her
friend Helen Williams was to do. Ancestor worship,
that oriental curse of occidental women, constrained her
to yield obedience to a prosy, if amiable, father. He

3. The antique vase from which the poems were drawn to be read
aloud.

wanted to see her white hands engaged upon the needlework at which she was so exquisitely skilful; but it irked him to see her lovely auburn head bent over a book, or bowed above a goose quill and the pages of a poem. Her connection with the Bath-Easton group, ridiculous as they may have been, gave her a new interest in life, and fixed within her the resolve to write, in spite of all opposition.

The diversions at Lady Miller's villa were a welcome change, after the amenities of Lichfield tea parties, where everyone knew everyone else. There were good clothes and good eating, and good talk, to satisfy a fastidious lady's taste. There were new faces, new minds, new inspirations. The social values, too, were unexceptionable. Lady Miller lacked just enough of aristocratic *aplomb* to make her guests feel in a subtle way her superior. Her title covered a multitude of deficiencies. Miss Seward developed rapidly in such an environment. She had been too much with her own people; her every action had been subject to the scrutiny of a Canon Residentiary. At Bath-Easton she let herself go. She reveled in a new sense of freedom, and gave rein to her facility for writing verse. Severe as may be our critical judgment of the result, we may at least congratulate her on having found an outlet for her emotions, and a means of manifesting her individuality.

Again and again she won the myrtle wreath, and received it from Lady Miller's hand, as graciously, no doubt, as it was given. Those who saw her at Bath-Easton and heard her read aloud did not forget her.

They went away and talked about her poems and her beauty and her voice. She was gaining a reputation beyond Bath and beyond Lichfield, and she did not shrink from sending her already-sanctioned verse to the London journals.

THE first piece of Anna Seward's work to attract the attention of the literary world was her *Elegy on Captain Cook*.[4] Capt. James Cook, after his voyages and discoveries, his invasion of the tropics and of the ice fields around the Pole, had been killed by savages in the Hawaiian Islands, in January, 1779. The *Elegy* which Miss Seward wrote on this untimely death, and which was published by Dodsley (price one shilling and sixpence), was received with respect, even in London. It was honored by some little of the grudging praise dispensed by Dr. Johnson, who rarely had a kind word for contemporary poetry, and seldom deigned to favor anything written by a woman. After Miss Seward's death, a rumor was circulated to the effect that Dr. Darwin had rewritten this poem on Captain Cook, and that all that was good in it was due to him.

We wish we could say that there is no evidence to support these assertions. But in the second part of the *Memoirs* of Richard Lovell Edgeworth, prepared for the press by his famous daughter, Maria, a letter to Walter Scott is printed,[5] from which an extract must

4. It was reviewed as a new book in the *Monthly Review* of June, 1780.
5. *Memoirs of Richard Lovell Edgeworth, Esq.*, II, 268.

here be shown: "Miss Seward's Ode to Captain Cook stands deservedly high in the public opinion. Now, to my certain knowledge, most of the passages, which have been selected in the various reviews of that work, were written by Dr. Darwin. Indeed they bear such strong internal marks of the Doctor's style of composition, that they may easily be distinguished by any reader, who will take the trouble to select them. I remember them distinctly to have been his, and to have read them aloud before Miss Seward and Dr. Darwin, in presence of Sir Brooke Boothby, who will corroborate my assertion."

These are hard sayings, and it is difficult to refute them. The letter was written in 1812, three years after the death of Miss Seward, and ten years after the death of Dr. Darwin. In view of the known antagonism which existed between Miss Seward and Mr. Edgeworth, after his marriage to Honora Sneyd, we may allow ourselves to wonder whether the passing of thirty-two years might not have left a confused remembrance regarding the verses in question; whether, in other words, the wish might have been father to the accusation. Edgeworth bore a fair reputation for truthfulness, and he probably did not write what he did not believe. Nevertheless, it is possible that a mere discussion of phrases with Dr. Darwin (Miss Seward loved an argument on poetic diction) may have remained in the memory of Edgeworth as an actual revision of the poem. At this distant date, it is difficult to solve so metaphysical a problem, and Edgeworth's statement must be taken for what it is worth.

Another bit of evidence which may be taken with a grain of salt is that recorded in the Percy correspondence, in Nichols' *Illustrations of the Literary History of the Eighteenth Century*.[6] The Bishop of Dromore,[7] Ireland, writing in the third person to Mrs. Jane West,[8] says, "Dr. Anderson has informed the Bishop that Sir Brooke Boothby . . . affirms, on his own knowledge, that Darwin either originated, or wrote over almost anew, the greatest part of the elegy on Captain Cook, which he never reclaimed."

This is hearsay evidence of the long-distance variety, readily accepted by the Bishop, who, as we shall see, was strongly prejudiced against Miss Seward, for political and other reasons. Sir Brooke Boothby is in Miss Seward's *Letters* reported to have been "dissipated," and possibly was not altogether clear in his mind, after a lapse of thirty years, but ready to affirm the worst regarding the prophet in her (and his) own country.

A few excerpts from the *Elegy on Captain Cook* may suffice to show the character of the poem. Those readers familiar with the poetic style of both Dr. Darwin and Miss Seward, may, as Mr. Edgeworth suggests, disentangle the lines which should be attributed to each!

> From the rude summit of yon frozen steep,
> Contrasting Glory gilds the dreary deep!
> Lo!—decked with vermeil youth and beamy grace,
> Hope in her step, and gladness in her face,
> Light on the icy rock, with outstretched hands,
> The Goddess of the new Columbus stands.

6. VIII, 429.   7. Percy.
8. A prolific writer of the period.

Round her bright head the plumy peterels soar,
Blue as her robe, that sweeps the frozen shore;
Glows her soft cheek, as vernal morning fair,
And warm as summer suns her golden hair;
O'er the hoar waste, her radiant glances stream
And courage kindles in their magic beam.
She points the ship its mazy path, to thread
The floating fragments of the frozen bed.
While o'er the deep, in many a dreadful form,
The giant Danger howls along the storm,
Furling the iron sails with numbèd hands,
Firm on the deck the great Adventurer stands;
Round glitt'ring mountains hears the billows rave,
And the vast ruin thunder on the wave.
Appal'd he hears!—but checks the rising sigh,
And turns on his firm band a glist'ning eye,—
Not for himself the sighs unbidden break,
Amid the terrors of the icy wreck;
Not for himself starts the impassioned tear,
Congealing as it falls;—nor pain, nor fear,
Nor Death's dread darts, impede the great design,
Till Nature draws the circumscribing line.
Huge rocks of ice th' arrested ship embay,
And bar the gallant wanderer's dangerous way,—
His eye regretful marks the Goddess turn
The assiduous prow from its relentless bourn.

. . . .

Now the warm solstice o'er the shining bay,
Darts from the north its mild meridian ray;
Again the Chief invokes the rising gale,
And spreads again in desert seas the sail;
O'er dangerous shoals his steady steerage keeps
O'er walls of coral, ambushed in the deeps;
Strong Labour's hands the crackling cordage twine,
And sleepless patience heaves the guardian line.
Borne as fierce eddies black Tornado springs,
Dashing the gulphy main with ebon wings;
In the vex'd foam his sweeping trail he shrouds,
And rears his serpent-crest amid the clouds;

> Wrapp'd in dark mists with hideous bellowing roars,
> Drives all his tempests on, and shakes the shores.
> Already has the groaning ship resign'd
> Half her proud glories to the furious wind.
> The fear-struck mariner beholds from far,
> In gathering rage, the elemental war;
> As rolls the rising vortex, stands aghast,
> Folds the rent sail, or clasps the shivering mast!
> Onward, like Night, the frowning Demon comes,
> Show'rs a dread deluge from his shaken plumes;
> Fierce as he moves, the gulphèd sand uptears,
> And high in air the shatter'd canvass bears.

WE have now come to the personal history of the year 1780, which was to bring three shocks and sorrows into the already saddened life of Anna Seward. We may first take up the later life of Honora Sneyd who was fast sinking into the grave.

The new Mrs. Edgeworth, though young and inexperienced—having led a gay and sheltered life—took upon herself some arduous responsibilities when she married. She assumed the care of four children, one boy and three girls, among whom was included Maria—the future novelist—six years old. Maria accompanied her father and Honora to Edgeworthstown, where the now contented bridegroom could settle down on his neglected estates. The tenants were, as may be supposed, "in a wretched state of idleness and ignorance." The buildings were decaying, the lands blighted and weed grown. The landlord set to work with a good will, and soon had woodchoppers, plowmen, carpenters, and landscape gardeners at work, improving the shabby house and the run-down plantation. English servants brought order and comfort into the home. Visits to and from relatives and neighboring gentry kept this remote country life from becoming too tedious.

After three years of sojourning in Ireland, the Edgeworths visited England, taking a house at North Church, in Hertfordshire. Honora became the mother of two children, Richard Lovell (called Lovell) and a girl named after herself. Miss Seward says that Edgeworth neglected his wife, and treated her inconsiderately. This seems unlikely, inasmuch as he was renowned for a genial manner and an amiable disposition. He did, it is true, leave her in England, in failing health, while he went back to Ireland to attend to a lawsuit and other business; but it is not probable that he left her unattended or unprovided with means or comforts. This appearance of neglect could easily be construed by Miss Seward as indifference and cruelty, since her injured feelings had made her sensitive and critical.

Upon the return of Edgeworth from Ireland, he and his wife went to the home of Mr. Sneyd, Honora's father, in Lichfield, so that the advice of the admired Dr. Darwin would be available. The worthy Doctor drew her blood away with futile persistence. The progress of Honora's disease (a decline, or perhaps pulmonary consumption[9]) was slow, and she was devotedly attended by her sister Elizabeth, to whom Mr. Day had vainly turned for consolation when Honora had rejected him.

9. Miss Seward says that five of Honora's sisters died of consumption.

Sonnet XXXI of Anna Seward's *Poems,* written at this time, is entitled, "To the Departing Spirit of an Alienated Friend" [Honora]. It has some bitter lines relating to Edgeworth:

> . . . His flight
> The rashly chosen of thy heart has ta'en
> Where dances, songs, and theatres invite.
> Expiring sweetness! with indignant pain
> I see him in the scenes where laughing glide
> Pleasure's light forms;—see his eyes gaily glow,
> Regardless of thy life's fast ebbing tide;
> I hear him, who should droop in silent woe,
> Declaim on actors, and on taste decide!

Sonnet XXXII is entitled, "Subject of the Preceding Sonnet Continued."

> Behold him now his genuine colors wear,
> That specious false-one, by whose cruel wiles
> I lost thy amity; saw thy dear smiles
> Eclipsed.

These sonnets, though of inferior merit as verse, show plainly the resentment which Miss Seward felt and continued to feel toward Edgeworth, in spite of his statement that their acquaintance was for him "a source of never failing pleasure."

Honora died in May, 1780.

During her married years, which seem to have been happy, Honora was as universally admired and praised as she had been during her girlhood with the Sewards. It is certain that she was surpassingly beautiful and notably intelligent and sweet-tempered. Maria Edgeworth remembered her with affection, and paid grateful tribute to the care and training which she received at Honora's hands. Well may Anna Seward have mourned in twice losing this lovely creature from her life, once by marriage and again by death. Six years later, visiting Honora's neglected tomb at King's Weston, she wrote:

> Six years have passed.
> On that unshrined yet ever-sacred spot,
> By faithless Love deserted and forgot,
> Six bloomy springs their crystal light have showed.

All through her life the poetess made frequent reference to Honora, never ceasing her lamentation for that too early death, and the alienation which made it doubly bitter.

Honora left two children. The girl, Honora, showed remarkable promise as a writer, but faded at sixteen, and died as a result of that decline so common to young women in her day. For some years after her passing, manuscripts of a translation from the French were handed about as evidence of her precocity. The boy, Lovell, grew to manhood, and was the victim of an odd misadventure. While traveling on the Continent, he was caught in the swirl of the war with France, and was interned as a British subject at Verdun. He spent eleven years a prisoner, chafing under his deprivations and his protracted separation from his family. Eventually he returned to England and lived out a somewhat ineffectual existence on his own estates.

Long remembered and much lamented, Honora Sneyd ("The most beloved as a wife, a sister, and a friend, of any person I have ever known," says Edgeworth) passed out of earthly record and into the mysticism of legend. If all that has been said be true, we may well regard her with wonder, marveling not at the perfervid phrases with which she has been described.

We here briefly sketch the later career of Edgeworth. Less than eight months after the death of Honora, he married her sister. As he says in his *Memoirs,* "She recommended it to me in the strongest manner, to marry her sister Elizabeth." Edgeworth and Elizabeth Sneyd were married on Christmas Day, 1780, in St. Andrew's Church, Holborn (London), in the presence of Mr. Elars (brother of the first Mrs. Edgeworth) "and his lady," and the faithful Mr. Day. The marriage was a happy one, and blessed with many children. Edgeworth and his wife divided their time between England and Ireland, where the patriarchal family life at Edgeworthstown was quiet and harmonious. Edgeworth was always busy, teaching his children, looking after his estate, taking part in local politics, studying chemistry and mechanics, and interesting himself in various pieces of engineering work. As his daughter Maria grew up and showed a literary talent, he collaborated with her in her educational and moralistic writings, exerting perhaps too much pressure of his will upon her, so that she seldom or never wrote with a free hand. Mrs. Elizabeth Edgeworth died in the autumn of 1797. On the 31st of May in the next year, Edgeworth married a woman more than twenty years younger than himself, a Miss Beaufort, daughter of his old friend Dr. Beaufort. She survived her husband. He died in June, 1817, expressing great gratitude at the last for an active and happy life.

Major André

Engraved from a Pen Sketch by himself, while before
a glass the day previous to his execution, Presented by B. Noyes.

MAJ. JOHN ANDRÉ

Pen Sketch, drawn by himself on the day before his execution.

ON July 31, 1780, Mrs. Seward died after an illness of many months. Like numbers of good home-keeping women, she seems to have had no history beyond the record of birth, marriage, and death. She was of "acknowledged beauty, even in waning age," as her daughter said, and had a "high and generous spirit." That she discouraged Anna's ambition we know. She probably desired above everything else to see her disturbingly literary daughter married to a comfortable fortune. In both her living and her dying, she seems to have been a less coercive influence than the Rev. Thomas Seward, who was for thirty-eight years an exacting guardian, and for ten years a burdensome charge and care.

THE autumn of the same year that saw the death of Honora Edgeworth and Mrs. Seward witnessed the doom of Major André. He had received his commission in March, 1771, when he was twenty years old. He went to Germany on military business (connected with the raising of the mercenary regiments for the British army), and was there when Honora was married in 1773. He did not return to England till late in the year. He joined the Armies in America, and experienced the varied fortunes of war. He was taken prisoner (1775) and released again, shared the gaieties of British official life in Philadelphia, and was confidentially attached to Generals Grey and Clinton as aide de camp. He seems to have been everywhere respected and admired for his ability, modesty, and personal charm.

He managed the correspondence between General

Clinton and Benedict Arnold, taking the name of John
Anderson and pretending that the letters concerned a
mercantile transaction. On September 20, 1780, he was
sent up the Hudson in the sloop *Vulture,* under the
pretense of looking after the sequestrated property of
Col. Beverly Robinson. On September 21 he had a
secret meeting with Arnold, who revealed to him the
nature of the defenses at West Point, and agreed to
help the British in an attack. The *Vulture* had been
compelled by an American attack to drop down the
river, and André could not gain access to her. He was
seized by three militiamen on the lookout for stragglers,
was tried by court-martial as a spy, and convicted despite all efforts to save him. He was hanged at Tappan,
on October 2, 1780.

The terrible news stirred Anna Seward to a transport
of rage which clamored for some vehement expression.
In the heat of her pity and anger, she wrote the poem
by which she is best remembered—the *Monody on the
Death of Major André.*[10]

The poem, which is written in vigorous couplets,
traces the story of André's life to its wretched close. The
noble character of the young man, the treachery of
which he was the victim, and the horror of his fate
might well have moved a less ardent friend than Anna
Seward to an elegy.

Her apostrophe to Washington is an almost savage
denunciation:

10. Published by Jackson of Lichfield.

Oh *Washington,* I thought thee great and good,
Nor knew thy Nero-thirst of guiltless blood!
Severe to use the pow'r that fortune gave,
Thou cool determin'd murderer of the brave!
Lost to each fairer virtue, that inspires
The genuine fervor of the patriot fires!
And you, the base abettors of the doom,
That sunk his blooming honours in the tomb,
Th' opprobrious tomb your hardened hearts decreed,
While all he ask'd was as the brave to bleed!
No other boon the glorious youth implor'd
Save the cold mercy of the warrior-sword!

. . . .

Remorseless Washington! the day shall come
Of deep repentance for this barb'rous doom!
When injur'd André's memory shall inspire
A kindling army with resistless fire;
Each falchion sharpen that the British wield,
And lead their fiercest lion to the field!
Then, when each hope of thine shall set in night,
When dubious dread, and unavailing flight
Impel your host, thy guilt-upbraided soul
Shall wish untouched the sacred life you stole!
And when thy heart appall'd, and vanquish'd pride
Shall vainly ask the mercy they deny'd,
With horror shalt thou meet the fate thou gave,
Nor pity gild the darkness of thy grave!

Washington, says Miss Seward, was greatly chagrined
at being the subject of such reproachful lines. A few
years after peace had been made between England and
America, he sent an officer to call upon Miss Seward,[11]
to assure her that "no circumstance of his life had been
so mortifying as to be censured in the Monody on
André, as the pitiless author of his ignominious fate:

11. *Letters,* V, 143 *et seq.;* also VI, 4.

that he had labored to save him," and that he requested her perusal of the papers which he was sending. Among the papers was "a copy of the proceedings of the court-martial that determined André's condemnation"; a copy of a letter from General Washington to General Clinton, offering to give up André in exchange for Arnold; a copy of Washington's letter to André, adjuring him to conceal nothing of the "selfish perfidy" of Arnold; and a copy of André's "high-souled" reply. After reading all these papers, Miss Seward was "filled with contrition" for the "rash injustice of her censure." Her previous admiration for Washington was restored, and she ever afterward spoke of him in the highest terms, full of respect and veneration.

With a journalistic instinct which would have done more for her if her financial security and her sense of female propriety had not been so shackling, she offered her poem[12] to the public at the time when feeling ran high and the death of the noble-souled young major was the topic of every tongue. Immediately she reaped the reward of timeliness. In the *salons* of London her lines were read and quoted; and in distant country houses her name was repeated beside the hearth.

This taste of fame was sweet to one who had hungered for recognition, and for a justification for being. She was beginning to feel keenly the inferiority of her single state. The unmarried woman of her day was the

12. The *Monody on the Death of Major André* was reviewed in the *Monthly Review* for April, 1781. It was printed in Lichfield and sold by Cadell for 2s. 6d.

butt of unseemly jests, and the victim of vulgar and indecent sneers. Anna Seward was proud. She knew herself superior to the majority of her married friends. The fact that she might have married did not mitigate her sense of incompleteness nor the mortification of suspected ridicule. Success could minister to her wounded vanity. To proclaim herself more clever than the ordinary married woman was to vindicate herself. Renown could wipe out her reproach. The charge of egotism has been made against her. It was probably, as it usually is, the bluster of chagrin, trying to distract attention from failure by exaggerating success.

Miss Seward's monodies were in the spirit of the day, which delighted in epitaphs and memorials. Every person who had any claim to consideration as a *littérateur* was besieged by lamenting relatives to write rhymed eulogies of the departed. Sometimes these were inscribed on suitable monuments, sometimes passed from hand to hand, or printed in local periodicals. Anna Seward was pestered with requests for these mournful outbursts of the muse. "People teaze me with applications to write epitaphs upon their favorite friends," she wrote to Mrs. Stokes. "Of frequent compliance there would be no end, and I could wish never to attempt another." Her collected works show how often she complied with these demands.

The transition from an epitaph to a monody is a short step, though the resulting ode may be unduly long. Dr. Darwin said of Miss Seward that she invented the epic elegy, in which a form of narrative was combined with

lamentation. She was undoubtedly influenced by Lord
Lyttelton's "Lucy" Monody (1747). At any rate, the
monody, as she made use of it, was suited to her poetic
powers. It allowed scope for the lofty language which
she loved, and for the emotional fervors and lyrical
license which fulfilled her notion of poetic diction. The
high-flown and overwrought style which ruins most of
her work was not so deadly in these monodies as
elsewhere. They may therefore be called her best productions. Moreover, they brought her into public notice,
secured for her the real boon of many agreeable friendships, and opened the way for that exchange of letters
which was the chief pride and diversion of her later
years. Never dreaming of the cool indifference of posterity, she believed herself worthy of lasting fame, and
saw, with her mind's eye, her precious poems enshrined
as British classics.

The year 1780 closed, with its record of sorrow and
disaster. Yet life began to take an upward trend. Depression was not so prolonged as it had been when
Honora married. Anna Seward now had her father to
care for. He was beginning to show that decay of the
mental faculties which settled year by year into complete imbecility. But she was mistress of the Palace,
with the task of directing the household, and sustain-
ing social prestige. She knew which of her old friends
could be trusted, and she was quick at making new
ones. She had resources within herself. Her capacity for
enjoyment had increased. She was known outside Lichfield, and respected (as well as envied) within it. She

felt the importance of her place in the world, and the consequence of her opinions and actions. She thirsted for more glory, for a closer acquaintance with the acknowledged great. She was well, she had courage, maturity, power to endure. She had piety, too, of the eighteenth-century kind, a belief that suffering must be submitted to, because it is sent by an obscurely motivated Higher Power.

We may remark here that she also had John Saville, her dearest friend and the object of her deepest affection.

CHAPTER IV

1781–1783

THE BARD OF EARTHAM

D URING the next year, Miss Seward was called
upon for another monody, into the composition
of which went sincere personal regrets. This
was for Lady Miller, the "Laura" of the Bath-Easton
assemblies, who had given the aspiring poetess a lift
toward Parnassus. She died on June 24, 1781, and was
buried in the Abbey Church at Bath. As was natural,
Miss Seward was asked to write an epitaph, and responded with one fairly felicitous, inscribed on the
monument in the Abbey Church, Bath.

> Once, in this now cold breast, those virtues shone,
> Which tender thought, and lasting record claim;
> Then, 'mid the wrecks of time, devoted stone,
> Uninjured bear thy Miller's spotless name!
>
> When clos'd the numerous eyes, that round her bier
> Have wept the loss of wide-extended worth,
> O, gentle stranger! may one generous tear
> Drop, as thou bendest o'er this hallowed earth!
>
> Are truth, and science, love, and pity thine,
> With liberal charity and faith sincere?
> Then rest thy wandering step beneath this shrine,
> And greet a kindred Spirit hovering near!

Sir John Miller erected a handsome monument in the
church, with Miss Seward's lines engraved upon it. The

poem *To the Memory of Lady Miller* came later, and was published by Robinson.

The author felt some misgivings concerning this poem, because of the contrast which it might offer to her previous monodies, both of which had had illustrious men for their subjects. She rightly surmised that in comparison with Major André and Captain Cook, Lady Miller, however estimable and benevolent, might seem like an anticlimax. Nevertheless, a wish to rise to the occasion, and to do justice to her friend, impelled her to draw as best she could on her sources of inspiration—the memory of happy times at Bath-Easton, and a regard for the friendly hostess who had crowned her with the myrtle wreath. The result was not much in the way of literature, though it met the need of the time and soothed the conscience of the poetess.

Miss Seward confessed her indebtedness to Lady Miller in these words:

> Though all unknown to Fame its artless reed,
>   My trembling hand, at thy kind bidding tried
> To crop the blossoms of th' uncultured mead,
>   The primrose pale, the briar's blushing pride,
> And on thy vase with true devotion laid
>   The tributary flowers—too soon, alas! to fade.
>
> Safe through thy gentle ordeal's lambent flame,
>   My muse, aspiring, dared the fiercer blaze[1]
> Which judgment lights before the hill of Fame,
>   With calm determin'd hand and searching gaze;
> But for thy liberal praise, with awful dread,
>   Far from thy burning bars my trembling feet had fled.

1. Of the reviewers.

The author then passed in review the chief competitors for Lady Miller's myrtle wreath: the Rev. Mr. Graves of Claverton; the Rev. Mr. Butt; Mr. Jerningham; the Rev. Mr. Whalley, long a friend of Miss Seward, and author of a much-admired poem, *Edwy and Edilda;* Mr. Anstey, author of *The New Bath Guide,* a poetical satire; and last in order of climax, William Hayley, "the first poet of England," as he was at that time thought to be. The stanza relating to Hayley is as follows:

> Bright glows the list of many an honour'd name,
>   Whom Taste in Laura's votive throng surveys;
> But HAYLEY flashes in a type of flame,
>   Trac'd by a sunbeam the broad letters blaze!
> Rapt Britain reads the long-recording fire,
>   Claps her triumphant hands, and bids her realms admire!

This poem, inferior, as its author knew, to the *Elegy on Captain Cook,* and the *Monody on the Death of Major André,* was noncommittally reviewed in the *Gentleman's Magazine,* which was ever kind to Miss Seward, printing most of her shorter poems, and commenting favorably, if not always enthusiastically, upon her work. In passing we may note that in the same volume of the *Gentleman's Magazine* to which we turn for this review, we find, somewhat earlier, the following estimate of Miss Seward as a poet:

There is . . . a poetess of the age, in whom almost every poetical excellence seems to be united. I need not tell you, that it is Miss Seward; produce me any female writer who equals that lady; "et eris mihi magnus Apollo"—her merit is so universally acknowledged, that I trust that I shall not be suspected of flattery, even to a female!

The *European Magazine* reviewed the poem on Lady Miller at considerable length, giving copious extracts and remarking, "It gives us very sincere pleasure, which we partake in common with our readers, to find the virtues of the late Lady Miller perpetuated by so excellent a poet as Miss Seward." The review was followed by an account of the life of the author, concluding with the words, "After these little anecdotes which we have collected with the care that distinguished excellence deserves, it is superfluous to pronounce the object of them, one of the most shining ornaments of the British Muse."

What wonder that the Lichfield poetess thought well of herself, after reading such tributes as these, paid to her by two of the best magazines of the day?

With the passing of Lady Miller, one of Miss Seward's pleasantest affiliations was withdrawn; though now the patronage so welcome at an earlier day was no longer needed. The Swan of Lichfield was coming into her own.

It was in 1781, also, that the cathedral city suffered the loss of Dr. Erasmus Darwin, of whose eminence it had been wont to boast. Marriage, not death, claimed the gallant Doctor.

A few years before, the Doctor, long a widower, fell ponderously, but none the less sincerely, in love, with a lady still in marriage bonds. This was a Mrs. Chandos-Pole, wife of a colonel, whose children he had successfully treated when they were suffering from an overdose of drugs administered by a reckless physician in a town near by. The Doctor seems to have made little attempt to conceal his passion, hopeless and irregular as it appeared; but the event proved that he had not sighed in vain. The Colonel fell ill, and presently died. The widow was instantly besieged, if report is to be credited, by half the eligible men of all the country round.

The Doctor, who was now fifty years old, besides being ugly, fat, lame, clumsy, and afflicted with a stammer, would scarcely have been judged an eligible suitor at all. Mrs. SchimmelPenninck says, "His figure was vast and massive, his head was almost buried on his shoulders, and he wore a scratch [wig], as it was then called, tied up in a little bob-tail behind." It is evident that he was not a figure likely to prove fascinating to a young and popular widow. For some time Mrs. Pole showed a natural reluctance to regard him as a possible *parti*. But her good sense prevailed, and she consented to marry him; never, it was believed, regretting her whimsical choice out of the ranks of her besiegers.

Gossip would have it (as gossip always will when an unmarried woman and a widower are on friendly terms) that Anna Seward had hopes of becoming the second Mrs. Darwin. The author believes this gossip to be (as its kind usually is) nonsense. Miss Seward seems never to have liked Dr. Darwin very well—he was, as she said bluntly, "sometimes friendly but never amiable." Moreover, it is certain that by this time her heart was fixed upon that object which for years it was to love with growing intensity, and for which it was eventually to break.

The new Mrs. Darwin (married a year after Colonel Pole's decease) was outspoken in her dislike of Lichfield. One discerns a hint of jealousy in the haste with which she compelled her husband to uproot himself from his surroundings and bundle his family off to Derby. Her petulant, though indefinite, abhorrence of the agreeable little cathedral town was reason enough to the love-blinded Doctor to rout him of his pleasant home and profitable practice. It is not on record that he ever complained of this expulsion. With philosophical ease he adapted himself to his new environment. He continued to heal the sick (or to do what he could toward that end), to grind out his verses, and draw around him a host of congenial friends, many of them distinguished for their wealth, intellect, or social station.

Dr. Darwin lived on in Derby, with an ever widening range of practice, till his sudden death in 1802.

An agreeable interlude of 1781 was the visit of a famous man from the outside world, the "bard of Eartham," William Hayley. He and Anna Seward had begun their acquaintance by letter. "He had been highly pleased," Hayley says of himself, "with Miss Seward's elegy on Captain Cook, and he sent her a few verses in praise of her publication, which engaged him in a long familiar correspondence and friendship with that celebrated lady."[2]

2. *Memoirs of William Hayley,* I, 241.

Deducing from the published *Poetical Works* of Miss
Seward, we find that she wrote a highly adulatory ode
upon the appearance of Hayley's *The Triumphs of
Temper*. This *Ode to Poetic Fancy* contained eight rap-
turous stanzas proclaiming the "magic" of "Hayley's
lay."

Hayley replied with epistles in prose and rhyme; and,
in the exchange of courtesies, sent Miss Seward a drawing of himself by Romney, his intimate friend. Miss
Seward rewarded both bard and painter by an *Epistle
to Mr. Romney. Being presented by him with a picture
of William Hayley, Esq.* It begins:

> Ingenious Romney, in thy liberal heart
> We feel thy virtues rivals of thy art;
> Indulgent wilt thou then accept my lay,
> Though faintly gilded by poetic ray,
> When it would tell how much to thee I owe
> That on these walls thy Hayley's features glow?

We refrain from quoting the long apostrophe to the
artist, and the ecstatic hymning of the bard's supremacy.
The lines below reveal the fact that the poetess had
never met the original of Romney's sketch:

> Though ne'er beheld the actual form he wears,
> My spirit thus thy Hayley's fame reveres;
> Marks his dear Muse his charming strains extend
> And boasts the privilege to call him Friend.
> But when in vain my grateful wishes sought
> His living image in the stores of thought,
> Thy pencil, *Romney,* the desire supplies,
> And bids me see the generous Bard I prize.

After this indirect acquaintance, it was natural that
the two poets should wish to see each other. In Decem-

ber, a somewhat unpropitious time, Hayley came to Lichfield to visit Miss Seward. He stayed two long, beatific, almost delirious, weeks, at the end of which "unforeseen business called him away."

We may imagine the pride with which Miss Seward presented this celebrated man to her coterie. He might be called the first-fruits of her literary success. It was that alone which had drawn him to Lichfield, and which inspired the friendship which had already begun, and which was to be increased a hundred fold upon their meeting.

William Hayley may need some explanation in the twentieth century. In the eighteenth his name was literally a houschold word. Born in 1745, of well-to-do parents, he spent his childhood in acute illness which threatened to destroy his mind. The nursing of his mother saved his life and mentality. He went to Cambridge, married early, and retired to his villa at Eartham in Sussex, to live on his patrimony and write verse. He tried his hand at the drama, not very profitably, and wrote, in 1777, his *Epistle on Painting,* inspired by his acquaintance with Romney. Other shorter poems followed. The great success of Hayley's life was *The Triumphs of Temper,* a small book of light verse, after the manner of *The Rape of the Lock*. Serena, heroine of *The Triumphs,* was, for twenty or thirty years after her appearance in 1781, as well known a character as Portia or Clarissa. The book was in high favor as a gift. Parents gave it to their daughters. Husbands bestowed it upon brides and matrons. The model of good behavior which it presented was thought to have a beneficial effect on ladies subject to tantrums. We cannot resist quoting here a letter to George Romney, from Emma Hart, newly married (1791) to Sir William Hamilton:

> Tell Hayley I am always reading his *Triumphs of Temper*. It was *that* made me Lady Hamilton; for God knows I had for 5 years enough to try my temper, and I am affraid if it had not been for the example Serena taught me, my girdle would have burst;3 and if it had, I had been undone, for Sir William more minds temper than beauty. He therefore wishes that Mr. Hayley would come to Naples that he might thank him for his sweet-tempered wife. I swear to you I have never been once out of humour since the 6th of September4 last.

After the production of *The Triumphs of Temper*, Hayley wrote his *Poetical Epistle on Epic Poetry* of which Southey says in his article on Hayley in the *Quarterly Review:* "A greater effect was produced upon the rising generation of scholars, by the Notes to his Essay on Epic Poetry, than by any other contemporary work, the Relics of Ancient Poetry alone excepted."5

Hayley wrote also an *Essay on Old Maids,* a *Life of Cowper,* and a *Life of Romney;* as well as his own *Memoirs* and an account of his son, Thomas Adolphus Hayley. Of his prose works, the *Life of Cowper* is the best.

It is difficult to make a modern reader understand what a personage Hayley was in the years following the appearance of *The Triumphs of Temper*. He was, as

3. This is a reference to the plot of the poem.
4. Her wedding day.   5. XXXI, 283.

Southey tells us in his *Quarterly* article, "for many years the most fashionable of living poets," "the popular poet of the day," "King of the bards of Britain." "He lived for some years in the possession of unrivalled popularity."

This, then, was the man who sought Miss Seward out, and spent two weeks in her home. An extract from one of her early letters to him gives a notion of what Anna Seward felt: "How charming is your poetical gallantry! If all the testimonies of it bestowed upon my flattered self, were collected and given to the world, the garlands of Swift's Stella and Prior's Chloë would fade before mine. My pride, my heart exults in these distinctions, conferred by the transcendant English bard of the present aera."

The encounter of two such enthusiasts as Hayley and Miss Seward must have resulted in some very pretty fireworks of compliment and epigram. Dr. Mansel, Bishop of Bristol, seems to have been the author of a bit of fooling, which was intended to characterize this historic meeting.

> "Prince of poets, England's glory,
>   Mr. Hayley, that is you!"
> "Ma'am, you carry all before you,
>   Lichfield's own, indeed you do!"
> "In epic, elegy, or sonnet,
>   Mr. Hayley, you're divine!"
> "Madam, take my word upon it,
>   You yourself are all the *Nine!*"[6]

6. Reported by Maria Edgeworth, from the memory of a Mr. Ward, who visited her in 1816, and who said he had passed some time in Lichfield, and had known Miss Seward. Nichols, however,

In letters written to his wife, who was studying singing with Rauzzini at Bath, Hayley gives some clear glimpses of his hostess and her environment.[7]

"As to the person of this female genius," he says, "I can not give you a better idea of it, than by saying she is a handsome likeness of those full-length pictures which you have seen of your namesake, Queen Elizabeth, where the painters gave her majesty all the beauty they could consistent with the character of her face. The Muse laughs at herself as fat and lame; yet the connoisseurs in woman would still pronounce her handsome."

"Behold me seated, my dear Eliza," he goes on, "in a very noble and comfortable house of the church, where divinity and poetry form a very uncommon and agreeable alliance! . . . I am now scribbling in a very elegant room, with a bed-chamber adjoining, in a detached part of the house, which are very politely consigned to my private use." It is evident that Hayley was impressed, as well he might have been, with the dignity and beauty of the Canon's house. He had a poetic word to say about it, in an impromptu poem to "that fair Seward, whom the Nine inspire." Hayley was enchanted with the voice of Saville. "He is equally astonishing in the grand and the pathetic, the humorous, and the tender," wrote the delighted guest. The crowds of

says that these lines were written by Professor Porson. See Nichols' *Illustrations of the Literary History of the Eighteenth Century,* VIII, 360 n.

7. *Memoirs of William Hayley,* I, 243–252.

callers did not please him so well. "A country town is a scene so very unfit for poetical studies," is his comment, "that I am amazed the Muse can write here at all; for notwithstanding the reports you heard at Bath,[8] she has a multitude of female visitors, and a host of divines." The Bard soon wearied of the social demands made upon him, and "resolved to make a hasty retreat to the dear solitude of Eartham." He had received pleasure and given it, and instinctively chose the right moment for his departure.

These two weeks of confidences, exchanges of opinion, comments on recent books, and retailing of harmless literary gossip (for Hayley was the kindliest of men) were a season of exultant happiness for Miss Seward, who had long withered in a winter of discontent. They placed her within the magic circle of authentic authors. Henceforth, she might reasonably esteem herself one of the dwellers, as she would have put it, on Parnassian heights.

Miss Seward accompanied Mr. Hayley on his homeward way, as far as Coleshill, and on the return journey in the chaise, wrote sixty-four lines of regret at the departure of this new friend. Later, when her fingers had been warmed over the ample fires of the Palace, she added a few more lines, to round out the poem (an *Epistle to William Hayley, Esq.*). We may be sure it was dispatched without delay, with excited visions of letters and laudations flying back from Eartham, when the bard should be once more at home.

8. For an explanation of this phrase, see p. 186.

THE year 1782 was a notable year for Miss Seward. In April appeared a biography of her in the *European Magazine,* an indication that her works had attracted enough attention to make her a personage worth noticing. She must have felt that she had at last "arrived." From this account (covering two-and-a-half pages) have been drawn most of the biographical fragments which have since that time been used in any story of her life. It prints the poem which she is said to have written at Dr. Darwin's behest; and gives other evidences of her precocity. The attempts of her father and mother to stifle her poetic talent are also described in detail. Her meeting with Lady Miller is noted, and the influence of that patroness is given its full value. These picturesque touches have done noble service for a hundred and forty years.

A pleasure which long remained a valued memory to Miss Seward was her visit to Mr. Hayley and his wife at Eartham.

We of the present day have no idea of the miseries of travel in England in 1782. Going anywhere required such a superhuman effort that many people never had the courage to travel. We can only marvel at those who actually got about, and can sympathize with Parson Woodforde's sister, who "trembled like a leaf" when she first ventured into a stagecoach. In summer, heat, dust, flies, cramped quarters, rough roads, crowded hostelries, drunken drivers, and swarming highwaymen were a few of the outstanding discomforts of a trip, whether it was taken by coach or chaise. In winter, snow or rain, freezing cold, pitch holes full of mud, drifted hillsides, broken springs, and the same drunken drivers and bold marauders made any sort of journey a torment. Miss Seward probably mitigated the evils of travel by going in her own chaise. She speaks in her *Letters* of having a new one made.

In the summer of 1782, Miss Seward (and presumably a maid, since she usually took one with her) braved the terrors of the road, and set out on a journey of one hundred and fifty miles, into Sussex. As a preliminary note to his account of this visit, Mr. Hayley wrote: "The summer and autumn of this year 1782 afforded them [the Hayleys] much social delight from a succession of guests, whose talents were highly entertaining. Their first visitor was Mr. Saville, the celebrated singer of Litchfield. They were charmed with his powerful style of singing, and his extreme sensibility, with the ease and modesty of his deportment. The grateful account which he gave of his reception, when he returned to his fair friend at Lichfield, Miss Seward, induced that lady . . . to venture on the same distant excursion, and she gratified her friends of Sussex with a visit of several weeks."9

A special lure, if any were needed, was the fact that George Romney was making his yearly visit to Eartham. The possibility of his painting her portrait may have occurred to Miss Seward; though to do her justice, her admiration for Hayley was sufficient to bear her up during the trials of a longer journey.

This visit has been the subject of some derisive com-

9. *Memoirs of William Hayley*, I, 277.

ment by various writers on Miss Seward and Mr. Hayley. It gave, we may concede, an excellent chance for more of the mutual admiration which Dr. Mansel's (or Professor Porson's) verse describes. The humor lies in the fact that both authors set too high a value on each other and themselves. This error has not been confined to Sewards and Hayleys.

As a matter of fact, the little group of earnest thinkers spent at Eartham a long-remembered space of cordial intimacy. We may recall them from the past: the handsome mature Miss Seward, in her rustling silks, flowing tissues, and lace headdresses; the truly good-hearted Mr. Hayley, his face revealing his eagerness to promote the well-being of others; the erratic, bedeviled Mr. Romney, suspicious of the world in general, but finding here a transient repose; the chattering and giggling Mrs. Hayley, meaning well, but unable to restrain her tongue; and with her, little Tom, child of mystery, not yet two years old, the idol of his father.

There was a constant murmur (broken by the shrill laugh of Mrs. Hayley) about literature and music and art. Miss Seward and Hayley were born readers, who had spent all their lives among books, which were as vital to them as persons. Romney, an almost illiterate man, knew little, in the academic sense, except his own art, to which he commonly gave every waking moment. He had traveled, however, and he had met many people of rank and power. He had ideas, and he could discourse with unexpected eloquence when he was roused. The endless discussions of the others may have bored him at times; but he could always turn to his sketching and his study of light and shadow. He allowed himself to be enticed from his crayons and colors, to walk about the carefully landscaped gardens of the villa, and share the chat or banter of Hayley and the ladies.

Inside the house, there were dallyings over the bard's collections of books and portraits and *objets d'art,* to which Romney, grateful for friendship, had contributed perhaps too generously. There were solid British meals, served on the faultless mahogany and Wedgwood of the day. There was not much flowing of wines, for Hayley himself drank nothing stronger than coffee, and did not encourage tippling.

In the course of the meal, or after it was over, when the fire in the library was lighted, fragments of biography would come out, on the impulse of increasing friendliness. Yet each one concealed something in his own bosom: Miss Seward her chagrin in admitting the frustrations of her life; Hayley the memory of his *liaison,* which had brought him little Tom; Mrs. Hayley the knowledge that she had lost her husband's love; Romney the remorse with which he must remember his wife, whom he had deserted nearly twenty years before. Outwardly all was animation and social ease; within were the repressions of middle age, and sometimes heaviness of heart.

Miss Seward, says Hayley, was a lady whom Romney "greatly admired for her poetical talents, for the sprightly charms of her social character, and for the graces of a majestic person." During her sojourn at

Eartham, the Bard informs us, ". . . the pen of Hayley, and the pencil of his friend Romney were most cheerfully employed in delineating her various endowments."[10] How many portraits of the Swan were begun or finished during her stay has never been made quite clear. Romney was in the habit of beginning pictures with great enthusiasm and then throwing them aside, never to be completed. Hayley succeeded in getting a finished painting of Miss Seward which he hung in his library, and on which he, of course, wrote some verses.

Romney, it would seem,[11] began at least a second portrait of Miss Seward when she was making this visit at Eartham, but did not complete it. Perhaps he worked a little more upon it when she visited his studio on her return journey; possibly he added some touches, or drew a new portrait when she was in London in 1786. Miss Seward seems to say distinctly that it was painted in 1786.[12] It certainly was not finished till 1788, when Romney sent it to Mr. Seward as a gift.

Miss Seward stayed six weeks at Eartham, and departed reluctantly from this congenial house, where flattering attentions attested her genius (as she would have said), as well as her good manners and good looks. Like the true swan, she burst into song before she went.

10. *Memoirs of William Hayley*, I, 277.

11. See Arthur B. Chamberlain, *George Romney*, p. 120. See also *post*, p. 162.

12. In a letter to Mr. Seward of Birmingham, December 9, 1806, she alludes to Romney's full-length portrait of her "drawn in 1786." She refers to the one given to her father, because she offers to show it to Mr. Seward. *Letters*, IV, 174.

Her poem, which may be read in her collected *Works,* is entitled, "To William Hayley, Esq. On Leaving Eartham, his seat in Sussex, Sept. 1782."

On her way back to Lichfield, Miss Seward stopped in London, to visit her Quaker friend, Mrs. Knowles. Together they visited the studio of Romney, who had probably returned to town. "When we found ourselves in the full blaze of the Romneyan creation," says the Muse, "all words are too weak to paint my wonder and delight. It was the gaze of astonishment; it was the thrill of rapture. Mrs. Knowles, who if she has less *enthusiasm,* has much more judgment, asserts the superiority of Romney's powers to those of any other painter."[13]

During this visit to London, Miss Seward renewed other acquaintances, and met a good many important people. Mrs. Knowles, who was a brilliant woman,[14] could introduce her to a circle of eminent friends. Miss Seward called upon an elderly gentleman, whom she had known in her youth in Lichfield, but whom she had not seen for twenty years. This was Mr. Mence, who had been priest vicar of Lichfield Cathedral when Mr. Saville became a vicar choral. Of Mr. Mence she says, "His mind retains all its original fire and exquisite sensibility, which, joined to the finest voice that ever warbled from the human throat, *made* him and *keeps* him still the most glorious singer in the world." Mr. Mence was "the sublime model" on which Mr. Saville

13. *Memoirs of William Hayley,* I, 281.
14. See p. 121, for her encounter with Dr. Johnson.

had "formed his vocal harmonies." He was the only singer to whom Miss Seward would award the merit of transcending her beloved "Giovanni"—Mr. Saville.

Thus did the Lady from Lichfield enjoy to the utmost her opportunities in London and return to her Close with memories enough to brighten the foggy darkness of the ensuing winter.

IN 1783 Miss Seward made one of her frequent visits to Buxton, a favorite resort of her father. Dr. Johnson said that Mr. Seward went to Buxton because he loved to lord it in a limited group, where he could show his learning and gift of talk better than he could in a larger and more sophisticated circle. During the progress of the combat between Miss Seward and Boswell in the *Gentleman's Magazine*[15] it was remarked[16] that the lady's dislike for Dr. Johnson was probably caused by the Lexicographer's slurs upon her father. Mr. White, her cousin, wrote, taking a part in the "Benvolio" controversy in the *Gentleman's Magazine:* "When she saw these false traits of Mr. Seward given in the dark shades of Johnsonian malignance, she said 'My poor father shares the almost general fate of those who were so unlucky as to have any personal acquaintance with Dr. Johnson.' "[17]

During the visit of 1783, Miss Seward met at Buxton

15. See p. 203.

16. *Gentleman's Magazine* (September, 1794), p. 815.

17. A letter from the Rev. Mr. White, Sacrist of Lichfield Cathedral, to the *Gentleman's Magazine,* dated October 21, 1794. The phraseology sounds suspiciously like Miss Seward's.

Mrs. Granville of Calwich, who was to introduce her into the Dewes and Granville group (relatives of the celebrated Mrs. Delany), from whose society she was, in times to come, to receive so much delight.

CHAPTER V

1784–1785

SCOTCHMAN, SWAN, AND BEAR

IT was in 1784 that Miss Seward began transcribing her letters into the thick volumes which at her death were sent to Constable of Edinburgh for publication. Long weary hours of composing and copying went into those thirteen books of manuscript. There were no typewriters at hand to lighten the burden of the writer's task; and it was only in her latest years that Miss Seward appears to have employed an amanuensis. The volumes bequeathed to Constable were, she says, not one-twelfth of the letters she wrote during the period from 1784 to 1807.

In December, 1784, Samuel Johnson passed out of this stage of life into one, we hope, more kindly and serene.

During the last year of his life, Johnson spent a considerable time in Lichfield with Lucy Porter. Miss Seward saw him constantly. In a letter to Miss Weston, October 29, 1784, she speaks of her "almost daily habit of contemplating a very melancholy spectacle"—Johnson in his last days, ill, suffering, and terrified. "It is by his repeatedly expressed desire that I visit him often; yet I am sure he neither does, nor ever did, feel much regard for me; but he fain would escape, for a time, in any society, from the terrible idea of his approaching dissolution. I never would be awed by his sarcasms, or his frowns, into acquiescence with his general injustice to the merits of *other* writers; but I feel the truest compassion for his present sufferings and fervently wish I had power to relieve them."

"A few days since," she goes on, "I was to drink tea with him, by his request, at Mrs. Porter's. When I went into the room, he was in deep but agitated slumber in an arm-chair. Opening the door with that caution due to the sick, he did not awaken at my entrance. . . . Upon the servant entering to announce the arrival of a gentleman of the university . . . he awoke with convulsive starts,—but rising, with more alacrity than could have been expected, he said, 'Come, my dear lady, let you and I attend these gentlemen in the study.'"

Regarding the comments upon Johnson in the months following his death, Boswell remarks, "Many who trembled at his presence were forward in assault when they no longer apprehended danger." Though this statement may not literally apply to Miss Seward, it is true that she seemed to relieve her feelings and loosen some pent-up emotions by saying and writing exactly what she thought about the dead lion. She wrote a "character" of Johnson for the *General Evening Post*[1] (December 27, 1784), pointing out his failings, and protesting against awarding him unmerited adulation. She did not sign this article with her own name, "because," as she said, "my friend, his daughter-in-law [stepdaughter],

1. This "character" is given in the Whalley *Memoirs*, I, 415.

Mrs. Lucy Porter, would resent the fidelity of the portrait."[2]

This is perhaps as suitable a place as any, in which to explain (somewhat tediously it is granted) the mental attitudes which characterized the relations of the poetess and the Doctor.

"Johnson hated me," Anna Seward wrote to George Hardinge in 1786. Very likely he did. Johnson hated a good many people, or at least he found a good many irritating and contemptible. The six volumes of Anna Seward's *Letters* give ample evidence that there was no love lost between the Singing Swan and the Great Bear. The reasons for their animosity (which was probably stronger on her side than on his) may have gone back to a time before Anna Seward was born.

As we have said, Mrs. Seward, before her marriage, was Elizabeth Hunter,[3] daughter of the Rev. Mr. John Hunter, Vicar of St. Mary's and Head Master of the Free School in Lichfield, which Samuel Johnson attended as a boy. This Mr. Hunter married in 1726, as his second wife, Lucy Porter, sister of Henry Porter, a "mercer" of Birmingham. The second Mrs. Hunter's niece, another Lucy (daughter of Henry Porter), made a long visit at the home of her aunt (Mrs. Hunter) in Lichfield. Sam Johnson, who was often a guest at his master's table, met Lucy Porter frequently. Miss Seward says that he "fancied" he was in love with her. She also

2. *Letters,* I, 35.
3. For Miss Seward's account of the relationship between Johnson and the Hunters, and of his early attachment to Lucy Porter the younger, see *ibid.,* III, 348 *et seq.*

says that he addressed to her some excellent verses, notably the *Sprig of Myrtle* poem, the occasion of too much controversy, which need not here be augmented. The fact seems to be that they were, in the first instance, written for Edmund Hector.

Elizabeth Hunter, daughter of young Johnson's schoolmaster and host, was, Miss Seward says,[4] the poet's confidante, since he showed her the verses before he presented them to the object of his infatuation.

"Disgusted by his unsightly form," says Anna Seward, "she [Lucy] had a personal aversion to him, nor could the beautiful verses he addressed to her, teach her to endure him. The nymph, at length, returned to her parents at Birmingham, and was soon forgotten."[5]

Elizabeth Hunter, afterward Mrs. Seward, could have been accurately informed concerning this poetic courtship, in which the big Johnson boy is reported to have sought the favor of the pretty flaxen-haired damsel, destined, by an odd trick of fate, to be his stepdaughter. It is not unlikely that Mr. Hunter would have encouraged his niece in her pouting and flouting. The chagrined young poet would have been only human if he put away in his heart a grudge which was to find petulant expression in later years.

4. Miss Seward says that she often heard the story from her mother. For a debate on the subject of the poem, see the Letters from the *Gentleman's Magazine,* collected by Nichols in his *Illustrations,* VII, 345, 348, 357, 361, 363. See also *Gentleman's Magazine,* LXIII, 875, 1009, 1098, and LXIV, 32.

5. Anna Seward's *Letters,* I, 44. This letter is addressed to James Boswell, who dismissed as unauthentic most of the information furnished him by Miss Seward, for his *Life of Samuel Johnson.*

Be that as it may, the two young people were soon separated. But after some muddled years, Sam Johnson found himself in Birmingham as the guest of his friend Hector, and was still sufficiently interested to seek out Miss Lucy. "Calling upon his coy mistress there," says Miss Seward, "he found her father dying." He lingered at the sick man's bedside, helped to settle the estate when Porter died, transferred his affections from daughter to mother, and married the widow, Elizabeth Porter (*née* Jarvis). It may be remarked here, not irrelevantly, that the widow's share of the estate was £800, of which Johnson took possession.

The Hunters in Lichfield would have heard of these goings-on, to the last detail. From a worldly standpoint, Samuel Johnson was perhaps as undesirable a bridegroom as ever put his name on a marriage register. The relatives of the deceased and supplanted Henry could not be blamed if they spoke their minds with more vigor than politeness when Mrs. Elizabeth Porter stepped off with the slovenly, penniless son of old Michael Johnson, vendor of books and small wares in Lichfield Square and Uttoxeter Marketplace. Echoes of these unflattering comments can scarcely have failed to reach Johnson himself; neither can these comments have been forgotten. They must assuredly have been heard and repeated by Elizabeth Hunter, who was shortly to become Mrs. Seward. After the unproductive experiment at Edial (in which most of the £800 was lost), and the rash advance on London, caustic remarks would not have grown less frequent when the ill-

MRS. THOMAS SEWARD (Elizabeth Hunter)
by Pickering, 1755
Courtesy of the Johnson Birthplace Museum, Lichfield.
Photograph by W. Morrison, Lichfield.

assorted pair were discussed at Lichfield tea parties. Sam had left his wife behind him, perhaps with the Hunters.[6] He came back at length, and took her with him to London, where she was no better off. Ill tidings did not perhaps travel so fast in those days as they do now; nevertheless, they traveled. Hunters, Porters, and Sewards, secure in their prosperity, heard from time to time of the bad bargain which Betty (or Tetty) Porter had made in her marriage. She starved in a garret, and wore clothes fit only for a Seward rag bag. "She lived thirty years with Johnson," says Miss Seward; "if shuddering, half-famished, in an author's garret, could be called living."[7] Somewhat slowly, as is the way of good news, came rumors of successes, and of a vast project in hand—something about a dictionary; but before the big success could come, poor Tetty was dead,[8] and the fatuity of her romance remained unrefuted in Lichfield.

For Johnson, in London, the hard barren years had gone on—years of privation, of agonizing toil, of thwarted ambition. In Lichfield they had been serene, prolific, and conventional years. Miss Elizabeth Hunter, after being sought by several eligible men (two, at least, of whom became Bishops[9]), had married Mr. Thomas Seward, poet and scholar, former tutor of Lord Charles Fitzroy, and rector of Eyam, who presently became Prebendary of Salisbury and Canon Residentiary of

6. Possibly with his mother and Miss Porter.

7. *Letters,* II, 348. Mrs. Johnson lived with Samuel Johnson about sixteen years.

8. Mrs. Johnson died in 1752.   9. See p. 4.

Lichfield. Mr. Seward and his wife and two young daughters, Anna and Sarah, had gone to live in the Bishop's Palace, no less, where in his schooldays Johnson and another bright boy, David Garrick, had been patronized and entertained by Gilbert Walmesley. Lucy Porter, still unmarried, boarded with the widowed Mrs. Johnson, in the house where the bookshop sustained a feeble existence.

The Seward girls were growing up to be handsome misses—the elder, a precocious poetess, praised and encouraged by the rising young physician, Dr. Erasmus Darwin. Johnson, in process of becoming the dean and tyrant of British letters, heard of the happy hospitable life of the Sewards, or saw the members of the family themselves on his infrequent[10] visits to his birthplace. The Rev. Mr. Seward, whose memory had not yet failed him, carefully refrained from appearing dazzled by the tardily achieved glories of Michael Johnson's son. He was not, his daughter tells us, of that herd that "paged his heels, and sunk in servile silence under the force of his dogmas, when their hearts and their judgement bore contrary testimony."

Time went on, bringing the brief and pitiful period of Sarah Seward's engagement to Johnson's stepson, Joseph Porter. This came in 1764, at the time when the Lexicographer, after his straitened years, had received his pension and was enjoying the luxurious latitudes of

10. It is not known how often Johnson visited Lichfield between 1737 and 1762. See Boswell's *Life of Samuel Johnson,* ed. Hill, Appendix B, III, 512.

rich men's houses. He heard of the events in Lichfield, no doubt, afar off, absorbed in the savoring of his un- accustomed elegance, not especially caring what hap- pened to Joseph Porter.[11] Coming back to Lichfield, to visit Lucy Porter, who had now inherited money,[12] he would have heard the story rehearsed, and would have met again the beautiful daughter of the Sewards. She was a brilliant girl, well read, to be sure, but lamentably uninstructed in the classics, woefully ignorant of Greek and Latin. Nevertheless, her shrewd brown eyes could see quite through him. She refused to be awed by his bluster, and looked at him with calm disdain, ever re- membering his origin and his history.

"There was perhaps," says Walter Scott, "some aristo- cratic prejudice in their [the Lichfield group's] dislike; for the despotic manners of Dr. Johnson were least likely to be tolerated where the lowness[13] of his origin was in fresh recollection."[14]

Miss Seward wrote to Mrs. Piozzi in 1788, "I always visited and received visits from Dr. Johnson, on every residence of his in our town, excepting only the few days in which you were here with him."[15] The reason for her not calling at that time was that there was "a

11. Johnson wrote kindly but casually of Porter in several of the letters to Miss Porter which have been preserved.

12. From her brother, Captain Porter, of the navy, who died in 1763.

13. Johnson said that the Rev. Cornelius Harrison of Darlington was the only one of his relatives "who ever rose in fortune above penury or in character above neglect" (*The Intimate Letters of Hester Piozzi and Penelope Pennington*, ed. O. S. Knapp, I, 105).

14. *Poetical Works*, Biographical Preface, I, x.

15. *Letters*, II, 43.

slight shyness" between her and Lucy Porter, her friend
from her earliest years. Anna Seward passed some
alarmingly harsh judgments upon Dr. Johnson in her
Letters and in various newspaper articles; but it is only
fair to say that she knew him as thoroughly, during the
last twenty years of his life, as anyone in Lichfield,
barring Lucy Porter herself. She was well aware, she
says,[16] that he disliked her, "notwithstanding the coax-
ing regard" which he always expressed for her. As the
years went by, and Anna Seward became the center of
the Lichfield coterie, and began to win her laurel
wreaths at Lady Miller's villa, and to be mentioned in
the public press, Johnson must have been well informed
of her pretensions as a writer, though she studiously
avoided all reference, in his presence, to her literary
works.

"He always spoke with strong dislike of all our celebrated female writers," she says, "except Mrs. Piozzi."
This method of reaching her indirectly, she suggests,
was the only way in which he could wound her, since
she was silent upon the subject of her poems. "Once,"
she says, "perhaps as a reward for the unobtrusive disposition of my muse, he paid an high compliment in
my presence, to my Elegy on Cook. . . . I blushed,
curtsied, and instantly turned the conversation into a
different channel."[17]

Boswell says: "I showed him some verses on Lichfield,
by Miss Seward, which I had that day received from
her, and had the pleasure to hear him approve of them.

16. *Letters*, II, 44.   17. *Ibid.*, p. 45.

He confirmed to me the truth of a high compliment which I had been told he had paid to that lady when she mentioned to him the Columbiads, an epic poem by Madame du Boccage: 'Madam, there is not in it anything equal to your description of the sea around the North Pole, in your ode on the death of Captain Cook.' "[18]

These two instances of expressed approbation are worth recording; for the Doctor was chary of his praise. It is clear that he treated Miss Seward with far less amiability than he did the other "female celebrities," Fanny Burney, Hannah More, Elizabeth Carter, Helen Maria Williams, and Mrs. Thrale. It is not too fanciful to suspect that everything about Miss Seward annoyed him: her old father, who pampered himself and posed as a *littérateur;* her secure social position; her palatial home, her good looks, her fine clothes; her reputation as a poetess; her self-esteem (which may be admitted); her acquaintance with the great (so easily earned he must have thought, with so little talent, when his prodigious powers had gone so long unrewarded); her too-intimate knowledge of his own affairs—the half-discerned sense of superiority with which she always kept in mind the poverty of his youth.

So often she refers to his malice and envy that these characteristics must have been especially vivid in her remembrance of the Doctor. "In the course of many years' personal acquaintance with him," she writes, "I never knew a single instance in which praise (from

18. Boswell's *Life of Samuel Johnson,* ed. Hill, IV, 331.

another's lips) of any human being except Mrs. Thrale was not a caustic on his spirits, and this, whether their virtues or abilities were the subject of encomium." Miss Seward had high enthusiasms and great loyalties. It angered her to have to sit silently by and listen to his sweeping condemnation of her favorite authors and friends; or, if she ventured to protest, to be beaten down by invective and contempt. She winced under the sharp thrust of ridicule with which he punctured her harmless vanities, distended by the breath of flattery and uncritical praise. She retaliated by writing openly of Johnson's rudeness and injustice whenever the opportunity offered. There is evidence that, though she was revolted, she was not always intimidated by his roarings, and that when she chose to brave his displeasure, she could give him as good as he sent. Boswell presents one example of her temerity. The occasion (1778) was the meeting of a "literary party" at the bookshop of Mr. Dilly, in London.[19] "I am willing to love all mankind," thundered the Doctor, *"except an American."*

"Miss Seward," Boswell tells us, "looking to him with mild but steady astonishment, said: 'Sir, this is an instance that we are always most violent against those whom we have injured.'[20] . . . He was irritated still more by this delicate and keen reproach; and roared out another tremendous volley, which one might fancy could be heard across the Atlantic."

19. Miss Seward gives an account of this meeting at Dilly's, on pp. 97 *et seq.,* of Vol. I of her *Letters,* but does not mention the above encounter.

20. She referred, of course, to his pamphlet, *Taxation no Tyranny.*

It was upon this same occasion that the conversation with Mrs. Knowles occurred, relative to the gentle Jenny Harry—convert to Quakerism—in which, according to Miss Seward, Johnson displayed the most shocking self-righteousness, and rudeness. His remarks, as reported by Miss Seward, from notes which she says were taken at the time, abound in coarse phrases, such as: "I hate the odious wench, and ever shall hate her"; "Well may I hate the arrogance of a young wench, who sets herself up for a judge on theological points." The quiet self-possessed Quaker lady, Mrs. Knowles, paid no heed to his ranting, but answered him fearlessly, as Miss Seward had done a little while before.

From Anna Seward, we get a notion of what Johnson could be at his worst. He possibly allowed himself more license in Lichfield than elsewhere. He may have felt disposed to show his home town how important he had become. The people who had snubbed or patronized him in times past could now discover, either in person or by proxy, how magnificent a figure had been (potentially) the poor ill-looking, ill-dressed lad who had touched the edges of their social circle, but had never been drawn completely within.

Miss Seward has been harshly censured for her references to the violent behavior of Johnson in company; but it is not difficult to find corroboration of her statements. Sir N. W. Wraxall says in his *Historical Memoirs:* "I will freely confess that his [Johnson's] rugged exterior and garb, his uncouth gestures, his convolu-

tions and distortions, when added to the rude or dog-
matical manner in which he delivered his opinions and
decisions on every point . . . rendered him so disagreeable in company, and so oppressive in conversation, that
all the superiority of his talents could not make full
amends, in my estimation, for these defects. In his
anger, or even in the warmth of argument, where he
met with opposition, he often respected neither age,
rank, nor sex; and the usages of polished life imposed
a very inadequate restraint on his expressions or his
feelings. . . . If not irascible, he was certainly dicta-
torial, coarse, and sometimes almost impracticable. Those
whom he could not always vanquish by the force of
his intellect, by the depth and range of his arguments,
and by the compass of his gigantic faculties, he silenced
by rudeness."[21]

The Margravine of Anspach wrote in her *Memoirs:*
"The great fault which I found with Johnson was the
inveterate blame and contempt which he threw on all
contemporary writers. . . . Johnson was bilious and
had the spleen."[22]

Fanny Burney wrote in her diary, "I was really quite
grieved to see how unamiable he [Johnson] appeared,
and how greatly he made himself dreaded by all, and
by many abhorred."[23] Again, she made note: "He has
been in a terrible severe humor of late, and has really

21. I, 143.
22. "Memoirs" of Lady Craven, Margravine of Anspach: in *The
Beautiful Lady Craven,* by Broadley and Melville, II, 114.
23. II, 163.

frightened all the people, till they almost ran from him."[24]

Adverting to incidents which occurred during Dr. Johnson's early life, and to his relations with the Sewards, we have now indicated some of the reasons why the Bear and the Swan disliked each other. The record of their animosities may be followed in the proper chronological place. This will include something of what came out after Dr. Johnson's death, specifically Miss Seward's correspondence with Boswell (in which the Scotchman abandoned all pretense of friendship), and her letters to various acquaintances, in which her desire to emphasize the flaws in the character of Johnson seems to amount almost to an obsession.[25]

FOR more than a year, Miss Seward had been working at her poetical novel, *Louisa,* which had been begun when she was nineteen, and laid aside, perhaps because of her father's interdiction. It was published in 1784.[26]

24. *Ibid.,* p. 177.

25. "I fear," says an anonymous correspondent in *The Gentleman's Magazine* (July, 1794), "Miss Seward's strictures on Johnson's veracity did not proceed from an exuberance of the milk of human kindness."

26. Mr. Frank H. Chase of the Public Library of Boston writes as follows: "The British Museum catalogue shows five editions, of which the first, second, third, and fourth, are all in 1784, and the fifth London, 1792. Our earliest edition was published in New Haven, Conn., in 1789, and is also called fifth. Apparently these two fifths were unconscious of each other's existence." Letter to the present writer.

The poem was reviewed in the *Monthly Review* of November, 1784.

Walter Scott gives 1782 as the date of this poem, as does
the *Dictionary of National Biography*. The *Gentleman's
Magazine* (obituary of Miss Seward) gives 1784. The
question seems to be settled by a letter from the authoress to her friend Dr. Whalley,[27] dated February 14,
1784. "My 'Louisa' is in the press here: I chose it for the
sake of correcting my own press. . . . The Lichfield
printer is very dilatory, so it may be long before the
poem comes out." On January 3, 1785, she wrote to Dr.
Whalley: "How provoking it is that you never got
Hayley's 'Plays,' nor my 'Louisa'! What does Lady
Langham say about them?—did she receive them from
Robinson?" These two books were lost in transit, and
Miss Seward eventually sent the Whalleys another copy
of *Louisa*.

"I know it is the best and ablest of my productions,"
she wrote to George Hardinge in 1786. "There may
certainly be a best, even when nothing is very good."
This modesty was possibly due to the position of Hardinge as Attorney General to the Queen. Later he made
himself so disagreeable by sharp criticisms of her diction, that Miss Seward petulantly refused to write to
him. "Parity," she told him, did not exist between them.
"It was vain to hope for this parity between a fastidious
Wit and a glowing Enthusiast. . . . My peace requires
that I should not be of your correspondence." Yet the
exchange of letters continued for some time longer.

27. *Journals and Correspondence of Thomas Sedgewick Whalley,
D.D., of Mendip Lodge, Somerset,* ed. Rev. Hill Wickham, I, 401,
414.

Hardinge was furious at the publication of Miss Seward's answers to his letters, in which he had scarcely shown himself at his best. After Miss Seward's death, he said spiteful and vulgar things about her, not much to his own glory.[28]

All this is parenthetical. *Louisa* was, we are told, "favourably received," and it ran through five editions. Sentimental stories about lovelorn and ill-treated "females" were greatly in vogue; and the age is as much to blame as the author for an artificial, far-fetched piece of bathos like *Louisa*. Weeping Clarissas were multiplied by a brood of lesser Richardsons; and the *Man of Feeling* and its imitators obtained a popularity which seems unbelievable to modern readers. *Louisa,* says Miss Seward, involves passions rather than incidents. In other words, it consists of a good deal more than plot. It contains a large proportion of description, with interpolations of apostrophe and other forms of maundering which appeal but slightly to the reader of today.

Louisa is in four epistles. "They resulted," says the author, "from an idea of its being possible to unite the impassioned fondness of Pope's Eloisa, with the chaster tenderness of Prior's Emma; avoiding the voluptuousness of the first, and the too-conceding softness of the second."[29]

The first epistle is from Louisa, the heroine, to her friend Emma, who lives in the East Indies. It is dated

28. In a letter written before her death, he refers to her as "the roan mare." See also Nichols' *Illustrations,* III, 815.

29. *Poetical Works,* II, 219.

October 21, 1779. Emma has been absent from England for four years. Louisa writes confidentially, "her bosom griefs to tell." Briefly, she has been engaged to marry Eugenio, a friend of her brother's, and now finds herself a victim of perfidy. Eugenio has gone away to win success in commerce. His letters grow infrequent and cease. Rumors say that he has found someone else to love.

> "Three wretched weeks [says Louisa] my throbbing bosom bears
> The wounding conflict of its various fears,
> While Rumour's voice inflames my grief and pride,
> And gives Eugenio to a wealthier bride.
> My trembling hands, the sick suspense to ease,
> From day to day the public records seize;
> While glances rapid as the meteor's ray,
> Eager amidst the crowded columns stray;
> Snatch at sad certainty from busy fame,
> Yet dread to meet my dear Eugenio's name.
> Now glooms on the stain'd page the barbarous truth,
> And blights each blooming promise of my youth!
> Eugenio married! Anguish and despair,
> In ev'ry pompous killing letter glare!"[30]

Louisa, deeply wronged, believes herself unable to survive the pain occasioned by loss and treachery. She contemplates suicide, but decides to live until grief alone shall slay her.

> Eugenio married, seals Louisa's doom,
> Her sure, though lingering passport to the tomb!

The second epistle is from Eugenio to Emma, on her return from the East Indies. It is dated April 15, 1781. He explains how he has been led to betray the fondness

30. *Poetical Works*, II, 233.

of Louisa's heart, and to desert his promised bride. One day, he says, he was wandering in a wooded park, and heard wild cries for help. He rushed to the spot from which the screams appeared to come. He found a beautiful young woman in the hands of such ruffians as prey (in the moving pictures) on woman's honor.

> "Alarm'd, the villains quit their struggling prey,
> And two, with terror struck, speed fast away.
> Fiercer the third, the arm of blood extends;
> The levell'd tube, in dire direction, bends!
> Yet no cold fear arrests my vengeful force,
> And his wing'd death-ball flies with erring course;
> But not descends my nervous blow in vain,
> The hidden lead[31] indents the murderer's brain;
> With one demoniac glance, as down he fell,
> The soul starts furious from its vital cell."

The assailants thus easily disposed of, the young man puts the young lady upon his horse, and takes her to his own home, under the "modest dome" of which his amiable parents are awaiting his return. He finds that Emira, whom he has saved, is the heiress to a vast estate. She immediately falls in love with her rescuer, and gives clear evidence of a desire to marry him. He resists her charms. But now, at a stroke, his father loses every penny of his money. He pleads with his son to marry the heiress and save his parents from blighting penury. The idea of their being saved by energetic work seems not to occur to anyone. Eugenio, in terrible suffering and despair, consents. Affairs progress at a rapid rate. Soon, without apprising Louisa of his intentions,

31. In Eugenio's cane.

he marries Emira and gains possession of her wealth. Having made the sacrifice, he resolves to let Louisa think that he no longer loves her. The delusion, he believes, will the sooner quench her love for him. Emma, to whom the letter is addressed, is requested to reveal his motives after he is dead.

The third epistle is from Louisa to Emma, dated April 21, 1781, and is "written the day after she [Louisa] had received from her [Emma] Eugenio's exculpating letter." Emma, it seems, has sent on Eugenio's letter without waiting for his demise. Eugenio is absolved from all imputation of evil. He is seen to be merely the victim of his noble nature.

> "Then did I read [says Louisa], and weep, and throb, and glow,
> Approve, absolve, admire, and sigh,
> Till pensive peace shone mildly in my eye."

Convinced of the innocence of her Eugenio, inasmuch as all his acts have been impelled by the purest motives, Louisa freely forgives him. Her health, she says, will now be restored by the knowledge that he has not proved "cruel, venal, false, and vain." She calls down upon him the blessings of heaven, and resigns him to his wife and family with the pious hope that he will ever remain as irreproachable and self-sacrificing as he has been proved.

The fourth epistle is from Louisa to Emma, dated April 25, 1781. Louisa is visited by Eugenio's father, Ernesto, who is greatly moved at seeing his son's deserted love. A long poetic colloquy ensues, concluded by Ernesto's words:

> "Honour'd Louisa! fair angelic maid!
> With every blessing be thy worth repaid!
> But time flies rapidly!—the least delay
> Ill suits the important message I convey;
> An hapless penitent adjures thee fly,
> To pardon and receive her dying sigh;
> O come with me, Louisa!—at thy gates,
> Lo! in the glen, the expecting chariot waits!"

Emira's story is short and painful, as her father-in-law relates it to Louisa. Realizing that she has no love from her husband, she becomes wild and dissipated. She feels no fondness for her "wee cherub-daughter." Resisting the admonitions of Eugenio, she rushes out from her home to gay debauched assemblages. She bestows her charms upon a "haughty lord, licentious, false, and vain." Paying the penalty of her evil behavior, she is about to pass away. She wishes to ask forgiveness of the woman whom she has wronged. Louisa, in her letter to Emma, relates the sad tale of Emira's last hour. She is readily forgiven by the angelic Louisa, and dies consoled. Louisa and Eugenio are, of course, united, with Eugenio's child as a bond of renewed affection between them. The poem concludes with an invitation to Emma:

> "Haste then to share our blessings as they glow
> Through the receding shades of heaviest woe!—
> As spring's fair morn, with calm and dewy light,
> Breaks through the weary, long, and stormy night,
> So now, as through the vale of life we stray,
> The STAR OF JOY relumes, and leads us on our way!"

Miss Seward took her story seriously, but the uneasiness of her preface shows that she feared the critics. It seems a foolish tale enough; and the manner was in agreement with the matter. Yet *Louisa* was accepted by the public, which was by no means made up of parlor maids, but of people of quality, who could afford to pay the price demanded. Critics carped, it is true. But five editions are fairly tangible evidence of success. The poem added laurels to those already won, and brought the reward of notices, letters, more friends who praised. These good things came to counterbalance the sorrows of the past.

"You will be kindly gratified," the author wrote the Rev. Mr. Whalley, "to hear that I receive the highest encomiums upon my poem, Louisa, by the first literary characters of the age.[32] I inclose the beautiful eulogium with which it has been honoured by Mr. Hayley. This eulogium has appeared in several of the public prints." Mr. Hayley was prepared to sacrifice criticism to friendship; besides, his was not a particularly penetrating mind. His warm "encomiums" made up for many gibes.

The review of *Louisa* in the *European Magazine,* which had usually been kind to her writings, hurt her feelings sadly. Severe not only to *Louisa,* but in retrospect to her other works as well, it alleged that "immorality, vulgarness, bombast, and even obscurity," pervaded all her writings. These slurs were hard to endure. Hayley's encouragement was, therefore, doubly welcome.

> The scoff of spleen shall miss its wounding aim,
> For Hayley praises, and his praise is fame.

32. A favorable review by Boswell of *Louisa* is quoted in the *European Magazine* for August 1, 1784, p. 106.

Thus the author of *Louisa* consoled herself for some unpleasantness on the part of the reviews. No wonder she wrote to Court Dewes of William Hayley, "Words are too weak to say how much I love, admire, and honour his genius and his virtues!"

CHAPTER VI

1785–1789

A GLITTERING WORLD

IN the spring of 1785 Boswell wrote to Miss Seward
for information and anecdotes concerning Dr. Johnson. She replied in a letter transcribed into one of
the volumes published after her death.[1] In this letter
she related as authentic the story of the dead duck,
later the subject of an exchange of letters in the *Gentleman's Magazine*. There were also an invidious description of Johnson's wife; and a colloquy between
Johnson and his mother on the matter of his marriage
to Mrs. Porter.

In this letter to Boswell, Miss Seward thus admon-
ished him:

> The genuine lovers of the poetic science look with anxious eyes to
> Mr. Boswell, desiring that every merit of the stupendous mortal may
> be shewn in its fairest light; but expecting also that impartial justice,
> so worthy of a generous mind, which the popular cry cannot influ-
> ence to flatter the object of discrimination, nor yet the yearnings of
> remembered amity induce, to invest that object with unreal perfec-
> tion, injurious, from the severity of his censures, to the rights of
> others.

A letter to Mrs. Knowles says:

> Mr. Boswell has applied to me for Johnsonian records for his
> life of the despot. If he inserts them unmutilated, as I have ar-
> ranged them, they will contribute to display Johnson's real character

1. *Letters*, I, 38.

to the public; that strange compound of great talents, weak and absurd prejudices; strong, but unfruitful devotion; intolerant fierceness; compassionate munificence, and corroding envy. I was fearful that Mr. Boswell's personal attachment would have scrupled to show those dark shades which truth commands should be employed in drawing the Johnsonian portrait; but these fears are considerably dissipated by the style of Mr. Boswell's acknowledgements for the materials I had sent him, and for the perfect impartiality with which I had spoken of Johnson's virtues and faults.[2]

Boswell afterward rejected the material which Miss Seward sent him, and "committed it to the flames."[3] Perhaps, however, at this time (1785), he had not begun to question the trustworthiness of her statements.

A month or so after the dispatch of the letter mentioned above, Boswell visited Lichfield, and called upon Miss Seward for the purpose of adding to his knowledge of Dr. Johnson. Boswell and the lady were by no means strangers. They had met both in Lichfield and London.[4] On this occasion, she did not find him, she says, so "candid and ingenuous" as she expected. She wrangled with him on the subject of Johnson's envious disposition. "He affected to distinguish, in the despot's favour, between envy and literary jealousy." The conversation between the two is not reported in full. It was probably at the time of this same visit that Boswell told Miss Seward (as she says) that Johnson's objection to

2. *Ibid.,* p. 47.

3. See *Gentleman's Magazine,* February, 1794, and Nichols' *Illustrations,* VII, 357.

4. Boswell first met Miss Seward in 1776, at her own home. See his *Life of Samuel Johnson,* ed. Hill, II, 467. He next met her at Dilly's bookshop in London, in 1778, *ibid.,* III, 284. He called on her in Lichfield, October, 1779.

the marriage of Mrs. Thrale was a purely personal one. "Mr. Boswell told me," she asserts, "Johnson wished and expected to have married her himself."[5]

On the whole, the visit of Boswell seems to have been a disappointment to Miss Seward, who had perhaps expected to have a larger part than was granted her in the biography which he was writing. Probably Boswell had become suspicious of her accuracy. The disaffection between him and Miss Seward may have begun at this time.

In the autumn of 1785 Miss Seward went to a musical festival at Manchester, where "the collected musical strength of the kingdom" was displayed, and where Madame Mara, "the new-risen star of the harmonic world," and John Saville of Lichfield took the leading parts in song. Miss Seward and her friend Miss Weston, afterward Mrs. Pennington, joined "a very agreeable party from Derbyshire," and spent some days in listening to the best classical music (a good deal of Handel), and meeting shoals of cultivated people. Toward Madame Mara, then undergoing a testing time before the English public, they turned an appreciative but critical ear. Mara could not entirely please; but for John Saville there was the most unqualified praise. "Our friend Saville," Miss Seward wrote to Helen Williams, "is to open the Messiah, and take all the principal tenor and contra-tenor songs. He unites poetic taste, and the vivid emotions of a feeling heart, and of a high and

5. *Letters*, II, 346.

kindling spirit, to a rich, extensive, and powerful voice, and the most perfect knowledge of his science."

This is only one of the eulogies which she pronounces on the subject of Saville and his singing. Of her heart's emotion concerning him, there can be no manner of doubt.

During this year and the next, Miss Seward made several visits, of a sort quite after her own heart, among the Dewes and Granville groups, whom she had met at Buxton in 1783. In December and January, 1785–86, she passed three weeks in the home of Mr. Court Dewes of Wellesbourne, near Warwick. Mr. Dewes was a wealthy bachelor of good family. He was related to the celebrated Mrs. Delany, whose niece, Miss Port (who married Mr. Waddington), visited Miss Seward in 1789, on her honeymoon trip. Curiously enough, Richard Lovell Edgeworth, when a boy at school in England (1752), had been invited to Wellesbourne for his Christmas holidays, and was mentioned in Mrs. Delany's letters of that period.

Miss Seward describes Mr. Dewes as "a little thin valetudinarian bachelor, with the complexion and air of a Frenchman; polite, learned, intelligent, sincere, and pious." He had, she says, in a letter of later years "the bestowing spirit of Mr. Day, without its acrimony; the politeness of Mr. E—— [Edgeworth], without its insincerity."

The village of Wellesbourne, where the Deweses and Granvilles lived, bordered upon the park of the Lucy family, whose deer are forever associated with the early life of Shakespeare. Miss Seward was thrilled at this contact with Shakespearean scenes; though the dead of winter was not the most favorable time to enjoy them.

The proprieties were well maintained by Mr. Dewes's brother, Mr. Granville, and his wife and children. Christmas entertainments, courtesies exchanged with congenial neighbors, card parties, home concerts, reading aloud, and exalted conversation "speeded the wintry hours of the day and night on smooth and rapid pinion." Miss Seward took with her, for reading aloud, Cowper's *The Task,* then new to the world, and, as she calls it, "the first very distinguished fire of a star lately arisen in our poetic hemisphere"; and Hayley's *Essay on Epic Poetry,* which had been out for some years, and had passed through several editions. She prided herself on knowing the new books of the most worth; and she never (at that time) missed an opportunity of rolling a log for her friend "the bard of Eartham."

She talked a good deal with Mrs. Granville about Jenny Harry, the Quaker girl (apostate), whose defense by Mrs. Knowles had aroused Dr. Johnson to such a pitch of insulting rudeness, in the memorable interview at Dilly's bookshop, that even Boswell was aghast. Jenny Harry had been a friend of Mrs. Granville before the latter lady, a Miss Delabere, had married. "Mrs. Grenville shewed me Jenny Harry's apologetic tract on quitting our church in favour of quakerism, at so vast a sacrifice of worldly interests," Miss Seward wrote to Mrs. Knowles. ". . . It occasioned us to comment with fresh indignation upon the ruffian-asperity of Dr. John-

son on this subject; for I had previously recounted to
them the conversation of that tremendous evening, as
Mr. Boswell calls it, at Dilly's, when you, with patient
and placid smiles, calmly and concisely refuted the
roaring of bigot rage, which induced his shuddering
friend's emphatic whisper,—'I never saw this mighty
lion so chafed before.' "

On this and other visits to Wellesbourne, Miss Seward
was greatly interested in hearing about Mrs. Delany
from the lips of her adoring relatives, and in seeing the
relics pertaining to that wonderful woman of the old
school. Particularly did she marvel, as others have done,
over the *hortus siccus,* for which Mrs. Delany is and
will be famous. This, she wrote to Mr. Saville,[6] was

contained in ten immense folios, each enriched with an hundred
floral plants, representing, in cut paper, of infinitely various dyes, the
finest flowers of our own and every other climate, from the best
specimens that the field, the garden, the greenhouse, and the con-
servatory could furnish; and with a fidelity and vividness of colouring,
which shames the needle and the pencil. The moss, the films, the
farina, every, the minutest part, is represented with matchless delicacy. It was at the age of seventy-five that this prodigy of female
genius invented her art, and gave it that last perfection which makes
imitation hopeless.

Always a fine painter, and not ignorant of the arts of chemistry,
she herself dyed her papers from whence the new creation arose. Of
this astonishing work Dr. Darwin has given a most erroneous description in his splendid poem.[7] He ought not to have taken such a
liberty.

It was hard for Miss Seward to tear herself away from
these sympathetic friends, though she was anxious about

6. *Letters,* III, 195 *et seq.*   7. *The Botanic Garden.*

her father, whom she had left in the care of her cousin, Mr. White, and the useful Mr. Saville. In the years which were now to come, visits such as these to the Dewes family were to count among the chief pleasures which Miss Seward enjoyed. She was received with flattering ardor, and entertained and fêted as an honored guest. Her opinions were listened to with deference; her remarkable conversational powers were stimulated and praised. Her lovely voice made her the center of attention when she was called upon to read and recite. Her vivacity, her store of information, her quick retort and apt quotation and reference, her interest in everything and everybody around her, her readiness to listen and please and admire, made her arrival welcome and her departure regretted. Miss Seward, it must be confessed, was a glutton for praise. These country-house visits brought her more gratifying tributes than she was likely to receive in London, where notabilities were as thick as blackberries, and "encomiums" were sparingly dealt out.

A few days after her return from this particular visit (ending in January, 1786), "through the snowy length of unjoyous roads," to the warmth of the Palace hearth, occurred the death of one of Miss Seward's oldest friends in Lichfield, Miss Lucy Porter. "Johnson's daughter-in-law [stepdaughter] dear Lucy Porter, was buried this evening," Miss Seward wrote to her Quaker friend, Mrs. Knowles. "The little asperities of her petulant humour had all softened down in her long illness, sustained with true Christian patience. Thus we saw her

passing slowly away from us, and saw it with considerable regret."

"Spite of the accustomed petulance of her temper,"
runs another letter, "I regret her as a friendly creature,
of intrinsic worth, with whom from childhood, I had
been intimate." It will be seen that the rude treatment
which Miss Seward had received from Dr. Johnson, and
her deep-seated dislike for him and his bad manners
did not prevent her from giving Miss Porter credit for
her true worth. It was characteristic of Miss Seward to
be loyal and generous to her friends—too generous,
sometimes, when their social or literary merits were
called in question. This fact is the better reason for
assuming that she did not consciously exaggerate when
writing of Dr. Johnson, however much her own emotional reactions may have been involved in her judgment.

THE "Benvolio" controversy in the *Gentleman's Magazine* engaged the attention of Miss Seward in the early
part of 1786. The occasion of the letters was the review
of Boswell's *Tour to the Hebrides,* which had appeared
in November. The first letter signed "Benvolio" which
Miss Seward sent to Urban's *Magazine* is dated January
10, 1786. At this date Miss Seward was at Wellesbourne,
visiting the Granvilles. The letter is too long to quote;
but it shows Miss Seward as a writer of excellent prose,
more vigorous than that of her private letters. Its object
is to offer a corrective to the extravagant praise lavished
upon Dr. Samuel Johnson, who had died a little over
a year before.

"Personally to have known the wonderful being," she wrote, "is to obtain the testimony of recollection for the fidelity of Mr. Boswell's anecdotes; since it cannot fail to parallel them; and they enable those who never conversed with him to see him as he was; to perceive the genius and absurdity, wisdom and folly, penetration and prejudice, devotion and superstition, compassion and malevolence, friendship and envy, truth and sophistry, which were blended in the large composition of that man!"[8]

"Over the malignance he records," another passage runs, "Mr. Boswell strives to spread a veil; but that veil is not impenetrable. Facts are stubborn things; and since they are fairly recited, partiality seeks to gild them in vain." Then follows a commentary on Johnson's injustices to Garrick, to Mrs. Montagu, and to the Scottish nation; the personal bias of his judgments; and the bigotry of his "toryism."

The next-to-the-last paragraph is as follows: "Of Mr. Boswell's Tour the following admirable compendium was lately given by the most illustrious literary character[9] now living, in a letter to one of his friends: 'It is a most amusing history of a learned monster, written by his shew-man, who perpetually discovers a diverting apprehension that his beast will play the savage too furiously, and lacerate the company instead of entertaining them.' " Boswell may well have winced at the word *shew-man,* but he made no public reply.

8. *Gentleman's Magazine,* LVI (February, 1786), 125.
9. Can this be Mr. Hayley?

The boldest passage in this letter of January 10 is the one which asserts that "Dr. Johnson's own veracity was too often the victim of his malevolent passions." Miss Seward's constant attacks on Johnson's "veracity," aroused Boswell, seven years later, to such a savage counter-thrust that the Lichfield lady must have regretted ever penning a line upon her celebrated fellow townsman.

Another long "Benvolio" letter, covering several pages, was written on April 12, 1786.[10] In it Miss Seward applied herself to discrediting the reputation which Boswell and Mrs. Piozzi had attempted to assign to Johnson for honesty, charity, and other virtues. She gave instances of his injurious sarcasm, his irritable temper, his delight in wounding the feelings of others, his ingratitude, and his indulgence in the most insolent rudeness. Referring to Mrs. Piozzi's book on Dr. Johnson, she says: "We recognize . . . the same human hornet, on sullen and sounding wing, in her drawing-room as we saw fastening upon the Scotch professors, and stinging them, in return for the honey with which they had fed him." He "eagerly sacrificed," she asserted, his veracity "to his hatred and prejudices"; and spoke yet again of his "MALEVOLENCE."

In the same issue of the *Gentleman's Magazine* are two letters from Boswell, not, however, in reply to Miss Seward. The first, dated March 9, alludes to a "noble lord," concerning whom some lines had been inserted in the first edition of the *Journal of a Tour to the*

10. *Gentleman's Magazine*, LVI (April, 1786), 302.

Hebrides, and omitted in the second edition. The second letter, dated April 17, deals with Mrs. Thrale's opinion of Mrs. Montagu's book on Shakespeare.

Miss Seward wrote another "Benvolio" letter on August 9, 1787, in answer to some protests (not written by Boswell) which had called her previous communications "malevolent." She defended herself with restrained eloquence. We quote one passage, leaving out others which would illustrate her vivacity as well: "If Johnson walked humbly with his God, he did not walk obediently, since his life was one continued disobedience to the humility commanded by the Scriptures, and to the great precept, 'Do unto others as ye would they should do unto you.' Ill could Johnson have borne the insults he afflicted."

One pertinent saying with regard to her sex is worth recording: "Respecting a misapplication of signature, be it remembered that souls are of no sex, and their effusions therefore may, at pleasure, assume a masculine or a feminine application."

Miss Seward took delight in writing these letters, giving vent to her indignation at hearing Dr. Johnson lauded as if he were a demigod, with no human faults. In her private letters, she more than once confessed with pride that she was the author of the "Benvolio" epistles, which had no doubt attracted a great amount of attention, on account of their animated and fearless style, as well as on account of the general interest of the subject. To Dr. Warner she wrote: "It gratifies my literary ambition not slightly, that you like me so much in my 'doublet and hose,' in the letters on Johnson's character, signed Benvolio. I was delighted by your recommending them to my attention as able, eloquent and convincing, without the least suspicion of the name or the sex of their author, so utterly exempted from the possibility of being meant as flattery."[11]

She publicly acknowledged the letters in the *Gentleman's Magazine* for December, 1793, and for October, 1794. In the issue for December, 1794, she wrote: ". . . The three letters signed Benvolio in the numbers for February and April, 1786, p. 129 and p. 302, and for August, 1787, p. 684, are *mine;* I avowed them at the time they appeared, to almost all my friends, and, I think, to Mr. Boswell. The only occasion on which I declined acknowledging them was in a literary circle in London, May, 1786, where I heard the two first, for the last was not then written, pronounced the most equitable balance of Dr. Johnson's good and ill qualities which had appeared. They were too highly spoken of to permit my owning them, as the company were chiefly strangers to me."

Of Miss Seward's contest with Boswell after the publication of his *Life of Samuel Johnson,* we shall have something to say on a later page. In passing, we may mention the fondness which Miss Seward showed for controversy. She engaged in a public debate (in print) with Mr. Weston regarding the reputation and claims of the "Sweet Swan of Twickenham"; also she debated the subject of pulpit oratory with Mr. Jerningham in the

11. *Letters,* I, 256.

columns of the *Gentleman's Magazine* for February, March, and April, 1801.

In May (1786) Miss Seward left her "aged nurseling," as she was fond of calling her father, and made one of her rare visits to London, where she lived in a "whirl" and "vortex" of social and intellectual delights. Of all she saw and heard we know but little. She was much with her friend Helen Maria Williams, the poet—young, ambitious, and impulsive—who had come to the city five years before, an ignorant aspiring girl, and now knew nearly everybody.

At the house of Miss Williams and that of the Mathiases,[12] there were "animated literary breakfastings," where "the belle esprits of both sexes" made those meetings brilliant with "genius, wit, and knowledge." She was forced to decline "countless kind invitations"; but, she says, "I was honoured by finding several literary parties formed on my account; and many were replete with every gratification to my spirit." It will be remembered that her monodies had attracted the attention of the reading public in London; that the poetical novel *Louisa* had had a remarkable sale; and that her "Odes" from Horace were just then appearing, month by month, in the *Gentleman's Magazine,* affording a sub-

12. Probably the family of T. J. Mathias (1754–1835), subtreasurer to the Queen, 1782 and following. He was for some time Librarian at Buckingham Palace. He wrote satires, edited Gray and other poets, and gained eminence as an Italian scholar. Or possibly this Mathias family was that mentioned by T. Harwood, historian of Lichfield, in a letter to John Wilson Croker, 1829. He says that Mr. Mathias was "a merchant in London, a friend of Captain Porter" (*The Croker Papers,* II, 44).

ject of both compliment and controversy. "I profess no unnatural stoicism to the praises of the learned and ingenious," she wrote on her return to Lichfield; "nor could I listen with undelighted ears to the warm approbation of my Horatian paraphrases, expressed in these circles." She did not hear the slighting remarks made by some critics, upon the poems, which, aside from their merits as translations, are pretty enough, gracefully and vivaciously expressed. In any case, her pleasing personality must have disarmed the most aggressive detractor, at least till she was out of sight. So she brought home memories of homage, and not of churlish cavilings.

We may stop here for further notice of these Horatian "Odes," which would have been the chief topic of any conversation with Miss Seward, when she entered a London drawing-room or found her place at a dinner table. She was totally without knowledge of either Greek or Latin; and she could not help being a bit nervous about these paraphrases, as she properly calls them; though she was bolstered up by the thought that many of her classically trained friends admired them. Mr. Grove of Lichfield and Mr. Court Dewes of Wellesbourne had "induced her," she explained, to paraphrase Horace's *Odes* from prose translations, to be furnished her by themselves or other competent scholars. They told her to read over the prose translations; to seize the leading idea; to write freely, not holding herself to literal phrasing; and to use any figure of speech, whether Horace used it or not, so long as it was consistent with the age in which he wrote. She found it amusing, she said, to put a few of the *Odes* into English, "while her hair was dressing," thus belittling the care which she lavished on all her verse and prose. As a matter of fact, she took endless pains with them. She felt that they would be subjected to unfriendly analysis, as indeed they were.

She reported appreciatively to Mr. Hayley the warnings of Dr. Vyse, one of the Canons of the Cathedral, who had been the tentative sweetheart mentioned earlier in these papers. "Nancy," said he, "take the advice of an old friend. Never again attempt translating Horace, since you do not know Latin." In spite of his air of angry earnestness (how men of that day did dislike to see a woman succeed!), she refused to promise, citing the encouragement of Mr. Grove and Mr. Dewes, "both accomplished scholars." Dr. Vyse was not the only one who thought her presumptuous, though it seems as if her method, frankly avowed, was legitimate enough. She did not, however, paraphrase the full number of *Odes*. She did not have time, for one thing; some of the poems were not interesting; and others were, as she truly said, "unfit for the female pen." The honor which they brought her (and it was not a little) shed an exultant glow upon those seventeen days in London, in 1786. The rewards of authorship are small enough at the best; and no one at this late day should begrudge her the treasure of her public plaudits, even though they seem to be somewhat richer than she deserved.

One of the pleasures of that stay in London was the

opportunity to attend the Handel Festival in Westminster Abbey. Miss Seward does not seem to have
gone up to London for the great Handel Commemoration Festival in 1784. This festival was repeated at intervals thereafter, and that of 1786 may well have been
as soul stirring as the earlier one. Her admiration for
Handel's music (apparently taken over from Mr.
Saville's) amounted to a passion. In a letter to Mrs.
Hayley, of 1795, she says: "The unusual opinions expressed in your last do not coincide with Giovanni's and
mine, to whom the choruses of Handel are dearer than
any other species of music."[13]

In writing to her cousin, Mrs. Martin, of the pleasures
of her trip to London, she says: "People universally
assert [of the Handel Festivals] that the world never
produced anything of equal effect in the art. Indeed, I
believe that, at these festivals, music touched her ne-
plus-ultra of excellence."[14] Then follows a long discourse on the qualities of the music, the characteristics
of the individual performers, and the rapture which she
felt in being privileged to listen to the "sublime harmonies" from Handel's "matchless genius." It is worth
noting that she had breakfast with Mr. John Bates, the
conductor of the band of more than five hundred musicians who gave vocal and instrumental performances in
Westminster Abbey. His wife, who sang for her, Miss
Seward thought far superior to Mara. "I observed to
him," she says, "that Mara put too much gold fringe
and tassels, upon the solemn robe of melody, 'I know

13. *Letters,* IV, 69.   14. *Ibid.,* I, 152.

that my Redeemer liveth.' Do not say gold, madam, he replied; it was despicable tinsel."

Another privilege long to be remembered was that of seeing Mrs. Siddons, for the first time in comedy. The play was *As You Like It*. Miss Seward made some shrewd comments on the performance, not all favorable to the majestic Rosalind. She thought the great actress's smile enchanting, her form magnificent, and her tears irresistible; but wisely came to the conclusion that a gay and impersonal character was not suited to "the Siddonian form and countenance." It would have been with some self-consciousness that she watched and listened; for the satellites of Miss Seward had not hesitated to compare her to the queen of the stage, and had asserted that their voices were peculiarly alike. She came away, no doubt, with many privately recorded hints for her readings of Shakespeare in country-house drawing-rooms or her own spacious *salon*.

The four years from 1786 to 1790, the year of her father's death, Miss Seward passed largely at home. She gave to the old man, now painfully feeble, both physically and mentally, the most conscientious care. It was her delight to provide him with every material comfort, with medical attention (Dr. Darwin's place had been taken by a Dr. Jones), and with all the distractions and consolations which his weakened mental state could support. A few excursions necessary for her own health, she made into Shropshire and Derbyshire; and once or twice she spent a week in Sheffield, when certain oratorios were being presented.

At Ludlow she enjoyed the society of Miss Weston, to whom she was then devoted, but from whom she was later estranged for a period of twelve years; and the Whalleys,[15] dear friends whom she visited more than once at their estate in the Mendip Hills. Ludlow, she said in the enthusiasm of this visit, was the most beautiful town she had ever seen. She took pleasure in tracing the ruins of Ludlow Castle, where Milton's masque of *Comus* was first performed. The extensive and minutely careful reading of Miss Seward, and the alertness of her mind, are shown by the fact that, wherever she went, she was always informed concerning the history of the region, and attentive to its literary meaning. The scenic beauties of her environment stirred her to raptures; but she understood the associations as well, and was often moved to celebrate them in verse.

By this time, Lichfield visitors were showing a flattering interest in the local poetess, whose fame had spread abroad. When, in 1787, Mr. and Mrs. Piozzi stopped at the Inn, on their way to or from Wales, it was the natural thing for the two literary women to become acquainted. Mrs. Piozzi had fallen somewhat from her high estate, but was still a prominent person, with her wealth, her memories of the Johnson circle, and her touch with the great world of rank and fashion. The Rev. Mr. Whalley, knowing Mr. and Mrs. Piozzi's

15. For an account of Mr. Whalley, see *Journals and Correspondence of Thomas Sedgewick Whalley, D.D., of Mendip Lodge, Somerset,* ed. Rev. Hill Wickham.

plans, sent a letter of introduction, which did not reach Miss Seward until too late; but her friends and cousins persuaded her that an unintroduced visit might not be a "liberty." To Mr. Parker, who laughed her out of her scruples, she felt indebted, she said, for "eight or nine radiant hours" in the society of the musician and his wife. They passed one evening with her, and she the next with them.

Mrs. Piozzi was all that Miss Seward had imagined her; and in truth she was as much charmed with Mr. Piozzi as with the woman who had been accused of lowering herself in her marriage. "Dr. Johnson told me truth," wrote Miss Seward to Mr. Whalley, "when he said she had more colloquial wit than most of our literary women. It is indeed a fountain of perpetual flow; —but he did not tell me truth when he asserted that Piozzi was an ugly dog, without particular skill in his profession. Mr. Piozzi is an handsome man in middle life, with a gentle, pleasing, and unaffected manner, and very eminent skill in his profession." Other passages in her letters do full justice to poor Piozzi, who had been maligned by gossips and their vulgar epithets. Possibly in defending him and Mrs. Piozzi, Miss Seward was thinking of the whispers concerning herself and Mr. Saville. To Mrs. Piozzi many references are made in later letters, of a highly complimentary nature, playing upon the epigram sent to Mr. Whalley—"Her conversation is that bright wine of the intellects which has no lees."

We may speak here, for the sake of convenience, of the further relations of Miss Seward and Mrs. Piozzi.

The next spring, Mrs. Piozzi sent Miss Seward a copy of her *Letters to and from the Late Samuel Johnson, LL.D. &c.* The dislike which Miss Seward felt for the late potentate of the literary world made it difficult for her to speak of the book without bitterness. She could not forbear some caustic remarks on the benignity of the *Letters,* adding that the editress had doubtless "expunged the malignant passages." She was hurt to perceive that she had no mention in the *Letters,* when so many other Lichfield people had been immortalized with a name or a line; she thanked Mrs. Piozzi (ironically, one imagines) for this suppression. She defended Miss Lucy Porter from the sneering remark of Johnson about her "hoary virginity," which she thought ill chosen. "Your epistles in this collection outshine your preceptor's," she wrote, "and are the gems of the volume." She referred with satisfaction to Dr. Johnson's praise of her own *Elegy on Cook,* which was almost the only scrap of recognition which she ever received from him. Her self-esteem demanded that Mrs. Piozzi should be aware of this bit of praise from such an exacting critic.

A week later she wrote to Mrs. Piozzi again, regarding some Della-Cruscan poems imputed to herself; and quite palpably exerted her utmost skill to show her power of poetic analysis and criticism, which was, we may grant, considerable. In the letters to Mrs. Piozzi is traceable a very human desire to prove herself the equal of her correspondent.

Baretti's coarse attack on Mrs. Piozzi in the *European Magazine* of 1788 aroused Miss Seward to an outburst of wrath against the "Italian assassin," as she called him, rashly referring to the trial for murder, in which he was acquitted. It was characteristic of Miss Seward, in whom loyalty was an eminent virtue, to feel a sense of outrage in reading such injurious reports, instead of half believing them and bandying them about, as is the way of the small-souled and envious. "The whole literary world should unite," she exclaimed, "in publicly reprobating such venomed and foul-mouthed railings."

It speaks much for the good nature of Mrs. Piozzi that her friendship with Miss Seward could survive the latter lady's frank criticism of her *Travels,* or, to give the exact title, *Observations and Reflections Made in the Course of a Journey through France, Italy, and Germany,* published in 1789.

One wonders that Miss Seward had the temerity to condemn the book so candidly, in a letter to its author. Most people would hesitate thus to excoriate a gift, but not so Miss Seward. It is in keeping with her qualities of openness and sincerity that she addressed her criticisms to Mrs. Piozzi herself. She would not write hypocritical praise to the author, and adverse opinions to others. It may be that, in the back of her mind, there was a sense of triumph in playing the schoolmistress to the famous Blue who had consorted as an equal with the wisest and wittiest in London. She was probably not conscious of this motive. She had carefully weighed the value of the book, and she intended to make her estimate clear, without fear or favor. She wrote:

> No work of the sort I ever read possesses in an equal degree the power of placing the reader in the scenes, and amongst the people it describes. Wit, knowledge, and imagination illuminate its pages,— but the infinite inequality of the style!—permit me to acknowledge to you what I have acknowledged to others, that it excites my exhaustless wonder, that Mrs. Piozzi, child of Genius, the pupil of Johnson, should pollute with the vulgarisms of unpolished conversation, her animated pages! That while she frequently displays her power of commanding the most chaste and beautiful style imaginable, she should generally use those inelegant, those strange *dids* and *does,* and *thoughs,* and *toos,* which produce jerking angles and stop-short abruptness, fatal at once to the grace and ease of the sentence;—which are, in language, what the rusty black silk handkerchief and the brass ring are upon the beautiful form of the Italian Countess she mentions, arrayed in embroidery, and blazing in jewels.[16]

There is much more of the same sort. Miss Seward justifies her unkindness by the statement that she "makes it a point of honour to speak her undisguised ideas, if she speaks at all, to her literary friends on their compositions." This is all very well. One should be honest at all costs. But Miss Seward herself could ill endure any strictures upon her own compositions, and suffered agonies of mortification when her own published works were assailed.

That Mrs. Piozzi bore no grudge after these rather severe censures upon her book, is shown by her letter to Mrs. Pennington (before her marriage Penelope

16. *Letters*, II, 337.

Sophia Weston) in which Miss Seward is mentioned
with kindness and good will. In August, 1791, she
wrote: "It appears so strange and so shocking to put up
my letter without speaking of Miss Seward, that I can't
bear it; nobody has such a notion of her talents as I
have, though all the world has talked so loudly about
them. Her Mental and indeed her Personal Charms,
when I last saw them, united the three grand Characteristics of Female Excellence to very great Perfection;
I mean Majesty, Vivacity, and Sweetness."[17]

No great intimacy developed between Miss Seward
and Mrs. Piozzi. They were not thrown much in each
other's way, and they evidently did not find each other
very congenial. One suspects that the shade of Dr. Johnson stood between them; and also that they felt the
constraint of their rivalry as conversationalists. Both had
been lauded by their respective groups of friends, as
adepts in the fine art of talking. Though each warmly
admired the other, there was a tacit understanding that
no close friendship was possible. Mrs. Piozzi showed
some kindnesses to Mr. Saville when he was in London
for his concerts; but it is not recorded that Miss Seward
was ever entertained in the Piozzi household either in
Wales or London. Occasional letters and the messages
sent by way of common friends constituted the chief
intercourse of the two literary ladies for many years.
Mrs. Piozzi long outlived Miss Seward.

One of the most flattering distinctions which Miss

17. *The Intimate Letters of Hester Piozzi and Penelope Pennington,*
ed. O. S. Knapp, p. 34.

Seward ever received was the visit to her, in 1787, of the Hero of Gibraltar, Lord Heathfield. When the great General came back to England, in a blaze of glory, Miss Seward wrote a high-sounding *Ode on General Eliott's Return from Gibraltar,* which was published in a quarto volume, early in June. Later in the summer, she was honored by a visit from the celebrated man, who was on a triumphal tour through the realm. His desire to wait upon her was a recognition of the "encomiums" which she had heaped upon him.

When it was known that the General was coming to Lichfield, elaborate preparations were made for his reception. He "frustrated" them, as Miss Seward tells us, by arriving on Sunday and departing the same day. Canon Seward was not well enough to greet the famous man when he called at the Palace; hence Miss Seward had to receive her guest and his attendants alone—unless her ever helpful cousin, Henry White, stood by her, as he probably did, to give her support and encouragement. Of the General's intended visit the poetess had had sufficient notice to have all her publications "elegantly bound," as the choicest gift she could offer. "He would not suffer his aide de camp to carry the book to the inn, but held it in his own hand as he walked through our streets," writes the much-honored lady. Truly, she must have felt her heart swell at such a tribute on her own ground and among her own companions, some of whom had seemed at times to entertain but small appreciation of her worth!

ONE of the diversions which Miss Seward enjoyed at

this period was her patronage of two boy prodigies, Thomas Lister and Henry Francis Cary. She met them in the spring of 1788. In a letter to William Hayley, she gives an account of them and their surprising performances.

Lister was the son of "a gentleman of family," living at Armitage Park, near Lichfield; Cary was the son of an officer[18] living at Sutton Coldfield. They were "just turned fifteen—their attachment and delight in each other generously enthusiastic." They had met each other at school, and had formed an "undying" friendship. Lister, on account of an impediment in his speech, had been thought unsuited for a university career, and had been placed with the banker of Lichfield, Mr. Cobb. Cary was at school in Birmingham, preparing himself for the University. For a time, the two boys were forbidden by their parents to write to each other, and were permitted to see each other only occasionally. Their parents had an idea that they devoted too much time to poetry, and that their friendship was of too feverish a nature. A sonnet written by Cary at the age of fourteen shows the warmth of his boyish feeling, as well as his mastery of the sonnet form:

To Mr. Thomas Lister[19]

Deem not the muse officious, if thy brow
    With her plain wreath to twine she fondly tries,
    Since, though Art marshalls not the varying dyes,
    Yet nature, sure, will bid the colours glow.

18. Capt. William Cary, who married Henrietta Brocas, and two other wives. Henry Francis, the translator, was born at Gibraltar in December, 1772.

19. *Odes and Sonnets,* published by Robson & Clarke.

Up the steep hill we, arm in arm, will go:
The hill of life—whether dark tempests rise,
Or golden suns illume the laughing skies.
Thus oft we fram'd the amicable vow,
What time the friendly star of evening pale,
That o'er the dim grove casts its silver gleam,
Led our slow footsteps down the devious vale.—
O! may these scenes prove no illusive dream!
Nor let our simple lives together fail
To flow, one lucid and unruffled stream!

Beginning with translations of Bion, Moschus, and Horace, the two boys had quickly ventured into original composition, with what was deemed a "miraculous" success. Before he had met Miss Seward, but while he was under the spell of her poetry (which he fervently admired), Cary had written and published his *Ode to General Eliott,* which, though actually commonplace, was considered a remarkable production for a boy of his age. "Cary, literally but just fifteen, is a miracle," wrote Miss Seward (June 5, 1788). "I never saw him nor heard of him until after his Ode to General Eliott came out. My acquaintance with him is not of four months' date." It had been reported that she had assisted the boy; but she refuted the suspicion with the words "Upon my honour, I never saw anything of his before it was sent away to be printed." It seems that Cary was visiting Lister at Armitage Park when he was received into the presence of the gracious poetess whom he had worshiped from afar.

Cary did not hesitate to attempt the most ambitious odes and sonnets, in the manner of Milton and Dryden. He became at once a regular contributor to the *Gentle-*

man's Magazine. In that periodical for September (1788), appeared a sonnet addressed to the two boys, which Miss Seward immediately assigned to Mr. Hayley. "I never," she wrote, "saw a more beautiful one of any origin, however splendid." She was somewhat taken aback, when she found that it was written, not by the bard of Eartham, but by Mr. Weston, "a self-taught genius," organist at Solihull, in Warwickshire. She was delighted, however, with a sonnet to herself by the same man, published in the *Gentleman's Magazine.* Here follows Weston's sonnet to the youthful prodigies:

To Messrs Cary and Lister[20]
Sonnet

Yet, yet your unpolluted stores with-hold,
　　Bright buds of genius, bursting into day!
　　Spite of propitious Phoebus' cheering ray,
Parnassian climes are chilling, *chilling* cold.
In vain ye glad th' enamoured breeze, unfold
　　In vain your rich luxuriant foliage, gay
　　With orient hues—that, blushing, ye display
Tyre's bloom imperial, streak'd with Ophir's gold!
　　Nor scent, nor beauty,—trust the warning verse,
Unconscious hapless pair! shall ought avail;
　　Envy, th' expanding blossom's cankering curse,
Shall gnaw,—detraction's instant blight assail
　　Your shrinking forms, and sportive scorn disperse
Your withered honours to the sighing gale.

Lister contributed some sonnets and other verses to the *Gentleman's Magazine,* over various signatures, though he does not seem to have written so prolifically as Cary. Miss Seward described Lister as "beautiful as a vernal morning," with an open countenance and clear

20. J. Weston, *Gentleman's Magazine,* September, 1788.

blue eyes. He was so good-tempered that he did not resent the oppressions of his parents, who feared that his passion for poetry might ruin his career. He endured his apprenticeship in Mr. Cobb's bank with touching patience; but by reading slowly aloud and making other faithful efforts, he so far corrected his speech that his father relented and sent him to Cambridge. He did not, however, fulfil the promise of his youth, and never achieved the fame of Cary. The two friends did not see much of each other after 1790, though they occasionally wrote to each other until 1805. Lister married a Miss Harriet Seal, whom Miss Seward described as a "sweet little creature." His second wife, whom he married in 1805, was a Miss Grove. Miss Seward called her "insipid," and said that she had "no mind." Lister was called to the bar and practiced law until the death of his father, when he went to live on the family estate at Armitage Park. He died in 1828. His son, Thomas Henry Lister, wrote a successful novel, *Granby,* and a play, *Epicharis,* which was produced at Drury Lane in 1829. Miss Seward, in her will, left to her "friend," Thomas Lister, Esq., of Armitage, the sum of five guineas, for either a mourning ring or some other token of remembrance.

"Cary's disposition is more saturnine [than Lister's]," Miss Seward remarked. "I think his genius is the stronger of the two." This guess was a wise one, proved true by the later history of the boys. During the next year, when he was sixteen, Cary published a small volume of odes and sonnets, with two introductory sonnets by his mentor, Miss Seward. She said of them in her letters that they needed the chisel—which was what a good many people said of her own. She found him a bit arrogant, though modest in outward demeanor; and disinclined to welcome her suggestions and criticisms.

Cary went to Oxford, as he had planned, and took orders in 1796. He was then presented by the Earl of Uxbridge to the vicarage of Abbots Bromley, a small village in Staffordshire. In the same year, he married an Irish girl, Jane Ormsby. His married life was harmonious, though marred by the affliction of the loss of his daughters. He became Vicar of Kingsbury in Warwickshire, not far from Sutton Coldfield. In 1808 he removed to London, subsisting on the returns from his livings (he was thenceforth an absentee vicar), a legacy from his father, and the proceeds of various pieces of literary work, the most ambitious of which was his *Lives of the Poets.* His health was bad, and at times his mind gave way under the strain of bereavement.

The great work of Cary's life was the translation of Dante, which brought him permanent fame. As early as 1790, Miss Seward was complaining that Cary was "debauched by Italian poetry"; and she was expostulating with him because he was leaving his Miltonic model for corrupt Italian masters. He answered her long argumentative letters with patience, but adhered to his own views, which he never changed. He began his translation of Dante with the *Purgatorio,* in 1797, but laid this work aside, and took up the *Inferno,* which was completed by the autumn of 1804. It was published in 1805, when Cary was thirty-three. "Our young friend Cary," Miss Seward wrote to the Llangollen ladies, "has published his translation of Dante's *Inferno*. It is thought the best which has appeared, and the sale goes on well." As a matter of fact, the sale was slow. Nothing daunted, however, he kept on with his chosen work, and on May 8, 1812, he wrote in his Journal: "Finished my translation of Dante's Commedia—began the 16th of January 1797." The three volumes, containing the complete translation, were published on the first day of January, 1814—at the expense of the translator. He was indebted to Coleridge, who spoke of him in his lectures, for the growing esteem in which his work was held. A new edition came out in 1819.

Gradually Cary widened his acquaintance in London, until he could claim friendship with many of the most eminent men of his day. He was a close friend of Charles and Mary Lamb; and we may here reprint Lamb's characterization of him in a letter to Bernard Barton: "Mr. Cary, the Dante-man, dines with me today. He is a model of a country Parson, lean (as a curate ought to be), modest, sensible, no obtruder of church dogmas, quite a different man from Southey— you would like him."

In 1826 Cary was appointed to a position in the British Museum, as Assistant Keeper of the Printed Books. He lived a studious, uneventful life,[21] prospering mod-

21. For a complete account of the life of Henry Francis Cary, see R. W. King, *"Parson Primrose," The Life, Work and Friendships of Henry Francis Cary (1772–1844), Translator of Dante;* also Henry

erately, educating his sons in a fitting manner, and winning solid renown for his admirable translation of his beloved Dante. When he died, in 1844, he was buried in Westminster Abbey, between Johnson and Garrick.

In the midst of the somewhat depressing duties of staying at home and nursing her invalid, came a pleasure which was to Miss Seward both vivid and lasting. This was the receipt of the picture of herself on which George Romney had been engaged, at intervals, for two years and perhaps more. Mr. Arthur Chamberlain thinks[22] that it was begun at Eartham in 1782, after the portrait painted for Hayley was finished. Some information is furnished by a wrongly dated letter written by the Rev. Thomas Seward to Archibald Constable.[23] The date as given is "Nov. 20, 1748." This is obviously incorrect. In 1748 the Sewards were living at Eyam, and Anna Seward was only six years old. The letter refers to the portrait which Hayley eventually hung in his own library, between the busts of Pope and Newton. Here follows Mr. Seward's letter:

My daughter has lately had the great honour of having her picture drawn gratis by Mr. Romney, at the request of her great poetic friend, Mr. Hayley, who intends to honour it with a place in his own library. . . . The picture is finished, and is most highly celebrated by all our acquaintance who have seen it in London. It is to visit Lichfield, and then, I hope, to be copy'd by the same excellent

Cary, *A Memoir of the Rev. Henry Francis Cary, M.A., Translator of Dante, with His Literary Journal and Letters.*

22. Arthur B. Chamberlain, *George Romney,* p. 120.

23. *Archibald Constable and His Literary Correspondents: A Memorial,* by his son, Thomas Constable, II, 29.

painter before it becomes stationary in Mr. Hayley's library. I expect it very soon. . . . The picture is a very large one, and Mr. Romney grows so eminent, that his price for pictures of such large dimensions is four-score guineas.

The question of date is satisfactorily settled by a letter from Miss Seward[24] to Mr. Thomas Sedgewick Whalley, dated December 4, 1782. She says: "Who do you think tapped at the dressing-room door, in about half an hour after you left it, and entered with a smiling countenance?—who but Dr. Darwin, verily and indeed? . . . I know well enough that Mr. Romney's art was the load-stone which drew hither that large mass of genius and sarcasm; that he had heard of the picture and wished to see it. He saw it with seeming pleasure and very warm praise." In a letter to Mr. Whalley, dated December 13, 1782, she says: "M. Cobb was in Romney's levée this morning." The picture was evidently in Lichfield for inspection during December, 1782, and was sent away, either to Hayley or Romney. This portrait, if it is the one which Hayley had in his library, is thirty by twenty-five inches in size, and shows the lady in a white dress, with her face turned aside, her hair puffed and bound with a ribbon.

Mr. Hayley probably treasured the portrait of the poetess until his death in 1820. "It made," says Mr. Chamberlain, "an unexpected appearance at a sale held by Messrs. Foster & Co., on October 25th, 1903. It was catalogued as by an artist of the English school, and was said to be a portrait of Mrs. Siddons. The vendor

24. *Journals and Correspondence of Thomas Sedgewick Whalley, D.D., of Mendip Lodge, Somerset,* ed. Rev. Hill Wickham, I, 381.

was a Wandsworth mechanic, and the picture came into his possession through his wife, whose father bought it some years earlier, with the other fixtures of a public house of which he became the landlord. At the time of the sale, it was almost completely hidden by several coatings of varnish and dirt, and the first bid was one of ten shillings. Eventually it was bought by Mr. Buttery, a picture restorer of Picadilly, for 350 guineas. After it was cleaned, it was found to be the portrait of Miss Seward, long lost to sight."[25]

The portrait which Romney gave Mr. Seward, in 1788, was also lost to view for a long time, though well cared for. After Miss Seward's death, though it was bequeathed to Charles Simpson,[26] it must have passed to Susan Seward, a cousin, who was much with the poetess in her later days. Miss Susan Seward married Major Burrowes,[27] "the heir to a large estate," and a very desirable match. The portrait was taken to Ireland, where the Burrowes family lived, and was unknown to the public until it was exhibited in Dublin in 1902. Mr. T. J. Burrowes sold it in 1920.[28] In Chamberlain's book on Romney, it is shown as Plate X.[29] The sitter has assumed a graceful position with her cheek resting on her hand, and her elbow on a table strewn with manuscript. In one hand she holds a roll of paper. The dress is black, cut square at the neck, with long sleeves and

25. Chamberlain, *op. cit.*, p. 153.

26. See *post*, p. 267.   27. *Letters*, VI, 490.

28. This information comes from Mr. Burrowes, of Stradone, county Cavan, Ireland, in a letter to the present writer.

29. See frontispiece to the present volume.

white cuffs. A sash encircles the waist. A light gauze silk headdress makes a background for the puffed but simply arranged hair. The ample form of the sitter was surely reduced by the charitable brush of the artist; for the waist is almost abnormally slender. Curiously, the neck and shoulders are those of a mature and rather heavy woman, while the waist is girlishly round and small. One conjectures that the artist painted the head, shoulders, and hands from life and then painted the torso and dress from a lay figure or model. The face is fine and high-bred, animated and pleasing, perhaps a bit self-conscious and self-satisfied. Miss Seward was delighted with it, and wrote of it as "a graceful, expressive portrait."

The arrival of the picture at the Palace in Lichfield was not entirely a surprise. In May, 1788, Miss Seward was writing to thank Mr. Hayley for exerting himself with Romney to procure for her and her father "the possession of that highly valuable present," the much-desired portrait.

On June 1 she wrote to Hayley, "I scarce know how to . . . express our gratitude for your having persuaded Romney to gratify my father, by his possession, before he dies, of the promised treasure."[30]

Regarding the receipt of the picture she wrote: "It arrived late last night; rich, adorned, and invaluable, by the Romneyan powers. My poor invalid was fast asleep in his bed—Lister and Cary, our young bards, were supping with me. They were on fire with curi-

30. *Letters*, II, 126.

osity, while the nails were drawing, and highly gratified with contemplating the most masterly portrait their young eyes had ever beheld. I placed it by my father's bedside at seven this morn. He wept with joy when I undrew the curtain—wanted to kiss it, and has talked and looked at it all day. I sent some verses to Romney, by this post, which but ill express my gratitude."[31]

Well may she have been grateful for the product of such an expert hand. It would bring an almost fabulous sum today. "I sent for the handsomest frame London could produce," she wrote to Hayley some months later. "It 'emblazes, with its breadth of gold,' the center of the dining-room, opposite the fireplace. I keep the one by poor Kettle, for which you know I sat at nineteen, as a foil to Titiano's, and am diverted with people taking it for my mother's picture, after they have looked at Romney's."

Mrs. Knowles, the Quaker lady who had dared to argue with Dr. Johnson, visited Miss Seward shortly after the picture arrived, and she thought it "one of the finest pictures she ever saw." Others thought it bore only a slight resemblance to the sitter. Perhaps these dubious ones were of the feline type who wished to remind Miss Seward that she had changed in the last six years, or that the artist had been too lenient with her bulk of solid flesh.

A word may be said here concerning other portraits of Miss Seward. The picture by Kettle, reproduced as a frontispiece for Volume I of her *Letters,* was painted, so

31. *Letters,* II, 126. The letter is dated June 1, 1788.

the inscription reads, in 1762. She says that she was nineteen at the time. As we have noted, she spoke disparagingly of it, and it does appear heavy and lumpish beside the more animated portrait by Romney. The Kettle portrait was sold at Christie's in 1924, with other pictures which had been owned by the late Sir Robert White-Thomson,[32] a relative of Miss Seward's on her mother's side. It was bought for eighty guineas, and is now in the National Portrait Gallery.

Miss Seward wrote to Mrs. T——,[33] the jealous wife of an early admirer, that she sat to Smart[34] for a miniature "twenty-five years ago," at which time she would have been twenty-eight years old. She sat to Meyer six years afterward. She adds: "Miers took immense pains with my picture; he made it a very fine one, but he did not make it like; and Smart's had still less resemblance. Both of them were long since given away." The Meyer miniature was bequeathed to the cousins White; it passed into the possession of the late Sir Robert White-Thomson, and is now owned by his son, the Right Rev. Leonard Jauncey White-Thomson, D.D., Lord Bishop of Ely.

An engraving was made of the Kettle portrait by A. Cardon, for the first volume of the *Letters*. A small en-

32. For this and other information regarding portraits of Miss Seward (other than those by Romney) the present writer is indebted to his Lordship, the Bishop of Ely, and to Alderman W. A. Wood, Honorary Secretary of the Johnson Society at Lichfield.

33. *Letters*, IV, 174. The letter is dated March 2, 1796.

34. John Smart, miniature painter (1741–1811). Mr. Saville also had his portrait painted in miniature by Smart, in 1770.

graving by Cardon is in the Johnson Birthplace Museum, in Lichfield; also a small oval engraving by Ridley, after Romney, and a photograph of the miniature by Meyer. The engraving by Ridley was published in the *Monthly Review* for February, 1797,[35] and one by Woolnoth was published in *The Beauties of Anna Seward,* which appeared in 1822.

The distracted Mr. Hayley had decided by 1789 that he could no longer endure existence with his "dear Eliza." Her half-mad whims and rages had become insupportable. Mr. Hayley, therefore, prepared to shift the burden which he had borne so long. He arranged to take her to the house of their "benevolent friend, Mrs. Beridge in Derby," and then to arrange for agreeable lodgings in that town. The details of this change accomplished, the poor bard felt so forlorn and dejected that he really needed cheering up. "When," he says of himself,[36] "he had passed through the very painful scene of bidding adieu to that most pitiable of mortals, with whom he had found it impossible to live, and equally impossible to be indifferent to her welfare; he sought and found some relief to his deeply-agitated heart, in passing a few social and confidential hours with his compassionate friend of Litchfield, Miss Seward, who had observed and pitied the nervous maladies and restless mind of the ill-starred Eliza."

The poet wished to urge Miss Seward to visit Mrs. Hayley at Derby, whenever occasion offered. This

35. Chamberlain, *op. cit.,* p. 154.
36. Hayley wrote his memoirs in the third person.

she seems to have done, since she frequently went to
Derby, where she had a number of acquaintances and
friends. Hayley appears to have stayed only a short time
at Lichfield on this occasion. He did not see Mr. Seward,
who was "barely alive," and not able to see or recognize
visitors. Miss Seward "was pleasant and cordial in the
highest degree."

We have the report of this visit by Miss Seward herself, in a letter to Court Dewes (May 3, 1789): ". . . I
walked out, and found, on my return, the illustrious,
the graceful Hayley, in my dressing-room. He is going
to Rome. . . . He said indispensable business called
him to town, and he set out the next morning. I travelled with him to Coleshill."

In spite of the sincere pleasure which this meeting
probably afforded to both Hayley and Miss Seward, the
fervor of their friendship had cooled during the years.
In 1786, writing to Mrs. Stokes, Miss Seward had said:
"You inquire after my correspondence with the illustrious H——. It is not what it was; but the deficiency
or cause of deficiency, proceeds not from me. I honour
and love him as well as ever; yet I feel that the silver
cord of our amity is loosening at more links than one."

Miss Seward continued to praise the works and worth
of Hayley, even though she complained of his neglect.
She kept up a correspondence with Mrs. Hayley, and
exchanged gifts with her. For Miss Seward, Mrs. Hayley worked a pocketbook with a lyre on one side and
a laurel wreath on the other. Hayley wrote, to accompany it, a poem beginning "Go thou embroidered

wreath and mimic lyre." The two women met occasionally at Derby and at the Palace in Lichfield. Though Mrs. Hayley was erratic and difficult, Miss Seward seems to have retained her affection, or at least her friendship, until the last. Mrs. Hayley died suddenly in 1797.

In 1789 died Thomas Day, whom we saw happily married in 1778, after the vicissitudes of his various courtships. Mr. Day lost his life through his devotion to a theory. He believed that horses—as well as other animals—would always respond to kindness, and that any evil behavior on their part was due to ill treatment. Having reared up a favorite foal, he essayed to break it himself, instead of employing a trainer. The horse threw him and struck him a fatal blow. Thus passed Thomas Day, philosopher and philanthropist, at the age of forty. "It is said," remarks Miss Seward, "that Mrs. Day never afterward saw the sun." She lay in bed with the curtain drawn, during the day, and went out only at night, to stray in the garden and mourn her loss. She survived her husband only two years.

In a letter to the *General Evening Post,* dated October 11, 1789, Miss Seward gave an analysis of the character of Mr. Day: "Mr. Day, with very first-rate abilities, was a splenetic, capricious, yet bountiful, misanthropist. He bestowed nearly the whole of his ample fortune in relieving the necessities of the poor; frequently, however, declaring his conviction that there were few in the large number he fed who would not cut his throat the next hour, if their interest could prompt the act, and their lives be safe in its commission. He took pride in avowing his abhorrence of luxuries, and disdain of even the decencies of life; and in his person he was generally slovenly, even to squalidness. On being asked by one of his friends, why he chose the lonely and unpleasant situation in which he lived? He replied, that the sole reason of that choice was, in being out of the stink of human society."

This singular man, who was in many ways in advance of his age, seems, in spite of his peculiarities, a high-minded and generous soul. One of his finest traits was his love for animals, and his detestation of cruelty. He deplored the almost universal custom of slaughtering animals and eating their flesh. He endeavored to inculcate in children habits of kindness and the ability to imagine the feelings of others, though the others might be only dumb beasts.

His educational theories, adapted from Rousseau, were rigorous, though in the main wholesome. He advocated simplicity in daily conduct, and a democratic perception of other people's point of view. He uncovered the fallacy of supposing wealth to relieve a child or a grown person from the demands of courtesy and fair play. Snobbishness, toadying, hauteur, arrogance, selfish absorption in one's own enterprises, and contempt for the rights of the rest of the world he relentlessly denounced for the sins that they are, without palliation or excuse.

The theories of Mr. Day, especially as revealed in his

Sandford and Merton, had an effect upon the rearing and teaching of children truly incredible at the present time, when books for and about the very young are numerous to superfluity. He deserves more credit than he gets; but perhaps he is more fortunate than the people who, in another sort of reversal, get more than they deserve.

THE BISHOP'S PALACE, LICHFIELD

HOME OF ANNA SEWARD. BUILT IN 1687

The wings were added by Bishop Selwyn, about 1870. Courtesy of W. Morrison, Photographer, Lichfield.

CHAPTER VII

1790–1791

A CANON'S PASSING

FROM 1780 to 1790, the year of her father's death, Miss Seward lingered on the plateau of middle age. The pain of the upward steps was at least in part forgotten; the downward not yet begun. We may pause and review her circumstances as she herself must have done from time to time.

Her domestic situation combined liberty with bondage. Her house she gloried in, loving it for itself and its associations. Its situation was ideal: for the front overlooked the Cathedral Close, and the rear gave a view across the valley of the Stow. "I sit writing upon this dear green terrace," she says in 1784, "feeding, at intervals, my little golden-breasted songsters. The embosomed Vale of Stow . . . glows sunny through the Claud-Lorrain tint which is spread over the scene like the blue mist over a plumb. How often has our lost Honora hung over the wall of this terrace, enamoured of its scenic graces!" Cypresses, junipers, lilacs, laburnums, and laurels bordered the turf, or dotted the grassy slope. Below the terrace lay the "sweet valley" of the Stow, a half-mile across, "bounded basin-like by a semicircle of gentle hills, luxuriantly foliaged."[1] There was

1. *Letters*, V, 78.

a lake in the bosom of the Vale, and beside it an old church with a gray and moss-grown tower.

No one, perhaps, whose windows have opened on such a scene, has felt more delight than Miss Seward in the beauty of a natural landscape. This outlook must have been one of the strongest reasons for living on in the house when all her family had gone.

The house, a veritable mansion, built in 1687, was handsome and spacious. There was a noble oak staircase, and on each side a vista of wide dignified rooms, where small-paned casement windows let in the light through old iridescent glass. In one of Anna Seward's early letters,[2] she wrote with justifiable content: "It is true I dwell on classic ground. Within the walls which my father's family inhabits, in this very dining-room, the munificent Mr. Walmesley, with the taste, the learning, and the liberality of Maecenas, administered to rising genius the kind nutriment of attention and praise. Often to his hospitable board were the schoolboys, David Garrick and Samuel Johnson, summoned. The parents of the former were of Mr. Walmesley's acquaintance; but those of the latter did not move in his sphere."

The Palace, where no Bishop had ever dwelt, was furnished in a manner befitting the clerical position of Mr. Seward; and it had doubtless accumulated the treasures of family bequests—furniture, hangings, porcelain, and plate. In appropriate spaces hung portraits, both old and new. The Peter Lely of a Seward

2. Introduction to *Poetical Works*, ed. Sir Walter Scott, p. xix.

ancestress was highly prized, partly for its resemblance to the living beauty of the poetical granddaughter. There was a portrait of Mrs. Seward as a girl; and there was one of the beautiful lost Sarah, by Kettle. The portrait of Anna, by Kettle, with its heavy mature look, was likely to arouse either mirth or indignation when the laughing, flashing-eyed original stood beneath it. The portrait of Canon Seward by Wright of Derby (painted in 1781) was voted more nearly a success. The charming portrait of Miss Seward, by Romney, may well have taken first place in the judgment of both father and daughter, because it bore the marks of being from a master hand. The furnishings and paintings are scattered now, and we can only vaguely reassemble them in thought.

The servants, a man, a lady's maid, a cook, and other necessary helpers, had stayed long, and were familiar with their tasks. In Miss Seward's letters we have no record of domestic upheavals, such as furnished the dramatic stuff of poor Jeannie Carlyle's. If there were lapses and vexations, they were deftly passed over and concealed. The lofty mind of Miss Seward needed not to make capital of her Abigail and her butler. The details of her dinners, suppers, and musical parties are lightly touched upon, elaborated with no *bourgeois* relish.

As to the Canon's financial situation, we may make some conjecture, since he received the income from a number of preferments, and had apparently made some good investments. Miss Seward, at his death, came into a clear income of £400; so that before his passing, when he was receiving the emoluments from his various offices, he must have been a man of plentiful means. Money was at that period worth several times what it is today, and even Miss Seward's $2,000, though she complained that it was inadequate, must have given her a comfortable living.

Miss Seward took a feminine pleasure in appropriate dress and accessories; and we may be sure that she was an imposing figure in her brocaded gowns, quilted silk petticoats, frilled pelisses, and wide plumed hats. The blemish of too much flesh she frankly deplored, despite her intelligent appraisal of her other good points. In speaking of a silhouette, the substitute of that day for the snapshot, she says that she has had several taken, but has kept none of them. "Men and women whose shoulders are on the large scale," she remarks, "appear with ten-fold their real clumsiness in those shadowy out-lines. Slenderness is essential to admit their presenting a resemblance which shall not be a caricature." She took pride in being told that she looked like Mrs. Fitzherbert, and she was not above expressing cordial pleasure in praises of her person. "I am charmed," she wrote, "that Mrs. Piozzi likes me well enough to dream that I have beauty."

From her earliest youth, Miss Seward lived in the midst of agreeable social activities. Mr. and Mrs. Seward were hospitable and entertaining; and were constantly in touch with numbers of friends, both at home and abroad. "I live in the mill-horse round of a provincial city's diurnal society," wrote Anna Seward. She complains frequently that social duties prevent her writing even the shortest poem. To do any literary work, she had to rise before daylight. She spent much time (some of it unwillingly) at the card table—"that universal leveller of intellectual distinctions." The balls, musical parties, concerts, teas, breakfasts, and dinners mentioned in her letters are too numerous to designate specifically. In November, 1796,[3] she wrote to Mrs. Stokes: "Lichfield has been of late wonderous gay. Six private balls were given, which I was persuaded to attend. Our public assembly, last week, proved rich in rank and titles, and I thought it pleasant." She subscribed to the assemblies and attended them to a late day. She was especially fond of concerts, both at her own house, and in the *salons* of others. In 1794, for example, she had a music-party of twenty-five in her own "saloon," at which there were "three violins, a violincello, Lady Fielding's harp, and an harpsichord." The singing of duets and glees varied the program of instrumental music. John Saville, was, of course, the heart and soul of these musicales. Large parties alternated with small groups of admiring friends who loved to hear her recite her own poems or those of her favorite authors. Mr. Hayley testified that her house was always full of clerics and chattering women.[4] Mrs. West wrote to the Bishop of Dromore that Miss Seward "lived at Lichfield in an elegant hospitable way."[5] It is evident that she led a

3. *Letters*, IV, 270.   4. See p. 101.
5. Nichols' *Illustrations*, VIII, 432.

busy life, with her domestic cares, her reading and writing, her visitors, her calls and balls, her breakfasts and suppers, and other social engagements, and her frequent journeys away from home.

A passage must now be given to one of the most important aspects of her career. Anyone who reads the poems and letters of Anna Seward attentively must see that the great love and passion of her life was for John Saville, vicar choral of her beloved Cathedral, and long her close friend and companion.

In a letter to Thomas Park, Miss Seward in speaking of Saville said that he had been her "almost next-door neighbor" since her twelfth and his twentieth year. "From that far, far distant period," she went on, "my esteem and friendship for him have never known abatement." Indeed, it had known increasing, until it had become an ardent and devoted love, permeating every act and instinct of her being.

Though he may not have been, as she thought him, "the brightest ornament of Lichfield," Saville was a considerable figure in the Close, enlivening with his music, and sweetening with his voice many public ceremonies and private festivities. There is little to be found concerning him. He was born at Ely, about the year 1736, came early to Lichfield as a cathedral singer, and remained there for forty-eight years, till the close of his life in 1803. He married, and had two daughters, one of whom died in a "strange" manner. The other, Mrs. Smith,[6] became a singer of sufficient repute to take im-

6. In 1803, Miss Seward spoke of Mrs. Smith's husband as a bankrupt, long deceased.

portant parts in concerts at Shrewsbury and Birmingham, and sing under Rauzzini at Bath. In that preten-
tious city, where audiences were notoriously critical, she
made a favorable impression. Miss Seward says that
Mrs. Smith was asked to sing in London, though her
father refused to permit her to do so, on account of her
delicacy and timidity.

Saville lived for twenty-eight years in a "little habitation," which was so small that there was no sleeping-
room for his daughter, when he happened to be ill and
needed other attendance than that of his old housekeeper. He later removed from this house, under what
circumstances we shall see. He was an enthusiastic
botanist, and gave all the spare time which he could
snatch to the cultivation of rare plants, of which he was
said to have two thousand specimens. His garden was a
sight to be shown to everybody's visitors. He was not,
however, a member of that triumvirate, Dr. Darwin's
Botanical Society. Miss Seward said that he refrained
from joining it, because he did not want to do the
writing and translating which would be put upon him.
"Therefore, as he used to say, 'I kept myself out of the
scrape!'"

Just when Anna Seward began to be conscious of her
infatuation for him, it is difficult to say. As early as 1770
he was spending a month with her and Honora Sneyd
and Mrs. Powys in Anna's blue boudoir, which they
left "only for meals." One assumes that at this time he
was to some degree a free man, though under the spell
of Anna's eyes. Miss Seward speaks of him with an

accent of proprietorship throughout the six volumes of her correspondence (beginning in 1784). Frequent are such expressions as "Giovanni and I," "Giovanni joins me in good wishes," "Giovanni thinks as I do," and "Mr. Saville wishes to be remembered." On a number of occasions Miss Seward went out of town with him and his daughter, for several days or a week at a time, visiting friends or attending a series of concerts.

Our knowledge of his character comes chiefly from the partial estimate of Miss Seward; but he seems to have been a man of education, breeding, and fine feelings. One glimpse which we get of him shows his sensitive nature, as well as the intimate quality of his place in Miss Seward's home. Miss Seward had a little dog, Sappho, a bright, lovable little creature, which made the old Palace, "so thinly tenanted," ring with her bark of "joy or watchfulness." One day in January, 1791, the dog fell dead in the presence of its mistress and her friend. The shock was a severe one for Miss Seward, and no less for Mr. Saville. "He doted upon her," wrote Miss Seward to Mr. Whalley; "and, being out of health, the absolutely agonized grief with which he took up her lifeless body, and the bitter tears which he shed whenever he entered the house, for many ensuing days, from missing the glad welcome of her bounding affection and gay sensibility, preyed on his body as well as his spirits. To this hour, he cannot hear her mentioned, nor look at the places where she reposed, without suffering visibly."[7]

7. *Letters,* III, 116.

Another picture of him may be transferred to our pages from one of Miss Seward's letters, written after his death. "Several years past, after a long drought, which threatened to destroy the harvest, a plenteous, yet soft, shower descended. The evening was warm, and the clouds, which had been many days of flattering gloom, had not increased in their lower. Some friends were with me in the saloon, the doors of which were opened on the lawn. The long-expected, long-desired rain dropt silently, yet amply, down. Mr. S. immediately stept to the door, and, with clasped hands and moist uplifted eyes, sang that superhuman strain ['He giveth rain upon the earth, and sendeth water upon the fields'; the words forming a part of an anthem]. We all caught his grateful piety, and shed those tears, which to shed, seems a foretaste of heaven."

To the sensitiveness of soul here displayed, Miss Seward attributed the marvelous expression which he put into his singing, so that it transcended that of most other musicians. Her admiration for his art was unbounded. "Mr. Saville's songs are always exquisite," she wrote; and "Of all our public singers, while many are masterly, many elegant, many astonishing, *he* only is sublime!"

"Other voices may be as fine, the skill and fancy of other singers as distinguished: but for all the graces and powers of touching expression, nor man nor woman ever sung as Saville sung."[8]

Similar remarks may be culled in large numbers from

8. Letter to Walter Scott, Anna Seward's *Letters*, VI, 209.

the pages of her letters. He read finely also, and was approved in recitation. On a certain occasion, late in his life,[9] when Miss Seward was entertaining a large "conversation party," he gave an impromptu proof of his powers. "Ah, with what grace and spirit did he recite by heart Courtenay's Character, in verse, of the complicated and stupendous Dr. Johnson! On his leaving the room soon after, during a few minutes, how did two gentlemen, strangers to him till then, praise the gracefulness of his address, the spirit of his conversation, the justness, the music, and variety of his recitation!"

After reading the *Letters* of Miss Seward, in which the most devoted regard for Saville is expressed, it is something of a shock to discover that he had a wife. He was separated from her, to be sure, on account of incompatibility of temper; but she appears to have spent at least a part of her time in Lichfield. There is only one reference to her in Miss Seward's published *Letters* (what was deleted in Edinburgh, after her death, we do not know): In 1806, three years after Saville's death, she says that she will never again enter "his latest habitation, now the home of his daughter and her mother."

It is in the letters to Dr. Whalley, published in 1863, that we find the most self-revelatory references to the Swan's romance. Miss Seward had begun her acquaintance with the Whalleys by writing a fervid letter in praise of "that enchanting poem," *Edwy and Edilda*.

9. *Letters,* VI, 110.

Mr. (afterward Dr.) Whalley replied in terms which marked him as an Enthusiast, as Miss Seward rightly called herself, and therefore a kindred soul. Before meeting the Whalleys, and when she was planning that they should visit her, Miss Seward wrote to them regarding Saville:

There was a time, a long extent of time, when I had occasion to remember that generous maxim of Dr. Young's, to which I steadily adhered:

"A friend is worth all hazards we can run;
How gallant, danger for earth's highest prize!
A world in purchase for a friend is gain."

The most diabolical machinations of spite and envy, the pleas of interest, and the interposition of misled authority were exerted in vain. The wishes of a noble heart, the affection of a most ingenuous sensibility, conscientious piety, with an awakened taste for every elegant science, these qualities constituted the counterpoising blessing. I preserved it at every hazard, and am rewarded with the entire approbation of my own mind on the subject, besides the delight I take in the virtues of my friend.[10]

On November 27, 1781, Miss Seward wrote again to Mr. Whalley regarding Saville. "During many halcyon years," she said, "Honora and I enjoyed this felicity respecting the friend I mentioned before. What joy did we not feel in convincing our wealthier friends that all the mental virtues and graces, with gentle and polished manners, might exist in a sphere of life considerably below their own! . . . At length, some nine years ago, the malice of our ceremonial beings, coöperating with the machinations of a shrewish, vulgar, and many ways

10. *Journals and Correspondence of Thomas Sedgewick Whalley, D.D., of Mendip Lodge, Somerset,* ed. Rev. Hill Wickham, I, 330.

unamiable wife, gained upon the easy nature of my father to estrange his heart from our friend, whose gentle disposition experienced the 'altered eye of hard unkindness' from him, and bled under the sense of it. No prospect of worldly disadvantage—and I was threatened with the highest—could induce me to renounce the blessing of a tried and faithful friend; but by ill-advised and mistaken authority, most of its sweetest comforts were mercilessly lopt away. You will love and esteem an injured man, of whom this frivolous world is not worthy. Were he prosperous, his virtues would ensure him your esteem; and half of them, when you shall come to know him, under the pressure of domestic sorrow, and of the neglect of the proud, would consecrate his claim to the amity of a heart like yours and that within its dearest recesses."[11]

Miss Weston, who was related to the first Mrs. Whalley, commented on this letter in the following words: "Poor thing! how naturally does she endeavour to prejudice you in favour of that friend, and how assiduously, and at the same time ingenuously, does she seek to lay open the nature and progress of her connection with him, and to remove from your mind any prejudices you might have imbibed from rumour on that account."[12]

These extracts make the situation clear. Anna Seward did not yield easily to the call of an unsanctioned and unprofitable love. In May, 1792, we find her writing to

11. *Journals and Correspondence of Thomas Sedgewick Whalley, D.D., of Mendip Lodge, Somerset,* ed. Rev. Hill Wickham, I, 344.
12. *Ibid.,* p. 362.

Mr. Whalley: "My whole sum of peace, and comfort, and earthly hope, long desperately set on one precarious die, often and often, but always vainly, have I struggled in the indissoluble toils of my affection." However, finding her struggles unavailing, she resigned herself to the demands of her affections, and with startling frankness confessed, on many occasions, her absolute and entire devotion to Saville.

That the two friends did not escape the barbed shafts of the gossips is sufficiently attested. An association such as theirs, in which the intimate details of everyday life were shared, must inevitably draw upon itself the mortifications of innuendo. In a letter to Mrs. Blore, discussing the *Notes on the Life of Dr. Darwin,* Miss Seward explained her omission of the name of Saville from her list of Lichfield celebrities: "He knew that my pure and disinterested attachment to his unblemished worth, had subjected me to unworthy reflections, and, therefore, no arguments, no entreaties of mine, could have obtained his permission to present the just portraits of his talents and virtues to general scrutiny."

In Nichols' *Illustrations of the Literary History of the Eighteenth Century,*[13] we catch an echo of the talk which went round in Lichfield concerning Miss Seward and Saville. Bishop Percy, in a letter to Mrs. West (above referred to), speaks of Miss Seward's "very improper attachment to Saville, one of the singing-men of Lichfield Cathedral." This attachment had "excited such censure among the most respectable clergy there," that

13. VIII, 428.

the Bishop was scandalized, even in his Hibernian retirement. His nephew, Dr. Percy, asserted that Dr.
Proby, the Dean of Lichfield (brother of Lord Carys-
fort), and his family had "ceased to visit her."

In the *Letters* of Miss Seward there are one or two
veiled allusions to this rude treatment and attempted
ostracism; but it is not likely that it amounted to much.
We have previously remarked Mr. Hayley writing to
his wife: "Notwithstanding the reports you heard at
Bath, she has a multitude of female visitors, and a host
of divines." What Mrs. Hayley had heard at Bath was,
of course, that Miss Seward had been slighted in society
on account of her love-affair with Saville. Hayley proves
that she was as popular as she had ever been. She never
seems to have lacked friends or companions among the
Lichfield people, although she sometimes complained
that she was misunderstood or slandered. Her relatives,
the Whites, Sewards, and Martins, stood by her loyally
and gave their sanction to her conduct.

There was certainly no furtiveness in her behavior;
and that there was any wrongdoing, in the strictly
moralistic sense, is highly improbable. The perfectly
open way in which the friendship was carried on, both
before and after the passing of Mr. Seward, justifies the
supposition that these two had made a mutual agreement to ignore the world and all its malice. They clung
to each other in spite of slander, and never wavered in
their devotion. Such a flaunting of affection may well
have shocked the good people of the Close; but it need
hardly signify anything improper. To Miss Seward,

Saville was her "soul's chosen friend," and no power on earth could tear her from him.

There was probably a good deal of personal feeling in what she wrote to Hayley upon his efforts to find a governess for his son Thomas: "Nothing but a considerable independent fortune can enable an amiable female to look down, without misery, upon the censures of the many; and even in that situation [which was her own], their arrows have power to wound, if not to destroy peace. Surely no woman with a nice sense of honor,—and what is she worth who has it not?—would voluntarily expose herself to their aim, except she has unwarily *slid* into a situation *where the affections, making silent and unperceived progress, have rendered it a less evil to endure the consciousness of a dubious fame, provided there is no real guilt, than to renounce the society of him without whom creation seems a blank.*"[14]

Here we undoubtedly have her own situation in a nutshell, and surmise need go no farther.

THE time was now approaching when the long-since superannuated Canon Seward was to loose his feeble hold upon the affairs of this world. Through his latest years, Anna Seward cared for her father with unremitting zeal, for which, almost to the last, he was able to express his gratitude. One of her letters gives a touching account of her return from a Christmas visit to the Dewes family in 1785–86. "Though in his bed, my dear father, watching for me, heard the hall door open

14. Italics here supplied by the present author.

on Monday midnight, and rang his bell. Hastening to him, I heard him say, as I entered his apartment,—'Is it my Nancy, my dear Nancy?' Our meeting was glad, even to rapture, on both sides."

When she waited upon him, though his mind was clouded, he did not fail to reward her with his "Thank you, my dear child, my darling, my blessing." She, in turn, gave him a love that was more than filial. "He seems," she wrote, "at once my parent and my child."

For a long time before his death, she felt a sorrowful shrinking from the inevitable change, suffering agonies when some more piteous paroxysm came on, and experiencing, by anticipation, all the misery of loss. He died in March, 1790, at the age of eighty-two. After his death, she wrote to H. F. Cary, her young *protégé:* "I have lost one of the most precious blessings of my existence, the revered, the so fondly loved, the helpless object of those sweet, though anxious cares, that were their own reward." Her letters abound in lamentations. Her grief was intensified by loneliness. All her nearest kinsfolk had been taken. Husband and children make the departure of an aged parent less of a calamity than it must be to a woman with no remaining ties.

Boswell, who had met Mr. Seward in his own home in Lichfield, said of the Canon that he was "a genteel, well-bred, dignified clergyman, who had lived much in the great world." This familiarity with persons of high rank had taken place in his younger days, when he was private chaplain to the Duke of Grafton and tutor to that nobleman's son.

Canon Seward was known among his acquaintances as something of a poet, and he had published verses (anonymously, by mistake) in Dodsley's *Collection*. He was the author of a tract on the *Conformity between Popery and Paganism*. With Mr. Simpson, he brought out in 1750 an annotated edition of Beaumont and Fletcher, concerning which Coleridge made the damning remark, "Mr. Seward, Mr. Seward, you may be, and I trust you are, an angel, but you *were* an ass!"

Miss Seward was much gratified in the year 1796, when Mr. and Mrs. Jebb of Chesterfield took her to visit Mr. Jebb's father, a centenarian, who had known Mr. Seward in his youth. "Madam," said the old man, rising to receive her, "I am glad to see you,—I remember your father, a sprightly bachelor.—I travelled from London with him, when he went to take possession of the living at Eyam. He was a *lovely* man, of fine person and frank communicative spirit. Soon after that period, he married a beautiful young lady, your mother, Madam. Mr. Seward, as you know, had travelled, and spoke admirably of the customs and manners of foreign nations."

Boswell says: "Johnson described him thus:—'Sir, his ambition is to be a fine talker; so he goes to Buxton, and such places, where he may find companions to listen to him. And, Sir, he is a valetudinarian, one of those who are always mending themselves. I do not know a more disagreeable character than a valetudinarian, who thinks he may do anything that is for his ease, and indulges himself in the grossest freedoms: Sir, he brings himself to the state of a hog in a stye.'"

This characterization of Mr. Seward aroused the indignation of his relatives and friends. It was reversed circumstantially by Mr. White, at the request of Miss Seward, in the *Gentleman's Magazine* for October, 1794; and by Richard George Robinson of Lichfield, in the same issue of the *Magazine*. Mr. Robinson, who said that he had known Mr. Seward for twenty-six years, speaks thus of his old friend: ". . . The implications that, as a Valetudinarian, he indulged himself in the grossest freedoms, is a gross misrepresentation of him. Mr. Seward's demeanour was always that of a gentleman. He was very fond of society, of which he was a very worthy and entertaining member; but his conversation was totally unaffected, and without the least tincture of the ambition the Doctor imputed to him. I will not omit this opportunity of adding another trait to his character, which is, that any of his friends might at any time confer on him a sensible pleasure by only pointing out in what way he could be of service to them."

The *Gentleman's Magazine* in Miss Seward's obituary, April, 1809, says: "Mr. Seward had graceful manners, great hilarity of spirit, and active benevolence." His urbanity put him at ease with persons of title and ecclesiastical rank; and his friendliness made him agreeable to the less distinguished. His house was a rendezvous for learned clerics, and for lighter-minded folk who found their level in card parties and merrymakings. The affection which he inspired in his daughter may or may not be a proof of his deserts (one remembers Miss Mitford's infatuation for her dreary cad of a father); but it is pleasant to think that Mr. Seward was, in most ways, at least, not unworthy of the sedulous attention and extravagant love which were his portion in his latter days.

WITH the death of her father, Miss Seward gained an undesired freedom. She might go and come as she chose; but neither the going nor the coming gave her the pleasure which they had given in her younger days. She was now nearly forty-seven years old, and was beginning to suffer those bodily ills which racked her through a great part of her remaining life. Her friends thought that she ought to give up the Palace, which was far too expensive and too much of a care for her means or strength. But she could not go. Pride, perhaps, had something to do with her staying, and the habit of living in a large way, which is hard for the self-conscious to reduce.

To some suggestions of Mrs. Piozzi, she wrote: "Ah, no, my dear Madam, Bath or London would be much too gay a scene for me. The local spells of the Close of Lichfield, formed by the remembrance of past happiness, are too powerful for me to break. My extreme attachment to this house, in which I have lived since I was thirteen years old, and the generous moderation[15]

15. Johnson spoke of the rent as "twenty pounds" (*per annum*); but Miss Seward told the Whalleys in 1790 that her house rent was £40.

of my episcopal landlord [Bishop Cornwallis], tempt me to try if I can not remain in it. It will require my utmost frugality to make my moderate income, not quite amounting to four hundred pounds per annum, support the inevitable expence of so spacious a dwelling. Bath and London journies are ill-calculated to such a plan. I must content myself with admiring and loving you all at a distance." It is needless to add that on no account would she have left, for more than a short stay, her "soul's dearest friend," John Saville.

She must have managed her expenditures wisely; for she always seemed to have money to spend, even in large sums, and she left a considerable estate at her death.

For her father, she erected in the Cathedral an impressive monument by John Bacon, R.A. She renovated his apartment, staining the paper a light green, and hanging fine prints in handsome frames. New neighbors—Archdeacon Lee, his wife, and three beautiful daughters—proved unexpectedly interesting, because of their musical skill. A new organ in the Cathedral was a source of diversion and pride. A visit to some gay luxurious people, at Colton, ten miles distant, brought laughter again to her lips. Mr. Saville and his daughter were with Miss Seward on this visit.

During the next spring, she spent several weeks with her dear old friend, Mrs. (or Miss) Mompessan, at Mansfield Woodhouse, where she was petted and soothed by her devoted hostess, of whom she wrote to Mrs. Powys of Shrewsbury: "She is many years my

senior, and, beginning to love me in the giddy, romantic, hoping, happy years of my teens, has never dashed
the over-flowing cup of her kindness with the bitterness
of neglect." Mrs. Mompessan, who came of an old
Derbyshire family, was an odd character, spirited, yet
"artless and amiable." With a small estate and £200 a
year, she lived in a sort of little Eden of her own cultivation. Miss Seward had visited her only once before—
when seeking consolation after the death of her sister
Sarah. The archaic simplicity of life in Mrs. Mompessan's old mansion, and the loving cheerfulness of
the feminine farmer herself, went far to restore Miss
Seward to her normally vivacious state.

From this sylvan retreat, she went on a sultry June
morning to Derby, where she was to give a day or two
to Mrs. Hayley, on the homeward trip. Mr. and Mrs.
Hayley had separated not long before this date, and the
lady with an ample allowance, which left her husband
in narrow circumstances, was living in lodgings among
a group of old friends. Mrs. Hayley received her guest
with "animated gladness, encompassed with youths of
genius—the rising hopes of Derby." The next morning,
"half the smart people of the town" came to call. The
afternoon and evening were passed at the home of Dr.
Darwin, who had long since departed from Lichfield,
with his exacting new wife. Miss Seward reports, "Mrs.
Darwin had an immense party to meet us, for whose
apprehended amusement she engaged me, by earnest
solicitations, to repeat odes and sonnets." Outbursts of
praise were recompense for the effort of speaking in the

torrid heat. Calls and parties followed. Mrs. Hayley invited in more than twenty people to tea and supper. The guest of honor, merry, buoyant, and sparkling, seemed quite herself again. To be the belle of a brilliant assemblage was revivifying wine to Anna Seward.

Later in the year, she visited her friends, the Whalleys, at their villa above Langford Court in the Mendip Hills. It was at this time that she made the acquaintance of Hannah More, who was living with her sisters at Cowslip Green. The famous bluestocking and *religieuse* was now in her forty-sixth year. Living in retirement, she was yet the center of admiration and activity. Her Sunday Schools had made her as well known as her literary works, which were numerous and well rewarded. "I like her infinitely," Miss Seward wrote. "Her conversation has all the strength and brilliance which her charming writings teach us to expect." Miss Seward returned the call and wrote a poem suitable to the occasion.

There cannot, however, have been much sympathy between the two women writers. Miss Seward hated the evangelical and the Methodistic. The conventions of the Church of England, with a trifle of personal latitude in matters of belief and skepticism, suited her exactly.

Miss Seward had written disdainfully of the pedantry in the poems of Miss More.[16] "[They] contain," she said to Mr. Dewes, "an affected and pedantic display of knowledge and erudition. . . . You have heard me sigh after the attainment of other languages with hope-

16. *Letters,* I, 143–144.

less yearning: yet I had rather be ignorant of them, as I am, if I thought their acquisition would induce me to clap my wings and crow in Greek, Latin and French, through the course of a poem which ought to have been written in an unaffected and unmingled English."

The association of Miss More with the Garricks, and the solid monetary success of her works made her a person to be respected. Miss Seward's poem, composed after visiting Miss More, is included in her collected verse. It lacks enthusiasm, and was possibly somewhat perfunctory. Miss Seward apparently tried to be honestly "thrilled" (her favorite word) by the endeavors of Miss More and her "sweet satellites," but found it hard to care much about these "glowing votaries of the sacred page."

Miss Seward's opinion of Miss More's religious bent is made sufficiently clear in a letter to William Hayley upon the receipt of his *Life of Cowper*. In this letter, dated March 7, 1803, she says: "I once heard Newton[17] preach a violently methodistical, and consequently absurd and dangerous sermon. Miss H. More and her sisters had requested for him the pulpit of the late pious and excellent Mr. Inman, their neighbor: Mr. and Mrs. Whalley were his parishioners, and I was their guest in 1791. When church was over Mr. Inman expressed deep regret for having, however reluctantly, granted Miss More's request. Now, said he, has this man, in one hour perhaps, rendered fruitless my labour of many years to

17. The Rev. John Newton (1725–1807), friend and counselor of Cowper at Olney. He was accused of "preaching people crazy."

keep my parishioners free from those wild, deceiving principles, which have turned the heads of half the poor ignorant people in this county. The result to poor Cowper of making Newton his comfortless conscience-keeper, ought to warn people of strong imagination how they listen to religious fanatics, presumptuously calling themselves evangelical preachers."[18]

18. *Letters*, VI, 65.

CHAPTER VIII

1792–1799

NYMPHS OF THE VALE

THE year 1792 was a hard one for Miss Seward, full of sickness, death, and gloom. Old friends were dropping away, and earthly ties were breaking. She felt herself alone in the world, and brooded over the deaths of her loved sister, long departed, and her mother, her father, and the matchless Honora. She was shaken with fears for her own health, and that of Mr. Saville. Her large empty house accentuated her loneliness. To Mrs. Hayley she wrote, "I sit sad and shivering and indisposed, by the fire." To Lady Blackiston, "Never have I known so long a depression of spirits."

Writing to Mr. Polwhele, on May 25, 1792, she spoke of the "illness of a friend, long, very long beloved; in whose sight, and whose prized society I have lived from my earliest youth; who knew and loved all those dear friends, of whom the grave has already deprived me; a friend, in whose clear spirit I never observed one cold shade of selfishness, one spot of depravity." This friend was, of course, John Saville. So ill was Saville at this time that he was obliged to cancel his engagement to sing in London; though the managers at Covent Garden "entreated him to keep his name on their lists," in case he should recover in time for his concerts.

In 1793, matters were no better. Very ill, Miss Seward permitted herself the gravest apprehensions. With the confidence in "waters" which she seems to have retained until the last, she went to Buxton, receiving little benefit. She went to Eyam, too, indulging her sorrow for the good days irrevocably past. She wept bitterly all the time that she was there, recalling vanished scenes in church and rectory. Back at home, she conformed her life to some extent to her old social habits; but inwardly she was melancholy and terror stricken. The year 1794 brought another cause of woe. A bodily injury[1] awakened in her a horror of lingering and torturing disease. This awful dread cast a shadow on all her later years.

In September, 1792, she had a visit from Honora Edgeworth's son. She wrote to her friend Mrs. Powys, "Ah! on Tuesday evening, for the first time since he was four years old, did I see and converse with all that remains of Honora in this wide world." Then follows an extended account of the appearance of the young man at her home, and his giving his name, "Lovel[l] Edgeworth."

"What a new and impetuous sensation did I that instant feel! . . . With an involuntary emotion, I seized his hands, the tears starting into my eyes, and I exclaimed, Good God! do I indeed see before me the only child of dear Honora."

When she had somewhat recovered, she walked with him over the house, showing him the rooms which Honora had called her own, pointing out to him a

---

1. Caused by a fall against a projecting corner of woodwork.

treasured silhouette, and the print of Romney's "Serena" which was said to be her exact counterpart at sixteen. She fancied he was like Honora; he had an engaging countenance; there was a "touching sweetness" in his voice. He stayed only half an hour, leaving her disturbed and reminiscent.

In November, 1793, young Edgeworth, then seventeen, was in Lichfield again, this time on his way to Derby, to consult Dr. Darwin. He was pale and hollow cheeked; he coughed incessantly. Miss Seward was chilled with apprehension. He came with the Sneyds to a supper party at her house, agitating her almost beyond endurance with memories and fears. As it turned out, these fears were premature. Lovell Edgeworth lived to involve himself in the strange misadventure at Verdun, when he was interned as a British subject, and condemned to an imprisonment which lasted for nearly a dozen years.

It is more than likely that the depression and misery which Miss Seward experienced during the two years 1792 and 1793 may have resulted from the contemplation of what was going on in France. The shock of hearing the terrible reports from across the Channel; the horror at the thought of atrocities committed; the fear of similar bloodlettings at home, were everywhere in England affecting sensitive minds and souls. Miss Seward was more susceptible than most people to those strong emotions to which the body inevitably reacts. That she should at this time find herself ill and suffering is not strange.

Her letters abound in eloquent passages denouncing the rabid ferocity of the French mob. It was in January, 1793, that she wrote that impassioned letter to her friend Helen Maria Williams which was published in the *Gentleman's Magazine* for February. She felt a real friendship for the rash Miss Williams, but a detestation of her ardor for the French cause, which had brought her, indeed, into the most perilous situations. "How often do I regret," wrote Anna Seward, "that you left our yet, and, I trust, long to continue, happy, country, for the regions of anarchy, tumult, and murder."[2] She confessed that she herself had once hoped that the democratic movement in France was the herald of new liberties. The hope was gone. What seemed to presage an advancement of mankind had proved only a retrogression to more horrible tyrannies than had been dreamed before. She railed against the "accursed French." "Behold them," she cried, "Bastilling the mildest and most indulgent monarch that ever sat upon their throne; . . . confiscating the property, and dooming to destitute banishment, those who had fled from the scenes of sanguinary tumult, and unpunished murder; where none could be sure that he, or she, might not prove the next victim; bullying and stigmatizing, with the most insolent contempt, every state, where the happier principles of subordinate government unite a people as one family!—destroying the freedom of their own press!—avenging, by proscription, all conversation which presumes to censure their fierce democratic sys-

2. *Letters*, III, 202.

tem!—menacing, with brutal indecency, in their conventional assembly, the few, *few* pleaders for mercy, who, conscious that their lives must probably expiate the generous attempt, deserve statues to their memory."

There was a great deal more, of the same sort. She apostrophized her friend with the words, "Fly, my dear Helen, that land of carnage!—from the influence of that equalizing system, which, instead of diffusing universal love, content, and happiness, lifts every man's hand against his brother!" It was a sincere and vigorous plea that she addressed to the reckless Englishwoman who had cast her lot with the French in an hour of extremest danger. In letters such as this, and the "Benvolio" epistles, Miss Seward showed a command of English of a moving quality much greater than that in her letters of a personal and sentimental sort.

Indulgence in emotions usually exacts a penalty. We are hardly surprised to find Miss Seward writing to one of her friends, "Never did I know what it was to be so ill as since I last wrote you."[3] From this time on, we hear of illnesses of various obscure types, recurring at intervals, and of persistent attempts to heal them by means of bleedings, drugs, and "waters."

In March, 1793, the *Gentleman's Magazine* printed a letter signed ****, enclosing and calling attention to some extracts from letters exchanged by Miss Seward and Mr. Hayley during the year 1782. These extracts were concerned with Dr. Johnson, and the "cool

3. *Ibid.*, p. 215, April 25, 1793.

malignity" which had prevailed in his *Lives of the Poets*. Miss Seward harped upon her favorite theme— the Doctor's injustice, and the "corroding envy" which had characterized his comments on almost all English verse writers.

One of the extracts, dated October 3 (1782), gives us a glimpse of the great Doctor in his native habitat: "*Immane Pomposo,* as Churchill calls him, has been in Lichfield 10 days. I am intimately acquainted with his daughter, Mrs. Porter, whose guest he is; and I have been accustomed to pay my respects to him. But my mind is sore about the envy he has shewn, and the real mischief he has done, to the literary fame of my favourite Bards in his late work. And under the influence of an unfashionable sincerity, I could not prevail upon myself to pay my usual homage at his shrine. . . . Till Tuesday last I saw not since he arrived this Champion of Poetic Defamation—that day he was my father's guest by invitation—and it became my duty to shew him every civility and attention—he will not bear the slightest dissent of opinion without becoming insolent. . . . A Gentleman who was of the party asked him if he had read your [Hayley's] Works. I rose from my chair, intending to leave the room while that theme lasted—but my apron entangling in his buckle, I could not disengage myself before I heard him say, 'Hayley, Sir, is a Man of Genius—but I have read nothing of his except his Essay on History.'—'How do you like that poem?'—Indeed it was not I who asked the question. 'I like his reproof to Gibbon—I esteem the man for it.'

'And is that all thou hast to say?' muttered I to myself—
but to his ear I kept an indignant silence."

Mr. Hayley answered mildly and jocosely, adding,
"All I hope is, that he will not live to write my Life."
Then follows a long and eloquent passage from one of
Miss Seward's letters, in which is given a studied bal-
ancing of Johnson's virtues and defects; and in which
the passionate (almost hysterical) dislike which the lady
felt for her great townsman is unreservedly displayed.

Miss Seward professed to be annoyed at seeing these
extracts from her correspondence laid before the public,
without Mr. Hayley's consent. She could not, she said
in a letter to the *Gentleman's Magazine* (April, 1793),
imagine who had had the effrontery to send them in
for publication. Yet we cannot help suspecting that she
welcomed one more opportunity (awarded through no
solicitation of her own) to speak her mind on the subject of Dr. Johnson's character and behavior.

In 1793 and 1794, when she was depressed and irritable,
Miss Seward engaged in an acrimonious contest with
James Boswell, in the columns of the *Gentleman's
Magazine*.[4] Raking up the quarrels of the past is an un-
pleasant pursuit, and these letters might be dismissed
with a word, were it not that they relate so nearly to
the greatest literary figure of the period, Dr. Johnson.
Miss Seward was rash in publicly exposing herself to
Boswell's attacks, and also in flatly asserting that John-

4. For Miss Seward's and Boswell's letters, see the *Gentleman's
Magazine*, LXIII, Part II, 875, 1009, and 1098; also LXIV, Part I, 32.

son, the idol of the Biographer, was lacking, at times, in strict veracity. Although she brought them upon herself, the covert sneers with which Boswell referred to her, when he had repeatedly professed friendship for her, and had been entertained in her home, were beyond question painfully humiliating.

In the *Gentleman's Magazine* for October, 1793, appears a letter from Miss Seward, beginning: "Mr. Urban, I have very recently seen a pamphlet, intituled, 'The principal Corrections and Additions to the first edition of Mr. Boswell's Life of Dr. Johnson.' It surprized me to see my name very impolitely introduced on the first page." She had taken offense at Boswell's repudiation of the material which she had furnished for his Biography, relative, specifically, to the *Myrtle* verses, and the dead duck. She wrote a letter covering a full page of the *Magazine,* defending her veracity and good intentions; hinting that Johnson at convenient times departed from strict truth; and complaining of Boswell's want of justice and "common politeness."

Possibly she thought that Boswell would remain silent, since he had passed over her "Benvolio" letters, written six or seven years previously. She reckoned without a full understanding of the man with whom she was dealing. In the November number of the *Gentleman's Magazine,* Boswell directed against her a rebuke couched in satirical terms which he may have felt to be moderate, but which she must have considered insolent in the extreme. This letter from Boswell, covering two double-columned pages of the *Magazine,* is too long to quote. Perhaps his most slighting insinuations were those implying that Johnson despised her. "I have withheld," he said, "his opinion of herself, thinking she might not like it. I am afraid it has reached her by some other means; and thus we may account for various attacks by her on her venerable townsman since his decease . . . some avowed and with her own name, and others as I believe, in various forms, and under several signatures. What are we to think of the scraps of letters between her and Mr. Hayley, impotently attempting to undermine the noble pedestal on which the public opinion has placed Dr. Johnson? But it is unnecessary to take up any part of your[5] valuable miscellany in exposing the little arts which have been employed by a cabal of minor poets and poetesses, who are sadly mortified that Dr. Johnson, by his powerful sentence, assigned their proper station to writers of this description."

Miss Seward would have done well to ignore Boswell's reply to her first letter, and let the matter rest. However, she rushed once more to the conflict with a long letter in the *Gentleman's Magazine* for December, 1793, elaborating her defense of her statements relating to the *Myrtle* poem; again insisting that Dr. Johnson was prone to disregard the truth; and lamenting the hypocrisy with which Boswell had pretended to be her friend, when he was now avowedly her foe. She closed her letter with the words: "Into a paper-war with a

5. Mr. Urban's. Sylvanus Urban was the mythical editor of the *Gentleman's Magazine.*

man, who, after professing himself my friend, becomes causelessly my foe, I will no farther enter. New instances of Mr. Boswell's heroic attempts to injure a defenceless female, who has ever warmly vindicated him, must ultimately redound more to his dishonour than hers, and will, I trust, produce no future intrusion upon Mr. Urban's publication from the pen of his friend and correspondent,

Anna Seward."

If she had thought Boswell malicious and insulting before, what must she have thought of him after reading the letter with which he retaliated, in the *Gentleman's Magazine* for January, 1794? The slurring remarks of the Scotchman were such that a gentlewoman could scarcely answer them without a serious loss of dignity; and the only thing which Miss Seward could do was to maintain the silence which she had promised. Boswell alluded invidiously to her age, her ignorance of classical and foreign languages, and her unenviable position as a minor versifier. He accused her of envy and malice. He called her sardonically "the fair lady," "our poetess," and "my fair antagonist." He referred to her familiarly as "Nancy Seward." He spitefully hinted at the derisive jingle about her and Mr. Hayley, in which she was characterized as "all the Nine"; and he did not fail to advert to the fact that she was, either in adulation or ridicule, dubbed "The Swan of Lichfield." His remark that "poetesses . . . have too often been not of the most exemplary lives" may or may not have been an innuendo inspired by her friendship with John

Saville. The general tone of the letter was offensive to the last degree; and specific phrases were cleverly contrived to carry a sting, though they might seem more harmless than they were. The letter was the work of an easy and practiced writer and skilled disputant, for whom, in the nature of things, Miss Seward was no sort of match.

She did not risk bringing upon herself any further attacks. To show that she was not entirely defenseless, she delegated to her faithful cousin, Mr. Henry White, the task of writing two other letters, dated March 19, 1794, and October 21, 1794. In a modest but dignified way, Mr. White refuted in the first letter an "absolute though doubtless unintentional misstatement" of Boswell's, relating to the Hunter and Porter families. In the second he answered in an equally restrained but convincing manner some suggestions made by one AE. V., in the *Gentleman's Magazine* for September, to the effect that Miss Seward's dislike of Dr. Johnson was caused by the Great Shah's disparaging remarks on her father, as reported by Boswell. AE. V. had pointed out "what was probably the ruling cause of Miss Seward's being so highly provoked against both Johnson and Boswell. For, may it not with reason be attributed to the Doctor's having, in language grossly contemptuous, exposed to his friend the failings and infirmities of the lady's father, and to the Biographer's having unwarrantably spread and perpetuated them? . . . Must not the fine feelings of a dutiful and truly affectionate daughter have been tremblingly alive in the perusal of this display of the character of her father in a book that was generally read, and a prevailing topick of conversation?"

That Miss Seward was deeply wounded by Johnson's aspersions on her father's good sense, there need be no doubt. However, she authorized Mr. White to say that AE. V.'s letter contained a "mistaken suggestion." "From no individual instance of false representation, and from no wound of personal feelings," says Mr. White, "arose her conviction of Dr. Johnson's propensity to defame; but from a countless number of imputations concerning the characters of others, groundless as that which Mr. Boswell has *generously* recorded concerning her father, at whose house he had been frequently entertained with the most friendly hospitality."[6]

This letter ended Miss Seward's part in a dispute into which she was unwise to enter. A number of other people, under a variety of signatures, added their comments to those of the chief antagonists, and much ink was spilled to little purpose, but probably to the great diversion of the intellectual public of the day.

DURING the years from 1790 to 1800, Miss Seward varied her home life by numerous visits to watering places or the homes of friends. Some of these visits we have recorded; but it would be tedious to speak of them all in detail. High Lake, or Hoylake, near Liverpool, became a favorite resort. She usually took a cousin or one of her Lichfield friends with her, and she also made many pleasant acquaintances at the hotels or pensions at which

6. *Gentleman's Magazine,* October, 1794, p. 876.

she stayed. People liked her, and many were impressed by her reputation as a poetess, and by her really fine talents as an elocutionist. One friendship led to another, and more doors were opened to her when she made a round of visits. In her turn, she was constantly entertaining her old friends or her new ones. Much of the time she was troubled by ill health, which medical prescriptions failed to remedy.

Of all the new friendships which she made, not one was to give her greater satisfaction than the intimacy which she formed with the celebrated Ladies of Llangollen, in Wales. In August, 1795, she was visiting her friends the Robertses at Dinbren, overlooking the Vale of Llangollen. From the elevation on which the house was situated appeared an enchanting view, such as those who have been in Wales must keep among their choicest memories. Somewhat beyond the immediate environment of the Roberts villa could be seen "the fairy palace of the two celebrated ladies," whom Miss Seward hoped to have the "honour and happiness" of meeting. This honor was the more to be desired since the two ladies maintained a strict exclusiveness, entertaining only those of rank and eminence who had been personally introduced to them by someone already known and approved. With almost juvenile exultation, Miss Seward reported to her cousins in Lichfield the attainment of her hopes. "By their own invitation," she says, "I drank tea with them thrice during the nine days of my visit to Dinbren; and by their kind introduction partook of a rural dinner, given by their friend,

Mrs. Ormsby, amid the ruins of Valle-Crucis, an ancient abbey, distant a mile and a half from their villa. . . . After dinner, our whole party returned to drink tea and coffee in that retreat, which breathes all the witchery of genius, taste, and sentiment."

Then follows a minute description of the villa of the recluses, its furnishings, and its exterior. One thing which particularly struck the enthusiast was the large Aeolian harp fixed in one of the windows. "When the weather permits them to be opened, it breathes its soft tones to the gale, swelling and softening as that rises and falls." The books in English, Italian, and French, the portraits and miniatures, colored lamps, souvenirs, and articles of virtu moved Miss Seward to a chant of admiration. The dairy house was a miracle of cleanliness and order, wherein the chief wonder was "a little machine, answering the purpose of a churn," which enabled the "Minervas" to manufacture half a pound of butter for their own breakfast, without soiling their hands. A dithyramb scarcely sufficed to do justice to the view from the house at twilight, when the evening star hung above the mountain and "the airy harp loudly rung to the breeze, and completed the scene of magic."

"You will expect," she writes, "that I say something of the enchantresses themselves, beneath whose plastic wand these peculiar graces arose." These two celebrated women were the Lady Eleanor Butler, and her friend Miss Sarah Ponsonby, who had fled from the gay Irish world to make a home together among the romantic hills of Wales. The report was that one or the other of them was being forced into an objectionable marriage, and that they resolved to run away from the conventional life of the nobility and be at peace. Accordingly, after one or two frustrated attempts, they left Ireland (about 1776) with their servant, Mary Carryl, and bought a simple cottage in Llangollen Vale. No inducements could ever draw them back. For fifty years they lived in their cottage, which they enlarged and beautified until it was a picturesque Gothic dwelling, prettily set in a landscaped garden. It was said, perhaps truly, that they never in all their fifty years at Plas Newydd left its roof for a night. They wore a semi-masculine costume, devoted themselves to gardening and reading, and received the *élite* of the social and intellectual world, who clamored at their gates. Lady Eleanor died in 1829, and Miss Ponsonby in 1831.

Miss Seward was prepared to find her two "Calypsos" both beautiful and elegant, though to speak truth they were by this time middle-aged, and, if their portraits are to be trusted, decidedly plain. To admit such facts would have been sacrilege. "Lady Eleanor," Miss Seward informs her cousins, "is of middle height"—not fat and red faced, but "somewhat beyond the *embonpoint* as to plumpness; her face round and fair, with the glow of luxuriant health. She has not fine features," it is true, "but they are agreeable; enthusiasm in her eye, hilarity and benevolence in her smile. Exhaustless is her fund of historic and traditionary knowledge, and of everything passing in the present eventful period." And so on.

Miss Ponsonby is less fully described. She is "somewhat taller than her friend, is neither slender nor otherwise, but very graceful. Easy, elegant, yet pensive, is her address and manner. . . . A face long rather than round, a complexion clear, but without bloom, with a countenance, which, from its soft melancholy, has peculiar interest. If her features are not beautiful, they are very sweet and feminine. . . . Such," carols Miss Seward, "are these extraordinary women, who, in the bosom of their deep retirement, are sought by the first characters of the age, both as to rank and talents. To preserve that retirement from too frequent invasion, they are obliged to be somewhat coy as to accessibility." The more, therefore, the glory to be received.

This exhilarating friendship with the recluses became one of the happiest circumstances in Miss Seward's life. The triumph which she felt in being welcomed into their circle was pardonable, surely, when others, greater than she, had felt their self-approval rising after they had been admitted to the Gothic villa at Llangollen. The ardors of Lady Eleanor, which "made cold-spirited beings stare," were matched by Miss Seward's own impassioned zeal for any cause which won her favor. Both the Ladies had listened with sympathy to the story of her life, and had expressed the deepest interest in her highly colored tale of Major André and Honora Sneyd. Their lifelong habit of reading, and their critical delight in poetry made the intellectual spinsters seem like congenial spirits who could be relinquished only at the cost of actual pain. Miss Seward quickly engaged them in correspondence. Then began an exchange of amenities which continued for a decade or more, and which seems to have been as pleasing to the anchoresses as to Miss Seward herself.

The poetess lost no time in putting her experiences into verse. She set to work upon her long poem, *Llangollen Vale,* and it must have reached the recluses in November; for early in December the author was writing to them: "I rejoice that my poem on Llangollen Vale meets a reception of such partial warmth from the bright spirits it celebrates, and whose praise I desire for it more than fame; yet I am conscious how largely that praise transcends its merits." Some people might be ungracious enough to say that any praise transcends its merit. This is scarcely true. Certain stanzas have a liveliness, a dash, and a technical finish which entitle them to a degree of commendation; though the poem as a whole is artificial, forced, and uninspired. Miss Seward, taking the material supplied her by Lady Eleanor's "exhaustless fund of historic and traditionary knowledge," followed the course of events in the valley, from the time of Owen Glendower to the date at which she wrote. A number of stanzas may be quoted, to show the nature of the poem:

> Lo! thro' the gloomy night, with angry blaze,
>   Trails the fierce comet, and alarms the stars;
> Each waning orb withdraws its glancing rays,
>   Save the red planet, that delights in wars.
> Then, with broad eyes upturn'd, and starting hair,
> Gaze the astonish'd crowd upon its vengeful glare.

Gleams the wan morn, and thro’ Llangollen’s Vale
　　Sees the proud armies streaming o’er her meads.
Her frighted echoes warning sounds assail,
　　Loud, in the rattling cars, the neighing steeds;
The doubling drums, the trumpet’s piercing breath,
And all the ensigns dread of havoc, wounds, and death.

.　　.　　.　　.　　.　　.　　.　　.　　.

High on a hill as shrinking Cambria stood,
　　And watch’d the onset of th’ unequal fray,
She saw her Deva, stain’d with warrior-blood,
　　Lave the pale rocks, and wind its fateful way
Through meads, and glens, and wild woods, echoing far
The din of clashing arms, and furious shout of war.

From rock to rock, with loud acclaim she sprung,
　　While from her Chief the routed legions fled;
Saw Deva roll their slaughtered heaps among,
　　And check’d waves eddying round the ghastly dead;
Saw, in that hour, her own Llangollen claim
Thermopylae’s bright wreath, and aye-enduring fame.

Then follow some inferior stanzas, pitched in a tone
of adulation so extreme that they seem likely to repel
rather than attract the “peerless twain” whom they celebrate. Miss Seward has been accused of “flattering” the
hermit pair; but it is obvious that one cannot flatter
people who cannot be flattered. She must have been
sure, before she left Plas Newydd, that this extravagant
laudation was acceptable to her close-wedded hostesses,
whose sentiments appear to have been as one in all important respects.

The Ladies sent Miss Seward a gift of fruit trees from
their own “umbrageous bowers,” as Miss Seward would
have said. “They will be the pride of my garden,” she
wrote, “and I shall watch their growth with solicitude,

as the pledges of an highly-prized friendship." Only a few days later came a drawing and the transcription of an article on the Sonnet, in Chambers' *Encyclopedia*. This drawing was engraved as a vignette for the *Llangollen Vale,* in its published form, and Miss Seward was concerned about the engraver's bill, which she wished to discharge. She sent each of the Ladies a letter case, netted with her own hands, and accompanied by a poem.

Llangollen Vale was published in 1796 (price one shilling and sixpence), together with "Eyam," "Time Past," "Hoyle Lake," "Wrexham," and six sonnets, selected from the centenary of sonnets which Miss Seward proposed to publish later. The little volume was reviewed in the *Gentleman's Magazine* for May, 1796, in a generally favorable manner. "There are few," says the reviewer, "to whom the lovers of poetry owe greater obligations than to Miss Seward, and we only lament that we have not more frequent opportunity of making her our acknowledgments." A number of long extracts are given, with polite phrases. "Yet," the reviewer concludes, "with all the praise which we freely bestow on Miss Seward, it is not without a due mixture of serious regret that we see her sometimes careless and sometimes affected, giving cause, on more occasions than one, for that kind of censure, which, with some justice, though too great acrimony, has been passed on the Della-Cruscan community. Miss S. should be superior to prettiness and conceits, which, whenever they occur, are disreputable to the claims of Genius."

In the same issue of the *Magazine* in which the review closes (it is continued through two numbers) is a long communication from Mr. Henry White of Lichfield, Miss Seward's cousin, defending *Llangollen Vale* from some scornful strictures made upon it in the April number of the *British Critic*. It is likely that the material used by Mr. White was supplied by Miss Seward; for it comprised a sheaf of poetical quotations from eminent authors, justifying her diction, which had been adversely criticized. Miss Seward was always amazingly ready with quotations, with which her mind had from childhood been stored. The *British Critic* had, to its own satisfaction, proved the poem to be pompous nonsense. Mr. White, to his satisfaction (and presumably Miss Seward's), proved it to be a gem of purest poesy.

An amusing tag to this controversy is a letter signed "Stephen Brown," in the August issue of the *Gentleman's Magazine,* taking sides with the *British Critic*. "What a dickens!" exclaims Mr. Brown. "Can not these fine lady-writers be satisfied with moderate praise? must it be heaped up and flowing over? Can not the admirers of the *Lichfield Swan* be content without *she carries all before her?*[7] From that love of justice which comes necessarily with declining years, . . . I was induced to look at the remarks of the British Critic on Miss Seward's poems, which have given offence to Mr. Henry White; and upon my honor, Mr. Urban, I think them very sensible, pertinent, and just, and what ought to satisfy said Miss Seward and her friends. . . . If Mr.

7. See the satirical verses on p. 99.

White's observations in your last Magazine are the result of his own reflexions, he will at least allow them to be inconsiderate. But if, as I can not help suspecting, he has lent his name to the suggestions of another,[8] he has acted yet more unwisely. Miss Seward might well and reasonably be satisfied with the portion of praise allotted to her in the review she dislikes so much; for, she may be assured, that thousands besides British Critic, although they will readily allow Miss S. the praise of ingenuity, do not think her the very first, best, and wisest of poetess[es] that ever wrote." The editor of the *Magazine* remarks in a footnote, "We must dismiss this controversy here." No doubt he anticipated another screed from the combined indignations of Miss Seward and Mr. White.

The sort of thing retailed above shows both what Miss Seward had to endure from the critics; and what her wounded vanity impelled her to do, in the way of trying to reply to reviewers, often cleverer than herself. It was, we fear, true that she was not content with "moderate praise." She longed to have it "heaped up and flowing over." The author has been surprised, in reading through the magazines of the day, to find how much commendation Miss Seward received, and how highly esteemed her works seem to have been in many quarters. She could not bear the slightest hint of disapproval. She liked to believe, as Mr. Hayley and others had taught her, that she carried all before her, and that she was indeed the first, best, and wisest poetess that

8. Miss Seward herself.

ever wrote. This eagerness for admiration, combined with a thin-skinned sensitiveness, can so destroy the peace of mind of an author that he (and especially she) had better be at the bottom of the sea with a millstone round his neck, rather than on earth trying to please a capricious public. Miss Seward made herself unduly miserable by paying both too much and too little attention to her critics. By paying them less attention, she might have been less harrowed by what she considered their unfairness and their cruelty; by paying them more, she might have amended the most grievous of her faults. The sense of superiority which came from her secure social position in ecclesiastical circles, and from the unwise praise of friends who succumbed to her personal charms, made her unwilling to admit the need of improvement. In the long run, the security of her position and the approbation of her friends may have been worth more to her than whatever excellence she might, under criticism, have attained as a poet.

THE correspondence with Miss Ponsonby and Lady Eleanor Butler was a source of delight to Miss Seward, as long as she was able to fulfil her part. It gave her an outlet for that emotional element in her nature, of which Robert Southey said, "She had a great deal of natural ardour, though it was often expressed in so artificial a way that it had the appearance of affected enthusiasm."

Mr. Saville and his daughter were received at Plas Newydd through Miss Seward's introduction in 1796.

Miss Seward herself visited there for three days in September, 1797, after having spent some weeks at Hoylake, in the ever returning hope of improving her health by sea bathing. The three days passed in the "Abyssinian Valley" renewed and strengthened the friendship begun two years before. Miss Seward speaks thus in a letter to Mr. Whalley: ". . . Swiftly flew three days of high gratification, scenic and intellectual, with the charming Rosalind and Celia of this lovelier Arden." In the letter written to the Ladies, immediately upon her return to Lichfield, she paid her homage to them in these phrases: "Be my beloved Miss Ponsonby and Lady Eleanor assured that I consider Llangollen Vale my little Elysium. It is nowhere that my understanding, my taste, and my sentiments luxuriate in such vivid and unalloyed gratification." This was literally true. It is likely that none of the country-house visits which she made, numerous as they were, gave her such a complacent sense of fulfilment as her short sojourns at Plas Newydd.

We may here complete the record of her association with the "mild enchantresses" of Llangollen. Letters and gifts continued to make their way from Lichfield to Wales, and from Wales to Lichfield. Miss Seward sent a framed print of Romney's profile picture, "Serena Reading," which bore an accidental resemblance to Honora Sneyd. Miss Ponsonby and Lady Eleanor sent a valuable seal ring, engraved with "Apollo's head and lyre." Books and manuscripts were frequently exchanged. In the autumn of 1799 Miss Seward stopped at Plas Newydd, on her return home from Hoylake. She spent four days of unalloyed bliss. She left a "Sonnet" of gratitude and compliment in a drawer in "the thatched shed by the brook at Plas Newydd." It is unnecessary to quote it, since it contains the sentiments already embodied in other poems addressed to her hostesses. In 1802, in company with Mrs. Smith, Miss Seward again visited the two friends at Llangollen, and composed a long poem in blank verse, by way of recompense for their hospitality. It was entitled, "A Farewell to the Seat of Lady Eleanor Butler, and Miss Ponsonby, in Llangollen Vale, Denbighshire, September, 1802." After the death of Saville in 1803, the letters to Llangollen (if we may judge by those printed) grew infrequent and almost ceased. So far as we know, Miss Seward never saw her adored Ladies again, which is the greater pity since her affection for them was such that, had they lived nearer, she might have found in them some consolation for her griefs.

Miss Seward was well over fifty when she was disturbingly reminded of an early love-affair—the one with Colonel T——. In 1796, it seems, she received a letter from the wife of Colonel T——, exhibiting a curious combination of jealousy and infatuation. Reading carefully through the answer which Miss Seward copied into her letter book (dated March 2, 1796), and also another letter dated June 19, of the same year, we infer that the Colonel married in 1775, and that he and his wife called at the Palace, failing to see her, since she was away on a visit. This was about ten years after the breaking of his engagement with Anna Seward, because of his limited means. We have seen that she had lost all her former affection for him, and that she retained no lingering regrets over the outcome of her affair of the heart.

The wife, on her own confession, had always been uneasy because Colonel T—— had never ceased to express his ardent admiration for his early love. Mrs. T—— had come to regard Miss Seward, whom she had never seen, as a sort of goddess, to be both feared and worshiped. She had made an effort to see the poetess in 1785, and had for the second time been unsuccessful. If she had seen her, Miss Seward writes, her illusions would have vanished. Miss Seward was horrified to hear that she had "through so long a period of former years" shed a "malign influence upon the destiny of an highly deserving pair." She strove in a kindly but vigorous way to awaken the wife from her foolish dream, and assure her of the truth—that she cared nothing for the man to whom she had once been engaged; and that the troubles and activities and affections of later years had driven all interest in him from her mind.

In June she had a strange visit from the man himself, which vouched for the reality of his "long delirium." "He inquired for me at the door," she wrote, "and sent up his name, Lieutenant Colonel T——. I was dressing. My man-servant brought his card up stairs. While he did that, my housekeeper, coming up the stairs from the kitchen, saw a gentleman whom she did not know, stand at the foot of the next flight of stairs, looking up with earnest melancholy eyes. Perceiving her, he went back into the hall; and when the man brought my message to request his going into the parlour, and to say that I would be down immediately, lo! he had vanished."

A letter from his wife, received later, asserted that Mrs. T—— had known nothing of this visit until she heard of it from Miss Seward. Mrs. T—— then asked her husband why he had acted so strangely. He should, she told him, have stayed and seen Miss Seward at last, since he had found her at home. He replied, "The momentary gratification must have been followed by regret and pain, that would sufficiently have punished the temerity of attempting to see her at all. I had no sooner entered the house, than I became sensible of my perilous state of feeling, and fled with precipitation." Miss Seward regretted, as his wife did, that he had not remained. He would have found her old and fat and lame, though not so lacking in charm as she herself asserted. "Small traces would have been perceived in me of that image so unhappily impressed on his mind, and which yet glows in the gay bloom of youth." The "insane constancy" of the man would, she felt sure, have disappeared in one "spell-dissolving interview."

She wrote to Mrs. T—— again (June 19), expressing her utter lack of any personal attachment to Colonel T——, and her hope that his ridiculous infatuation would yield to common sense. It was in these two letters to Mrs. T—— that Miss Seward revealed the inner history of her own loves—up to the time, at least, that she gave her heart irrevocably to John Saville. These letters furnish almost the only information which we have regarding those engagements of the affections (to use a Sewardian phrase) which are supposed to fill so large a place in every woman's life.

Her association with Mrs. T—— was not yet ended; indeed it had only begun. One evening in June, 1797, when Miss Seward was entertaining her friends the Zacharys in her upstairs book room, the servant announced a strange lady, who wished to see her alone. "Going down stairs to attend her," Miss Seward wrote to Mrs. Stokes, "I met Mr. Saville in the gallery, who whispered as he passed me—'Mrs. T——, or I am much mistaken.'" It was the unfortunate woman herself, who cried dramatically as Miss Seward came into the room, "At this instant, the vision of my life is realized!" Miss Seward soothed and cajoled her, and persuaded her to join the party upstairs.

The T——s had established themselves at least temporarily in Lichfield. Miss Seward does not speak of meeting the Colonel, but tells of calling on the wife and daughter, and of inviting them to her house. The daughter was about sixteen, a modest, well-educated girl, an excellent player on the harpsichord and piano-forte. Of Mrs. T——, Miss Seward speaks highly, adding, "All her own talents and accomplishments are wasted upon a cold and prepossessed ingrate, whose very virtues, by exciting her esteem, have embittered her regrets." How long the friendship between the two women continued the present writer has not discovered. Miss Seward had acted with tact, patience, and generosity, as she usually did in any situation in which the feelings of others were involved. In one of her letters to Mrs. T—— she analyzed herself impersonally, and the reader of her *Letters* feels that she spoke truly when she said, "I know that I have some talents; that I am ingenuous; that my mind is neither stained nor embittered by envy; that I detest injustice, and am grateful for every proof of affection."

ACCEDING to the request of Mr. Hayley, Miss Seward had faithfully kept up her association with Mrs. Hayley, difficult as it must at times have been. In December, 1797, came the news that Mrs. Hayley was dead. Miss Seward, seeing it in the papers, could only make conjectures as to the cause of her friend's death. She feared that Mrs. Hayley had died by her own hand—which was not the case. An "epidemic fever" had carried her off in about the fiftieth year of her age. Eccentric to the point of being unbalanced, Mrs. Hayley seems nevertheless to have been a worthy woman. The fact that she and her husband could not live together is no damning commentary on either. Mr. Hayley could never be accused of anything but kind intentions. He had endured the whims and oddities of his wife for years, and parted from her with reluctance. His provision for her was generous, and his anxiety for her welfare was ever active.

The chief source of our knowledge of Mrs. Hayley's

character (aside from her husband's *Memoirs*) is Miss Seward's letter to Mrs. Gell, dated December 3, 1797. "Nature," said she, "after striking off this one singularly characteristic impression, broke the mould in which she made Mrs. Hayley." She went on, with an extended analysis of the lady's personal qualities, shrewdly appraised. It is too long to quote in its entirety, yet some extracts may be made: "She had a Gallic gaiety of spirit, which the infelicities of her destiny could but transiently, however violently, impede. The short paroxysm of anguish passed, the tide of vivacity returned, and bore down everything before it. . . . With sportive fancy; with no inconsiderable portion of belles-lettres knowledge; with polite address, and an harmonious voice in speaking, and with the grace of correct and elegant language: with rectitude of principles, unsuspecting frankness of heart, and extreme good humour; she was, strange to say! not agreeable, at least not permanently agreeable. The unremitting attention her manner of conversing seemed to claim; her singular laugh, frequent and excessive, past all proportion to its cause, overwhelmed, wearied, and oppressed even those who were most attached to her; who felt her worth, and pitied her banishment from the man she doated on—in whose fame she triumphed, tenacious of its claims even to the most irritable soreness. Yet her rage for society, and excessive love of talking, were so ill calculated to the inclinations and habits of a studious recluse, as to render their living together inconsistent with the peace of either."

At this time, Miss Seward was not aware of the magnanimous way in which Mrs. Hayley had forgiven the unfaithfulness of her husband; even to the accepting of his illegitimate boy and caring for him with the affection of a mother. It was not until the death of Thomas Adolphus Hayley, in 1800, that Miss Seward knew the facts. She had supposed that the boy was the son of a young man named Howell, whom Mr. Hayley had made his *protégé,* and who was lost in a shipwreck, on his return journey from the West Indies. Whatever may have been Mrs. Hayley's idiosyncrasies, she deserves to be remembered for her loving charity, such as few women have been large-hearted enough to parallel.

Miss Seward had frequently read her sonnets aloud, with that wonderful voice of hers, which gave a dulcet elegance to anything she read, even to her own commonplace odes and lyrics. Her friends had urged her to publish her compilation of one hundred sonnets, written during the space of two decades, under the stress of varied emotions. The Ladies of Llangollen were particularly insistent that she should put these verses into print. "I am flattered extremely," she wrote to them, "by the conviction you express, that my centenary of sonnets and which form a sort of compendium of my sentiments, opinions, and impressions, during the course of more than twenty years, would be acceptable to the public. . . . I certainly mean they should one day appear. I know their poetic worth, and dare trust their fame to posterity:—assured that the Gothic mantle, now spread over poetic taste, will be cast away in time to come."[9]

After they had been printed (1799), she said of the sonnets in a letter to Miss Ponsonby: "If I do not extremely flatter myself, the Sonnets possess an inherent buoyancy, which give them the power of emerging in future. That expectation has often been ridiculed as the forlorn hope of the poet; but Spenser, Milton, Otway, Collins, and Chatterton, are instances that it is not always found vain." Alas! If she had known how cruel posterity could be, she would have despaired more darkly over the world's taste. She died in the full assurance that she could never be forgotten, and that her verses would live on as inevitably as Spenser's or Milton's.

These sonnets were very dear to the author's heart. She was proud of them, because they adhered to a strict form, the Miltonic, which seemed to her the only permissible model. She took great care to make them technically correct, to vary the internal structure by running sentences and phrases from one line to another, and to close with a strong sententious line. She did not always change the thought at the ninth line, but sometimes linked the whole sonnet together, making no special pause for the sestet. On the whole, the sonnets are pleasing and dignified. Taken individually, they seem distinctly praiseworthy, many of them admirably phrased and musically worded. But read in succession, they pall,

9. *Letters*, IV, 133.

their defects of thought and diction showing too numerously to command sustained admiration.

Probably the best of the sonnets is one which was the favorite of the author:

Sonnet XL

Dec. 19th, 1782

December Morning

I love to rise ere gleams the tardy light,
    Winter's pale dawn;—and as warm fires illume,
    And cheerful tapers shine around the room,
    Thro' misty windows bend my musing sight
Where, round the dusky lawn, the mansions white
    With shutters closed, peer faintly thro' the gloom,
    That slow recedes; while yon grey spires assume,
    Rising from their dark pile, an added height
By indistinctness given.—Then to decree
    The grateful thoughts to God, ere they unfold
    To Friendship, or the Muse, or seek with glee
Wisdom's rich page:—O, hours! more worth than gold,
    By whose blest use we lengthen life, and free
    From drear decays of age, outlive the old!

Sonnet XI has a spontaneous tone, and in the octave expresses a sincere love of nature, falling off to a more conventional thought in the sestet:

How sweet to rove, from summer sun-beams veiled,
    In gloomy dingles; or to trace the tide
    Of wandering brooks, their pebbly beds that chide;
    To feel the west wind cool refreshment yield,
That comes soft creeping o'er the flowery field,
    And shadowed waters; in whose bushy side
    The mountain bees their fragrant treasures hide
    Murmuring; and sings the lonely thrush concealed:

> Then, Ceremony, in thy gilded halls,
>   When forced and frivolous the themes arise,
>   With bow and smile unmeaning, O, how palls
> At thee, and thine, my sense!—how oft it sighs
>   For leisure, wood-lanes, dells and water-falls;
>   And feels th' untempered heat of sultry skies!

The *Gentleman's Magazine* for December, 1799, prefaced its review of the *Sonnets* with this characterization of the author: "Ingenuous as she is lovely, her conversation is the true portraiture of her inmost soul. Within a gaiety of manner commanding the profoundest respect is mingled the engaging complacency which fascinates all around her." Then follows a short but highly commendatory review, with well-selected quotations from the poems. If Miss Seward were as vain as her enemies asserted (which is not by any means likely), she might be pardoned for having a good opinion of herself and her works, after she had read a number of paragraphs like that given above.

Capel Lofft gave the sonnets "warm praise" in the *Critical Review,* prefacing his remarks by a "laboured dissertation" upon sonnets in general, which Miss Seward thought tiresome and unnecessary. But she "took thankfully," she said, Mr. Lofft's kindly estimate of her work, since critics were not always so lenient to her Muse. On April 30, 1799, Miss Seward wrote to thank Mr. F. N. C. Munday, author of *Needwood Forest,* for the sonnet on her late publication. "It is," said she, "truly Miltonic." We print the sonnet below:

On Miss Seward's Sonnets, with Particular Allusion to Her Twenty-first and Twenty-second.[10]

10. *Letters,* V, 217.

Critic, hast thou fastidiously proclaim'd
　Misjudging from such humble verse as mine
　The lyre's lost energy, the sad decline
　Of genius in this island, early nam'd
In classic heraldry, and foremost fam'd?
　From Greece, from Latium, came th' impatient Nine,
　Here to receive their laurels, and entwine
　Their shoots; rewards of Envy only blam'd.—
And here they still rejoice; here still abides
　Imagination in her mountains strong;
　While harmony beneath her stream divides.
And thou shalt blush, vain critic, for thy wrong
　Tasting these sweets which the Queen Muse provides,
　With rarest elegance of sex and song.

Another admirer, Mr. Christopher Smyth of Lincoln's Inn, sent a sonnet[11] of praise, a welcome poetic tribute of the many which Miss Seward received during her lifetime.

11. *Letters*, V, 266.

CHAPTER IX

1800–1808

THE CROWNING GRIEF

DURING the latter years of the century, Miss Seward became more and more concerned for the health of Mr. Saville. In December, 1801, he had a terrifying seizure of a paralytic nature. "On the first of December," Miss Seward wrote to Mrs. Powys, "I received an alarming summons to his house at day-dawn." Passing over the details of his illness, we find that he presently recovered under the ministrations of Dr. Jones, though he remained weak and inactive. At this time he was preparing to leave his own tiny house and take possession of "a neat little dwelling," which Miss Seward had been "fortunate enough to *purchase for him,* two doors below where he was living." This new home, however, was "unaired and wholly unfit for his reception." What was more natural than that he should be brought to Miss Seward's "thinly tenanted" Palace? "Dr. Jones," she says, "seconded my proposal that he should be brought here in a sedan [chair], where his daughter could be constantly with him, and sleep in a tent-bed in his apartment, and where he could have every necessary care and attendance."

He stayed for more than a month. No mention is made of his wife. What a choice morsel of scandal this must have been for the sedate clerical gossips of the

Close! How they must have rolled under their tongues the names of the brazen pair, and whispered their suspicions and surmises! In her letters at least, Miss Seward took no heed of slander. She and his daughter nursed the invalid through the cold winter weeks. Mrs. Smith gradually removed her father's books and other belongings to his new abode, and made it neat and comfortable. And then, on a Monday in February, Miss Seward and her cousin and his wife, and Mrs. Smith, went with Mr. Saville to take possession. They "drank tea and supt in his pleasant parlour." This house was larger than the other. "He has a good bed-chamber," Miss Seward went on, "a neat second room for Mrs. Smith, if he should again want her nocturnal nearness to his person, and a third for his new servant."

In spite of the cheerful housewarming, fear had not yet departed. Saville was feeble, Miss Seward shaken and apprehensive. Mrs. Powys came for a visit of three weeks. Then Saville and Miss Seward went to Warwickshire together to visit at the home of a Mr. Mitchell and his niece. Near the grounds of Mr. Mitchell dwelt an obliging choir of nightingales. On a "glowing and balmy evening," a party of seven people set off for the wild coppice where the birds were wont to sing. Miss Seward had prepared herself for the occasion by looking up poetical passages descriptive of the notes of "Philomel"; and her enjoyment, as usual, was the double one of experience and recollection. She did not say that she was disappointed; yet she did not think the

DR. ERASMUS DARWIN
BY WRIGHT OF DERBY
Courtesy of the National Portrait Gallery, London.

notes so pensive as the poets had led her to expect. They were not so pensive as the wood lark's, and not sweeter.

She took her usual summer trip—this time to Hoylake, where she stayed five weeks, hoping to restore her health by sea bathing. But twenty-one immersions failed to work the looked-for miracle. Mrs. Smith was with her on her journey into Wales, where she spent two weeks in the house of the Robertses and in the cottage of the Ladies of Llangollen. She was hardly a week at home, before she set off again for Birmingham, to enjoy a grand festival of oratorios—three days of Handel and Haydn, eight hours of music out of each twenty-four. In all, she was ten weeks absent from home. Though it had its miseries as well as its pleasures, this was the last summer which was to give her any lifting of the heart. In the next she was to receive the cruelest of blows.

BEFORE death struck where he could grieve the most, he threw a dart in another direction. In 1802 died Dr. Darwin, who, for the twenty-five years in which he had lived in Lichfield, had been an intimate friend of the Sewards.

We have seen that the Doctor married and removed to Derby, where he continued as active in his profession as before. He brought up three families: his own by his first wife; his second wife's children by Colonel Chandos-Pole; and his own second group of young people. His son Charles was a brilliant student, receiving, while still very young, an honorary medal from the

Society of Arts and Sciences. He died at an early age, as a result of some rash experiments made while he was pursuing the study of medicine.

In 1799 occurred the tragic death of the Doctor's son Erasmus, a man of mature years. He became a victim of melancholia, aggravated by worry over some unimportant accounts. On a gloomy December evening, he slipped away from his family, and threw himself into the river Derwent, which flowed at the lower end of the garden of the Derby house. Miss Seward says that the younger Erasmus was a sensitive and retiring person, who wished to enter the Church and avoid the harsh contacts of the world; that he was wounded by the rough irony of his father, and morbidly conscious of being the butt of paternal ridicule. She asserts, moreover, that the Doctor showed a hard and unfeeling spirit at the time of his son's death; that he spoke contemptuously of the dead man's cowardice, and after the funeral never referred to the lost son again. These statements were indignantly denied by the Doctor's relatives. The middle ground of fact seems to be that the Doctor concealed whatever grief he felt, putting into practice his theories concerning the folly of repining, sorrow, and remorse.

The one remaining son of Mary Howard, Robert Waring Darwin, was his father's pride. After studying medicine, he settled at Shrewsbury, where he attained "instant eminence as a physician." "He joined to a large portion of his father's science and skill all the ingenuous kindness of his mother's heart." Successful, prosperous, and admired, he lived a long and contented life, dying in 1848, at the age of eighty-two. He married Susannah, daughter of Josiah Wedgwood of Etruria, and had six children. The fifth of these was Charles Robert Darwin, the evolutionist. Charles Robert married his cousin, Emma Wedgwood; and his sister Caroline married the younger Josiah Wedgwood. The Wedgwood and Darwin pedigrees thus became inextricably involved. These marriages were highly approved by the heads of both families.

After the death of Dr. Darwin, his son Robert Waring, Miss Seward says, requested her to put into writing her recollections of his father, in order that they might be incorporated into a biography which the Rev. Mr. Dewhurst was to write. She accordingly set down a series of anecdotes relating to the period which Dr. Darwin had passed in Lichfield. After having spent some time on this piece of work, Miss Seward decided that it would do greater justice to herself if it were printed under her own name than it would if it were handed over to a biographer to use as he pleased.

In May, 1803, Miss Seward's faithful friend and cousin, Mr. Henry White, took her manuscript to London. Delay ensued, owing to the publisher's fear that some of the remarks in the book might cause offense to Dr. Darwin's friends and their families. Johnson had offered "an handsome price" for the book, but insisted on expurgations and changes, very annoying to the author. "Rather than break with him," said Miss Seward to Dr. Lister ". . . I have attempted that

softened colouring [which he demanded]." After a
good deal of demur and haggling, the alterations were
made, and the book came out in 1804. By the time it
appeared, Miss Seward was under the heavy shadow of
grief, and was too much occupied to take pleasure in
any plaudits which she received. The comment on the
book in the *Edinburgh Review,* which the author considered cruel and unjust, overbalanced the praise of
friends and other kindly critics. This review, which appeared in April, 1804, was sufficiently disagreeable,
though it was not actually unjust. To be sure, Miss
Seward had sought to disarm criticism by asserting that
she had made no attempt at a biography as such. She
wrote to Walter Scott: "To present a faithful portrait of
his [Darwin's] disposition, his manners, his heart;—to
draw aside the domestic curtain; to delineate the con-
nubial and parental conduct of his youth; the Petrar-
chan attachment of his middle life; . . . to analyze
his poetic claims; and to present singular instances of
philosophical love in the eventful history of one of his
distinguished friends;[1]—these, and these only must you
expect from my feminine Darwiniana."

The book might indeed be unpretentious; but its
modest intentions could scarcely excuse the fact that it
was planless and incoherent, and that it was padded
with a long, dull analysis of Dr. Darwin's *chef-d'œuvre,*
The Botanic Garden. The *Edinburgh Review* attacked
its faults with its usual lack of reserve. A few quota-

1. Thomas Day.

tions will suffice to show the nature of the remarks
which so incensed the author of the *Memoirs:*

After perusing this table of contents [previously quoted], the
reader will have himself alone to blame if he expect in this volume
any exact or orderly deduction of the facts of Dr. Darwin's life. Miss
Seward apparently spurns the fetters of vulgar, chronological narra-
tion. . . . After having followed her with patience through her
eccentric and capricious evolutions, we are unable to say that our
progress has been rendered more pleasing by this irregular variety,
or that it has afforded us any tolerable compensation for the want of
a distinct and intelligible narrative. . . .

Of this "sketch of the character and manners of Dr. Darwin," we
can only say, that it leaves no very distinct impression on the mind;
and *that* impression, such as it is, has not in our own case at least,
been extremely favourable. . . .

The long and elaborate analyses of these two poems [the two
parts of *The Botanic Garden*], which Miss Seward has thought fit to
give, will, by many readers, be considered as prolix and uninter-
esting.

And so on. There is much censure, and little praise
in the article. Miss Seward's own comment on the
methods of the magazine may be found in a letter to
Walter Scott, dated June 20, 1806: "Ignorance and envy
are the only possible parents of such criticisms as disgrace the publication which assumes the name of your
city. In putting them forth, their author is baser than
a thief, since to blight the early sale of an eminent work
by unjust criticism is to rob the bard of his remunera-
tion, while the arrested progress of his fame must in-
flict severer mortification."[2] She remarks that Jeffrey,
the editor, should be named Jeffries, such is his tyrannic
cruelty.

2. *Archibald Constable and His Literary Correspondents: A Memorial by His Son, Thomas Constable,* II, 25.

The *Edinburgh Review* published as a footnote to its critical article a retraction from Miss Seward, in which she publicly announced that she had been mistaken in at least one statement in her volume. The retraction, which must have been exceedingly humiliating to the lady, was as follows:

> The author of the Memoirs of Dr. Darwin, since they were published, has discovered on the attestation of his family and of the other persons present at the juncture, that the statement given of his exclamation, page 406, on the death of Mr. Erasmus Darwin, is entirely without foundation, and that the Doctor, on that melancholy event, gave amongst his own family, proofs of strong sensibility at the time, and of succeeding regard to the memory of his son, which he seemed to have a pride in concealing from the world. In justice to his memory, she is desirous to correct the misinformation she had received, and will therefore be obliged to the Editor of the Edinburgh Review to notice the circumstances in the criticisms of the book, since, unless a second edition should be called for, she has no means so effectual of counteracting the mistake.

This passage was printed at the request, and largely in the words, of Dr. Robert Waring Darwin, who resented the imputation of callousness which had been cast upon his father in Miss Seward's book. On the whole, the *Memoirs* did not bring much glory or happiness to the author.

THE record of declining years should not be a painful one; but too often it seems to be an iterated story of loss, renunciation, loneliness, and disease. In the case of Miss Seward, it is not all sad. Nevertheless, we must now chronicle what she assuredly would have called the crowning tragedy of her life.

On the second of August, 1803, John Saville died suddenly. At the time of his attack—in the early evening—he was hurrying to dress for a concert, to which his friends had already gone, Miss Seward among them. She had last spoken with him at four o'clock. The swiftness of his taking-off deprived her of a last look and sigh from her beloved. Her grief was terrible. It was that of a' widow, rather than of a friend. For weeks she was unable to leave her house; and it may truly be said that she never recovered from the blow of her bereavement.

The following notice appeared among the "Obituaries" of the *Gentleman's Magazine* for September, 1803:

[August] 2. Aged 68. Mr. John Saville, vicar-choral of the Cathedral-church of Lichfield. This melancholy annunciation of the loss of an excellent man, very generally known, and where known, always beloved, will excite the sympathy of Genius, and the tear of Friendship. Pre-eminent were his abilities as a vocal performer, from the rare union of feeling with science, of expression with skill. The Commemoration of Handel, and the remembrance of Saville will live together. From this well-merited praise Eulogy turns with delight to the virtues of the heart, and her tablet is not the record of Flattery when it exhibits him as pious, generous, friendly, ingenuous, intelligent, and sincere.

This sounds very much as if it were written by Miss Seward herself, though we have no clue to its authorship.

At first she roused herself sufficiently to be proud of the honor shown to Saville in the tributes of his funeral day. She took, too, a sad pleasure in settling his affairs, paying his debts and making arrangements for the comfort of his daughter and her children. "God gave me the means," she said; "my best use for life is to fulfil all that I am conscious he fervently wished."

The Dean and Chapter granted her permission to erect a monument to the memory of Saville, in the transit aisle of the Cathedral. This memorial, designed by Sir Nigel Gresley, cost her one hundred pounds, which may be translated into a much larger sum today. "It will cost me an hundred pounds," she wrote to an intimate friend, "and never, never could I part with money so willingly as for this *last* tribute to the memory of my dearest friend." The design she described as "simply elegant," meaning, no doubt, elegantly simple. Into a Gothic niche in the form of an oblong, fitted a slab of dark gray marble, recording the name and the dates, and displaying the long poetical epitaph. Above this oblong and entablature were pieces of broken marble, on which stood an urn with ascending smoke, to signify the departure of mortal life. The epitaph is given below:

SACRED TO THE MEMORY

OF

JOHN SAVILLE

*Forty-eight years Vicar-Choral of this Church
He died August the 2d, 1803, aged sixty-seven.*

Once in the heart, cold in yon narrow cell,
Did each mild grace, each ardent virtue dwell;
Kind aid, kind tears for others' want and woe,
For others' joy the gratulating glow;
And skill to mark, and eloquence to claim
For genius in each art the palm of fame.

Ye choral walls, you lost the matchless song,
When the last silence stiffened on that tongue!
Ah! who may now your pealing anthems raise
In soul-poured tones of fervent prayer and praise?
Saville, thy lips, twice on thy fatal day,
Here breathed, in health and hope, the sacred lay.
Short pangs, ere night, the fatal signal gave,
Quenched the bright sun for thee,—and oped the grave!
Now from that graceful form and beaming face,
Insatiate worms the lingering likeness chase.
But thy pure spirit fled, from pain and fears,
To sinless,—changeless,—everlasting spheres.
Sleep then, pale mortal frame, in yon low shrine,
"Till angels wake thee with a note like thine!"[3]

However fully this epitaph may have expressed the feelings of Miss Seward, we must confess that its images and phraseology leave something to be desired, to the eye and ear of the modern reader. The grim pleasure of setting up this memorial being over, nothing remained for the mourner but to reiterate the perfections of the deceased and bemoan his loss.

One of the circumstances connected with the death of Saville, Miss Seward must often have related. It is found in print in a letter to her old friend of Bath-Easton days, the Reverend Mr. Whalley:

Except these words—"The bell rings, and I must go to church," the following are the last I heard my dear friend speak: "Look at this beautiful engraving of a design for a monument to Handel. I know you dislike writing epitaphs after having written so many; but you must write one more for me, to occupy the blank space here left for an inscription."

I replied, "We will talk of that hereafter—but now play a concerto with me." He did so till the evening prayerbell rang, and he went cheerfully away—to return no more! Alas! I have written one

3. This last line is from Johnson's epitaph on Philips the musician.

more epitaph, obeyed the injunction of those almost latest words, though their meaning applied to his adored Handel. O Heaven, that they should prove an unconscious prophecy of his own impending fate!—so nearly impending!

The prostration of grief left Miss Seward little strength for any activity except the transaction of necessary business and the writing of letters. On December 15, she writes that all lesser considerations [than the death of Saville] have vanished from her thoughts: "Till Saturday seven-night, these gates have formed the impassable limits of my feeble steps. It was not till then that I could assume fortitude enough to pass the silent grave, in which my soul's dearest comforts forever lie, till it shall itself be emancipated, and seek, as I trust, the realms of pardon and everlasting peace."

Three months of being shut up in her silent Palace with her memories and her sorrows were scarcely conducive to mental poise. The letters of this period (though those printed are undoubtedly the most moderate that she wrote) are filled with outbursts of grief and rebellion. It is evident that Miss Seward was completely broken. Courage went out of her. Nothing mattered much, now that Saville was gone. The self-sufficiency, tending to arrogance, which had characterized her words and actions, was subdued to heartbroken weakness and wailing. She struggled a while, then sank and succumbed to anguish of mind, producing in its turn indefinite maladies of the body.

A LITTLE more than five years of life remained to her; but they were hardly worth the living, so filled were they with mourning, and with physical and mental suffering. From the time of Saville's death, Miss Seward cut down her correspondence, which heretofore had taken endless hours of hard labor; and yet enough remained to furnish an outlet for her emotions, and possibly a distraction from her miseries. The comments on her "Darwinian volume" must have claimed her attention, though not in the most agreeable way. She tried to read. Music she could not bear.

> Saville, the gates of harmony
> Eternally were closed to me,
> When thou didst pass the mortal Goal,

she wrote in her sorrowful poem called *To Remembrance*. In a letter to Mr. Archibald Constable, dated September 18, 1807, she says of a present of some books: "The collection of Scottish Ballads is indeed a truly valuable book—too valuable for me, who, after all the best days of my long life had been devoted to harmony now turn sickening from the sound—sad consequence of a sudden and dire fatality which from that hour, four years ago, in my heart, made *music* to awaken the nerves of anguish."

She inured herself to carry on a superficial conversation with, as she put it, "that herd of acquaintance, from whom it were folly to expect genuine commiseration." (Some, it may be, of the herd had even sneered at the passion of her lamentations and the blackness of her woe.) There were intermittent stages in her suffering and her "hopeless nerveless melancholy." She was able to go about a little, to find some pleasure in receiving or in visiting her real friends. When the next summer came on, she spent five or six weeks at her favorite resorts, Buxton and Matlock, with an attached young cousin, Susan Seward. It was at Matlock that she passed the anniversary of Saville's death. "Strange countenances shall not look upon me that day," she cried. On the "fatal second" of August, she wrote a frantic letter to Miss V—— (Vyse?), in which she counted off the hours until the stroke of his decease. Every letter of the period is dampened with her tears.

In illness and desolation, Miss Seward looked about for a companion, to stand between her and the emptiness of the great Palace, in which she insisted upon living. She was now sixty, and the vitality which gave her, till near the last, many of the aspects of youth, was slowly ebbing. Susan Seward, "with her fortune, merits, and accomplishments," seemed destined for early marriage. Some more dependable associate must be found, who could share the years to come, which might be many, in spite of disease and heartbreak. In a letter written to Mr. Charles Simpson, Miss Seward told her plans. This letter, in printed form, must have caused some chagrin to the woman whom it named; but in justice to the writer, it must be said that she did not expect it to be published until a long time after her death.

She had selected from among her acquaintances a Miss Fern, a woman no longer very young, whom she had known for years. This Miss Fern had suffered many things from a tyrannical father and a hostile step-

mother. She looked forward to a more endurable existence with her brother John; but he died in 1793, leaving her poor. We infer that her situation was still
uncomfortable, and that she was free to go to Miss
Seward when the request came.

In the letter to Mr. Simpson, Miss Seward discussed
Miss Fern and her affairs with painful frankness. Miss
Fern had once had beauty, so the letter said; but fourteen years earlier, it had been destroyed by a "cutaneous
eruption" which tarnished and muddled her once radiant complexion. Since that misfortune, she had lived
without lovers, though she was tall and finely formed,
and her features were good. Men admitted that she was
agreeable, but avoided her because she was without
money. Miss Seward believed that Miss Fern of the tarnished countenance would never marry. So she had
long been hoping to seize upon the lady when she
needed a "female" who might be at once her companion, nurse, and friend. What arrangement was made
does not appear; but a little later we find Miss Fern
reading aloud to the semi-invalid, writing her letters,
and accompanying her at tea-drinkings in Lichfield and
on jaunts to more distant regions. In June, 1805, Miss
Fern is spoken of as "my guest," but surely some pay-
ment would be made for her services. That she was
with the older woman to the last is shown by Southey's
letter discussing the disposal of Miss Seward's property.

Miss Fern was, said Miss Seward, "one of the few."
"Native strength of understanding and play of fancy;
wise and vigorous exertions in situations of teasing trial;

sweetness of temper, rectitude of principle, a liberal spirit, and ingenuous goodness of heart, combined, early in life, to form her character. Intimately acquainted with her during a long series of years, I never," Miss Seward went on, "with much to esteem, met with the slightest circumstance to disapprove in her conduct or manners." This is high praise. Miss Seward was fortunate in securing so worthy a companion for her dismal later years.

In February, 1806, we find her writing to Miss Fern, after the departure of some relatives who had stayed at the Palace seven weeks: "I trust you will hasten to resume your friendly influence over my many wants and few solitary hours. My health and my heart have need of you." This last sentence tells much of the character of Miss Fern, and the consolation which she was able to offer to her broken-hearted friend.

THE remaining summers were passed at watering places, or at the homes of friends. "It is nine years," Miss Seward wrote in 1800, "since I passed the three summer months at home." Her habit in this respect did not change until ill health made further excursions impossible. A visit to the Whalleys, at their high-seated cottage in the Mendip Hills was a renewal of the joys she had experienced there thirteen years before. This time she stayed ten days. The Mrs. Whalley of earlier days was gone, and a new lady reigned in her stead. The cottage had been enlarged until it had become an elegant villa, filled with beautiful things. A full-length

portrait of Mrs. Siddons, by Hamilton, was one object
worth noticing, among many. The scenery surrounding
the villa was magnificent. Miss Seward loved a grand
landscape, with panoramas of mountain and sea, and
here her taste was fully gratified.

She passed one morning with Hannah More, whom
she does not seem to have much liked or admired; and
Miss More and the Countess of Waldegrave came over
to Mendip Lodge for a day.

One of the pleasantest incidents of this visit to the
Whalleys was the reconciliation of Miss Seward and
Mrs. Pennington, once Sophia Weston. They had loved
each other, but had allowed hard feelings to separate
them for twelve years. Age and experience had softened
their spirits. Miss Seward wrote of Mrs. Pennington,
"She received me with tears of returning love, and our
reconciliation was perfect. She made me promise to stay
with her a few days on my way back to Winterbourn."
It was during this visit, too, that Miss Seward met at
Bristol, with deep emotion, two daughters of Richard
Lovell Edgeworth, Maria and Emmeline. She longed
to see them, not because they were Edgeworth's children, but because they had passed some of their childhood years with her "soul's dear Honora." They sought
her out, and "spoke with apparent delight" of her attentions to them in their infancy, and the hours they
had spent happily beneath her father's roof. They "drew
back the curtains of the past, on scenes both dark and
bright." She inquired for Lovell, Honora's son, and

heard that he was still, after some years, a prisoner of war at Verdun.

Miss Seward left a melancholy poem with her host when she departed from Mr. Whalley's house; *Addressed to the Rev. Thomas Sedgewick Whalley, on leaving his seat, Mendip Lodge, in Somersetshire, Oct. 10th, 1804.* It was filled with mourning for her lost Saville.

Miss Seward was now suffering from constant dizziness, and from undefined maladies which threatened to end her existence. With characteristic courage, she kept up as much as she could, pursued her studies and correspondence by means of a reader and amanuensis (probably Miss Fern), and continued her interest in the affairs of the day. Cards enlivened her hours of recreation. Callers and visitors were a distraction, possibly also an irritation and strain. Presentiments of her own decease were not wanting, among the gloomy recollections of sorrow and the ever recurring news of friendships broken by death.

The letter from Mrs. Jane West (already quoted) to the Bishop of Dromore says of these later days: "Her fortune was very handsome, and in her latter years she lived at Lichfield in an elegant hospitable way, much admired by strangers, patronising genius, and quarreling with all who contradicted her." This not very sympathetic account had been transmitted in a roundabout way to Mrs. West, who had little or no personal acquaintance with Miss Seward. As to the quarreling, there may have been something of the sort. Miss Seward was a sick woman, afflicted with what would now be given the name of high blood pressure, and kindred ailments which often seem to render the best-intentioned people extremely irritable and easily agitated. She had suffered much mental and physical anguish, for which she knew not how to find a remedy. She had been maligned by many persons, some of whom should have helped instead of injuring her; and others of whom she knew to be her inferiors in birth and culture. While she had been spitefully attacked,[4] she had also been assiduously flattered. She had probably developed both a "defence complex" and a fixed idea that she had an inalienable right to dominate. Neither of these states of mind is calculated to make a woman easy to live with.

One more revival of her association with Saville is recorded in June, 1806. Mrs. Smith received a legacy from a relative (a Mr. Pegge), amounting to five thousand pounds. Her daughter Honora, now married to Mr. Jager, had (no doubt encouraged by her mother's windfall) bought the "pleasant little mansion in the Vicarage," in which John Saville had lived from 1765 to 1772. One guesses that his wife had been with him during these years. Behind the house was a garden which Honora Sneyd had called "Damon's Bower."[5] Mr. and Mrs. Jager and Mrs. Smith invited Miss Seward

4. She had been accused of writing scurrilous ballads. See also *Letters*, VI, 289, for an account of an anonymous letter.

5. See Shenstone's poem, *Verses written Towards the Close of the Year 1748*.

and Miss Fern to have tea and supper in that "so con-
secrated mansion." The ordeal was trying to Miss
Seward, to whom it recalled the lost days when Honora
Sneyd was yet her "child of recompense." "The last
time till yesterday," she says, "that I was ever in that
mansion and garden, as appears by my journal book,
was the 2d of August, 1771, and on the 2d of August,
1803, its dear and excellent master was struck from
existence."[6]

The old days, she cries, rushed back on her soul,
"decked in gaiety and joy; in music and in song; in the
bloom, the smiles, of Honora Sneyd; in the grace and
in the accents of Saville; but O! how afflicting did the
contrasting sense of everlasting privation render them!"
Only two other houses could ever, she thinks, so power-
fully restore the past. One was probably the rectory at
Eyam; the other her "dear friend's latest habitation,
now the home of his daughter and her mother."[7]

In 1807, Miss Seward had some negotiations with Constable of Edinburgh regarding the possibility of his
publishing some or all of her works. Archibald Constable himself dined with her in April. He was a friend
of the Rev. Henry White, by whom he was probably
accompanied on his visit to the Palace. It may have
been the report which the publisher carried back to
Edinburgh that induced Walter Scott (not yet
knighted) to stop at Lichfield in the following May.

6. *Letters*, VI, 286.   7. Saville's wife.

He and Miss Seward had long been writing to each other. Scott himself had begun the correspondence.

On October 17, 1799, Miss Seward wrote to Mrs. Powys, regarding the disputed authorship of *Plays on the Passions:*[8] "A young poet, of the name of Scott, and a native of Edinburgh, has sent me poems of his in manuscript, Glenfilas, and the Eve of St. John; each of which bear the stamp of a genius fully responsible for the Plays on the Passions. I have not, however, any other reason to believe them his." In November she again refers to these poems in a letter to Mr. Thomas Park. Writing to the same gentleman in January, 1801, she speaks of the publication of the poems: "At length the tales of wonder are before the public, and contain Scott's Glenfilas, and the Eve of St. John, which I mentioned to you with such warm applause. . . ." The willingness which Miss Seward always showed, to welcome a new writer, is here exhibited. We may be sure that her "warm applause" went by post to the young poet named Scott, and that he was pleased and proud to win this recognition. Later, when he had been surfeited with praise, he found Miss Seward's somewhat boring. In the meantime, a good many letters had passed the Border, to and from each of the poets.

The first letter to Scott in the collection of Miss Seward's *Letters* is dated April 29, 1802. It is written to thank the Northern Bard for a copy of his *Minstrelsy of the Scottish Border*. She wrote a searching critique of the poems included, explaining that it seemed to her

8. By Joanna Baillie.

"that barren thanks and indiscriminate praise was an unworthy acknowledgement of the honour" conferred upon her "by the gift of these highly curious and ingenious books." Inspired by the Scottish verses, she wrote an imitation of them, called a *Ballad in the Ancient Scotch Dialect, Auld Willie's Farewell*. Scott thought so highly of this poem that he inserted it in the third volume of the *Minstrelsy*. Miss Seward says in a note to the poem in her collected works that Scott observed that "the stoutest antiquarian in Scotland could not, after perusing Auld Willie's Farewell, suspect that the writer had the misfortune to have been born *south* of the Tweed."

Scott was growing somewhat tired of this correspondence, though he might have been grateful (and probably was) for the persistent advertising of his wares that Miss Seward did among her friends. At the time that Saville died, she had a letter in hand, which she was writing to Scott. Half crazed by sorrow, she added some incoherent lines, announcing her determination to sink herself in an oblivion of woe. She told him that it was needless to answer her letter, for she had no heart left for her correspondence. Scott apparently took her at her word. After her death he wrote of this period to Miss Joanna Baillie (March, 1810): "The despair which I used to feel on receiving poor Miss Seward's letters, whom I really liked, gave me a most unsentimental horror for sentimental letters. The crossest thing I ever did in my life was to poor dear Miss Seward; she wrote me in an evil hour (I had never seen her, mark that!) a long and most passionate epistle upon the death of a dear friend, whom I had never seen, neither, concluding with a charge not to attempt answering the said letter, for she was dead to the world, etc., etc., etc. Never were commands more literally obeyed. I remained as silent as the grave,[9] till the lady made so many inquiries after me, that I was afraid of my death being prematurely announced by a sonnet or an elegy. When I did see her, however, she interested me very much."

It speaks volumes for the enduring charms of Miss Seward that nearly everyone who met her liked her immensely. No matter how ready a person might be to extinguish her with his contempt for her failures as a poet, let him only come within the radius of her personality and he was a helpless devotee. This fact was, no doubt, partly due to the irresistible way in which she took possession of those around her; but it was also due to the brilliancy of her conversation, and to something large and benevolent in her nature. Turning to Scott's "Introduction" to her *Poetical Works,* which he edited after her death, we may read his report of this visit:

In Summer, 1807, the editor, upon his return from London, visited Miss Seward, with whom he had corresponded occasionally for some years. . . . Miss Seward, when young, must have been exquisitely beautiful; for, in advanced age, the regularity of her features, the fire and expression of her countenance, gave her the appearance of beauty, and almost of youth. Her eyes were auburn, of the precise shade and hue of her hair, and possessed great expression. In reciting, or in speaking with animation, they appeared to be-

9. Two years elapsed.

come darker; and, as it were, to flash fire. I should have hesitated
to state the impression which this peculiarity made upon me at the
time, had not my observation been confirmed by that of the first
actress of this or any other age,[10] with whom I lately happened to
converse on our deceased friend's expressive powers of countenance.
Miss Seward's tone of voice was melodious, guided by excellent taste,
and well suited to reading and recitation, in which she greatly exer-
cised it. . . . Her stature was tall, and her form was originally
elegant; but having broken the *patella* of the knee by a fall in the
year 1768, she walked with pain and difficulty which increased with
the pressure of years.

We have noted Scott's confession that when he met
her in her own home, on that day in May, he "really
liked her"; and we may mention the fact, also, that he
was persuaded to stay two nights, when at first he had
firmly insisted that he had only a few hours to spare.
In a triumphant letter to Cary, Miss Seward described
"the proudest boast of the Caledonian muse," and gave
a vivid picture of his material self, as well as a shrewd
estimate of his inner being. He is, she says, "rather
robust than slender; but lame in the same manner as
Mr. Hayley, and in greater measure. Neither the con-
tour of his face, nor yet his features, are elegant; his
complexion healthy, and somewhat fair, without bloom.
. . . An upper lip, too long, prevents his mouth from
being decidedly handsome, but the sweetest emanations
of temper and of heart play about it when he talks
cheerfully, or smiles; and, in company, he is much
oftener gay that contemplative."[11] There is more, which
might be tedious in the quoting.

Miss Seward invited her relatives the Whites, and Mr.

10. Mrs. Siddons, of course.   11. *Letters*, VI, 338.

Simpson, the barrister, to take breakfast with the lion; and in the evening (Saturday) the party dined and supped with the Simpsons in their home. Every hour was a feast of wit and laughter. "Such visits," wrote Miss Seward with a sigh of satisfaction, "are the most high-prized honours which my writings have procured for me." She may be forgiven for her pride. Such a visit was more than the would-be wit of her traducers had ever procured for *them*.

It may have been during this stay of two days at the Palace that Miss Seward suggested Scott's becoming her literary executor, and the editor of her posthumous volumes, letters included. "This [request] I declined on principle," Scott's letter to Miss Baillie continues, "having a particular aversion at perpetuating that sort of gossip." That he was induced to grant a part of her request, we shall see later, when we come to the discussion of her will.

Scott went away, leaving the proudest and happiest of memories in Lichfield. He may have talked over with his publishers the plan of bringing out some of Miss Seward's works; for on June 2, 1807, Mr. John Murray, the London publisher, wrote to Archibald Constable: "I have received a very obliging letter from Miss Seward . . . in consequence of a few books which I sent her. The more, however, I consider her merit as an authoress, the more satisfied I am that it would be hazardous to offer any important sum for her works, either published or *ante*-posthumous, and I trust that you will not betray your usual circumspection, or rather judgment, for the mere honour of carrying the publication of an English poetess into Scotland."[12]

Miss Seward was, of course, unaware of this warning on the part of Constable's friend and colleague in London. She was now, seemingly, in constant pain from her maladies, and was convinced that she had not long to live. She began to think of putting her affairs in order for her departure. In July, 1807, she drew up a paper shown in facsimile in Volume I of her *Letters,* addressed to Mr. A. Constable, directing that after her death he should receive the "exclusive copyright of Twelve Volumes, quarto, half-bound," containing letters or parts of letters written during the years 1784–1807, inclusive.

"I wish you," she wrote, "to publish two volumes annually, and by no means to follow the late absurd custom of classing letters to separate correspondents, but suffer them to succeed each other in the order of time, as you find them transcribed. When you shall receive this letter, the writer will be no more. While she lives she must wish Mr. Constable all manner of good, and that he may enjoy it to a late period of human life."

Though she had made this provision for the publication of her letters after her death, Miss Seward had not given up all hold on life, and was still quite capable of making plans and demanding high prices for her collected works. On September 18, 1807, she wrote to Mr. Constable: "If I should ever be able to obtain leisure to

12. *Archibald Constable and His Literary Correspondents, A Memorial* by his son Thomas Constable, I, 375.

correct my miscellany of published and unpublished poems, of prose and verse, and master courage enough to expose them, during my life-time, to the oyster-knife dissection of the reviewers (almost to a man of them unacquainted with the usages, the licenses, and indeed all that constitutes the *beauty* of poetry and eloquence), *you* shall have the first offer of the copyright; and perhaps Mr. Scott will have the goodness to settle the terms."[13]

It seems that in the course of time, Constable actually proposed to Miss Seward that he should publish a two-volume edition of her poems, consisting of 1,000 copies. The negotiations were carried on through Scott. She replied as follows: "Mr. Scott informs me that you prefer to purchasing the whole collection of my works, already arranged for publication, that of a single edition of two volumes . . . to be filled by a republication of my Monodies, together with a selection from my Sonnets, and other published poems, the said edition to consist of 1000 copies, for which you would give £130. My life is too far advanced to make the plan of selling a single edition desirable to me. If I persuade myself to undergo the anxiety of republication, it must be with a copyright sale either of a part or the whole of my collection."[14]

The letter is very long, and may be condensed. Her works, published and unpublished, she says, would fill

13. *Ibid.*, II, 13.
14. *Ibid.*, p. 20.

six volumes of verse, and four of prose, besides thirteen[15] volumes of selected letters. "However, these volumes [the manuscript letters] are for future consideration, and for appearance distant, probably posthumous."

For "the entire copyright" she expected to receive six hundred guineas, and fifty copies for distribution. This appears to be a proposal for the publication of four volumes of poems only. But she preferred a different plan. She wished to sell the entire copyright of all which she "intended should form a complete edition" of her works (the thirteen volumes of letters excepted). "They would at least fill six and probably eight, volumes of verse, and four of prose. . . . For them," she says plumply, "I shall expect one thousand guineas, and fifty copies for presents."

It is evident that Miss Seward thought well of her works, and considered them a valuable piece of literary property. The reply which Mr. Constable made is not printed; but he refused the offer which Miss Seward made, and did so without "hurting her *amour propre*," as Thomas Constable says. She did not alter the terms of her bequest, in which her letters were transferred to Constable for posthumous publication. Thus, as far as we know, the negotiations with the Edinburgh firm were brought to a close. The correspondence with Scott continued almost to the time of Miss Seward's death.

15. The letter of bequest says twelve. See page 256. One remains in manuscript to this day. It is not certain whether the manuscript volumes of the published letters are still in existence.

IN writing to Miss Seward in August, 1807, Scott remarked: "I am very happy although a little jealous, withal—that you are to have the satisfaction of Southey's personal acquaintance. I am certain you will like the epic bard exceedingly."

In October of the same year, Southey, writing to Miss Barker, said: "This evening has brought me a letter from Litchfield and I am bound to make a visit there. . . . She [Miss Seward] is really a very staunch friend." This was true. For years Miss Seward had been exalting Southey to the clouds in her letters, and it may be presumed in her endless conversations with literary people. Such trumpeting of a young man's worth, especially if he be a youth supporting a family with a goose quill, is not to be disdained. Miss Seward was by no means a despicable critic. She not only read a new publication which interested her; she reread it, studied it, analyzed its methods, picked out and examined its words, learned long passages from it for parlor recitations, and quoted it in her letters. She wrote reviews, too, and no end of letters to her favorite periodicals, particularly the *Gentleman's Magazine*.

It is true that her first impression of Southey was unfavorable. That is, she deprecated his politics, though she discerned his literary promise. On reading *Joan of Arc,* published in 1795, Miss Seward burst into a rhythm of reproach, charging the youthful author with treachery and hatred toward his country. This unrhymed ode of denunciation is too long to quote. In 1807, Miss Seward retracted her harsh judgment on the views and motives of Southey, and wrote at the end of the poem, when she was preparing her works for the press: "Cooler reflection, and a long experience of the mischiefs resulting from the sanguinary system which this government has unwarned pursued through the last 14 years, have . . . convinced me that the deprecation in Joan of Arc of monarchical ambition and rapacity, under that proud and specious term, Military Glory, proceeded from benevolence to the Human race, and from a spirit of justice too firm to be warped by the vanity of national enthusiasm."

The *Philippic* on *Joan of Arc,* which to say truth was written in the days when older and wiser men thought that the French Revolution and Democracy were going to reform the world, reached the eye of Southey and roused in him the natural resentment of the young against their critics.

However, in 1798 Miss Seward was writing to Cary of "the rising splendours of Coleridge and Southey's muse." "I return your Coleridge, and have purchased one myself," she said. "It would disgrace a poetic reader not to have him on their shelves." This ready welcome of new and untried writers was ever a characteristic of Miss Seward. She did not fear to form her own opinions, nor to speak out before she had found what the London critics were saying. "Unpublished and unheard of compositions are the tests of the taste and judgment of the listener," she says. This is one of her astute remarks, unadorned by verbiage, which wins respect for her mind and heart.

To Southey she gave fully as high an estimate in these early days as to Coleridge. "Our rising stars, Coleridge and Southey," she wrote to Mrs. Jackson of Edinburgh, "are resplendent poetic stars, whose lights are unborrowed of that sun [Shakespeare]." And in the same letter these words occur: "In the epic Southey's Joan of Arc approaches, in genius, nearer the Paradise Lost than any other epic attempt in our language."

When, in 1802, a reference was made to her and her cousin Mr. White in an article in the *Critical Review,* Miss Seward concluded somewhat rashly that Southey was the author. She felt temporarily incensed, though her admiration for his best works did not decrease.

In July, 1802, she wrote a review of Southey's *Poems* which appeared in the *Poetical Register*.

In a letter to Miss Barker, written on July 9, 1802, Southey wrote: "I hear of a review of my own poems inserted in the 'Poetical Register' . . . by Miss Seward. They tell me it is like her poem to me [the *Philippic on a Modern Epic*]—praise and censure equally extravagant, sugared bile, oil and vinegar."

When *Thalaba* came out, she complained of its irregular meter, but was too much agitated by the death of Saville to give the poem much attention. With *Madoc* she was enraptured. "I have heard it four times read," she wrote to Cary, "and listened with delight which 'grew by what it fed upon.' . . . Madoc has more for the understanding and the heart," she continued, "than any composition without the pale of Shakespeare and Richardson." It would be tedious to enumerate the references to Southey in her *Letters*. Her praise was acceptable to Southey, who was young, ambitious, and eager for recognition. He began the correspondence with a letter to her in 1807,[16] by asking her to suggest alterations in *Madoc,* which she called the poem of her idolatry. The correspondence continued until her death.

In July, 1808, in writing to his friend C. W. Williams Wynn, M.P., regarding a recent circle of visits, Southey remarked casually, "We halted two days with Sir Ed. Littleton [*sic*], in Staffordshire, and there Tom and I parted . . . I to Lichfield where I made a short stay with Miss Seward." He was tantalizingly silent as to his entertainment:—how the rooms of the Palace were furnished, what entertainment was offered him, whom he met, and how progressed his friendship with Miss Seward. Many years afterward, however, he wrote more circumstantially of this visit, picturing, unfortunately, only his introduction to the authoress and not the remainder of the two days he spent under her roof.

In a letter to Mrs. Bray, written from Keswick, in 1833, Southey thus described his visit at Miss Seward's house:

I once passed two days at her house, having known her before only by letters. A lady[17] with whom I was very intimate and who

16. The date 1809 (see *Letters*, VI, 358) seems to be a misprint for 1807. The volume closes with a letter dated November 5, 1807, and no letters of 1808 and 1809 are given. In a note attached to this letter to Southey, Miss Seward says that she has never met him and has just begun a correspondence with him. He visited her in 1808.

17. Miss Barker, afterward Mrs. Slade.

had a quick sense of the ludicrous, carried me to her door, and was present at the introduction. . . . Miss Seward was at her writing desk; she was not far short of seventy, and very lame. . . . Her headdress was quite youthful, with flowing ringlets: more beautiful eyes I never saw in any human countenance; they were youthful, and her spirit and manners were youthful, too; and there was so much warmth, and liveliness, and cordiality, that, except the ringlets, everything would have made you forget that she was old. This, however, was the impression with which I left her. The first scene was the most tragi-comic or comico-tragic that it was ever my fortune to be engaged in. After a greeting, so complimentary that I would gladly have insinuated myself into a nut-shell, to have been hidden from it, she told me that she had that minute finished transcribing some verses upon one of my poems,—she would read them to me, and entreated me to point out anything that might be amended in them. I took my seat, and, by favour of a blessed table, placed my elbow so that I could hide my face by leaning it upon my hand, and have the help of that hand to keep down the risible muscles, while I listened to my own praise and glory set forth, in sonorous rhymes, and declared by one who read them with theatrical effect. Opposite to me sat my friend Miss Barker, towards whom I dared not raise an eye, and who was in as much fear of a glance from me as I was of one from her. The temptation to laugh at a time when you ought not is a terrible one. . . . However, I did overcome this temptation, and even contrive to make a becoming acknowledgment at the end, and to offer some worthless remark when pressed for a critical opinion; and when all was over, I thought as you will think that I had gone through more than St. Anthony.

CHAPTER X

1809–1811

THE END AND BEYOND

THE *Gentleman's Magazine* for March, 1809, records among its obituaries: "[March] 25. In the
Episcopal Palace, in the Close of the Cathedral
church of Lichfield, the justly celebrated Miss Seward;
'Wept, prais'd, and honour'd by the friends she lov'd.'"

In the April issue appeared a "Biographical Sketch
of the Late Miss Seward."

The later letters in the sixth volume of *Letters* show
Miss Seward in the miseries of disease. The last manuscript volume was never published; hence the letters
from November, 1807, to the time of her death (excepting those printed in the *Memoir* of Thomas Sedgewick
Whalley, 1863) have never been made public. They are
in the possession of the Bishop of Ely.

Walter Scott published[1] Miss Seward's last pathetic
letter to him, in which she bade him farewell, and consigned her precious works to his compassionate care.
He says:[2] "The arrangement of Miss Seward's fortune
was left under the charge of her residuary legatee,
Thomas White, Esq., residing in the Close of Lichfield,
and Charles Simpson, Esq., of the same city; the former

1. *Poetical Works,* Biographical Preface, I, xxxi.
2. *Ibid.,* p. xxxiii.

connected with her by relationship, and both still more by kindness and intimacy."

The following are Walter Scott's verses (not much better, it must be confessed, than some of Miss Seward's own elegies), which were inscribed on the tomb in the Lichfield Cathedral:

> Amid these Aisles, where once his precepts showed
> The heavenward pathway which in life he trode,
> This simple tablet marks a Father's bier;
> And those he loved in life, in death are near.
> For him, for them, a daughter bade it rise,
> Memorial of domestic charities.
> Still would you know why o'er the marble spread,
> In female grace the willow droops her head;
> Why on her branches, silent and unstrung,
> The minstrel harp is emblematic hung;
> What Poet's voice is smother'd here in dust,
> Till waked to join the chorus of the just;
> Lo! one brief line an answer sad supplies—
> Honour'd, belov'd, and mourn'd, here SEWARD lies:
> Her worth, her warmth of heart, our sorrows say:
> Go seek her genius in her living lay.

Believing that she had attained a secure place in the annals of English literature, Miss Seward had provided with minute precision for the distribution of her belongings and the publication of her works, both prose and poetry. Southey, somewhat disappointed, perhaps, that he was not remembered, and as nearly jealous of Scott as so generous a soul could be, wrote to Miss Barker (afterward Mrs. Slade) from Keswick, May 13, 1809:

Mr. White wrote me an intimation of Miss Seward's death. I was right in supposing her farewell letter to me was not written in so desperate a state as it purported to be, for she recovered that attack, and died of a different complaint. . . . Her will, the Wolseleys tell me, filled fourteen folio sheets, and Scott has a legacy of 100 l., for which he is expected to write her epitaph. A bequest of 500 l. for her own monument3 is the only foolish part of her arrangements, —that was a poor vanity: the very verger when he shows the monument, will relate it to her discredit. I am glad I have seen her; glad, too, that you were present at the first interview, and not in the slightest degree surprised that when it rains legacies, none should fall upon me. . . . Scott's legacy and her monument money should have gone to Miss Fern. . . . She might have left me a set of her works, or some piece of her plate, and I should have shown such a token with pleasure. Her papers, which are in Constable's hands, are very numerous; the letters alone would fill fourteen quarto volumes, of which two4 are to be published. . . . She was a woman of great abilities; and if ever I pass through Lichfield again, I shall feel with regret that she is gone.5

A letter to the present writer from Frederick A. Brabant, Esq., Solicitor, of Gray's Inn Square, London, throws some light on Miss Seward's will: "Miss Anna Seward drew up and engrossed her own will, and it is 152 folios of 72 words a folio in length. . . . She gave a great many annuities and directed that on the death of the last annuitant (which occurred in 1842), legacies should be paid to the grandchildren and great grandchildren of her cousins Grace Robarts and Mary Hall. The legal representatives of the deceased in 1903 paid the amount due to these grandchildren into Court, as they were unable to ascertain them."

By the terms of the will, mourning rings of the value of five guineas were to be given to Lady Eleanor Butler and Miss Ponsonby (the Ladies of Llangollen); Miss

3. The monument was for her father and his family.
4. Six were published.
5. *Letters of Robert Southey,* ed. J. W. Warter.

Cornwallis ("Clarissa"); Mrs. Mary Powys of Clifton; and Dr. William Hussey. To Mr. William Feary of Lichfield, and to Thomas Lister, Esq., of Armitage, the sum of five guineas respectively was apportioned, for the purchase of mourning rings or some other tokens. The following persons received mourning rings of the value of two guineas: Mr. and Mrs. Hussey Wyrley, Mrs. Thomas White, Mrs. Susannah Burrowes (Susan Seward), Mrs. Hinckley, Mrs. Martin, Mrs. Charles Simpson (wife of one of the executors of the will), and Mr. Ironmonger.

A curious fan, "of ancient date but exquisite workmanship," went to Mrs. Thomas White, together with the "best diamond ring," and the miniature portrait of the poetess. The miniature of Canon Seward, by Richmond, went to Mrs. Burrowes. To the Rev. Henry White went the portrait of Canon Seward, by Wright of Derby; also some drawings by the Rev. William Bree of Coleshill. The picture of the Swan herself, by Romney, was bequeathed to her executor, Mr. Charles Simpson. It eventually came into the Burrowes family and remained many years in Ireland.

The miniature of John Saville, "drawn in 1770, by the late celebrated artist Smart," probably the most treasured of Miss Seward's possessions, was given to Saville's daughter, Mrs. Smith, with a reversion to Mrs. Smith's daughter, Honora Jager. Miss Seward exhorted Mrs. Jager and her heirs to "guard it with sacred care from the sun and from damp . . ." that so the posterity of her valued friend might know "what, in his prime was the form of him whose mind thro' life . . . was the seat of liberal endowment, warm piety, and energetic benevolence." The mezzotint of "Serena Reading," from a picture by Romney, inscribed "Such was Honora Sneyd," went to Honora's brother, Edward Sneyd. To Mrs. Powys went the miniature of Honora, "drawn at Buxton in the year 1776,[6] by her gallant, faithful, and unfortunate lover, Major André, in his 18th year."

Servants in the house were to receive mourning garments, and ten pounds each in money. To her personal maid Miss Seward left all her apparel except her best laces and some treasured trinkets and articles of clothing. These went to Mrs. Elizabeth Smith.

The Palace, in which Miss Seward took so much pride, was not, of course, her own. It was let by the Bishop of the Diocese, until the time came when a Bishop arose who cared to occupy it himself. Of late years, it has proved too expensive for a private dwelling, and it is now used by theological students.

Miss Seward must have had a wealth of books, plate, and valuable furnishings, the accumulation of the years of her own and her parents' home-keeping. Many articles were sent to Ireland, to Mrs. Burrowes (Sarah Seward) where they long remained in Stradone House, the seat of the Burrowes family, in county Cavan. In 1921, Stradone House was destroyed by fire, and all of Miss Seward's books were lost, along with numerous other valuable objects. Some volumes may have gone,

6. This date must be wrong. It should be 1769.

on Miss Seward's death, to the Rev. Mr. Henry White, who was a collector of books and manuscripts.

The portrait of Miss Seward by Romney eventually returned to the relatives of the testatrix, and remained long in Ireland. Mr. T. J. Burrowes of Stradone sold it in 1920 to Messrs. Agnew of Bond Street. The White family received a number of family portraits. These were sold at Christie's in 1924, by the representatives of the late Sir Robert White-Thomson. The portrait of Anna Seward by Kettle went to the National Portrait Gallery (price eighty guineas). The portrait of Elizabeth Hunter (Mrs. Seward) was bought by a gentleman who presented it to the Johnson Birthplace Museum at Lichfield. The portrait of Sarah Seward, by Kettle, and that of Canon Seward, by Wright of Derby, were also sold, but have not been traced by the present writer.[7] Undoubtedly the much-loved White family received many personal belongings of the poetess, besides those mentioned on page 267. The Seward Bible, the miniature by Meyer (painted in 1777), a gold watch, a manuscript volume of her own letters, and a volume of letters from the Rev. T. S. Whalley, are all in the possession of the Bishop of Ely.

The Lichfield *Mercury* of May 18, 1928, gives a notice to the public regarding the will of Anna Seward, deceased: "An inquiry who are the persons legally and beneficially entitled and on what shares and proportions to the fund in Court standing to the credit of an ac-

---

7. Messrs. Christie, Manson, & Woods are not at liberty to disclose the name of the purchaser of the Canon's portrait.

count entitled 'In the Matter of the Trusts of the Will of Anna Seward,' so far as they affect the interests of certain of the grandchildren and great-grandchildren therein mentioned of Grace Roberts[8] and Mary Hall (subject to duty)."

Then follows a notice to the effect that all claimants to the fund are to attend personally or by their solicitors the hearing to be held on October 18, 1928, "for adjudication upon the claims." A list of persons believed to be competent to share the fund is given, beginning, "Grace Robarts, late of Mile End, London, is believed to have had twelve children."

On May 14, 1792, Miss Seward wrote a letter of condolence "To Mr. Robarts of London, on the Death of his Wife." In this letter the name Osorio occurs, which is also found connected with the Robarts name in the list published in the Lichfield *Mercury*. The *Letters* afford no further information concerning this group of cousins whom circumstances seem to have deprived of their due share in Miss Seward's estate.

WE have seen that Scott wrote a letter to Miss Baillie, in which Miss Seward's bequest (but not her £100) is mentioned with vexation. He went on: ". . . I am now doing penance for my ill-breeding [in neglecting a letter from Miss Seward] by submitting to edit her posthumous poetry, most of which is absolutely execrable."

Scott wrote a pleasingly noncommittal "Introduction" to the *Poetical Works,* and arranged them in a suitable

8. Robarts.

manner, with notes and comments. Lockhart says that "the book [three volumes] was among the most unfortunate that James Ballantyne printed, and his brother published, in deference to the personal feelings of their partner." By this he probably means that its sale was small. It would be; for most if not all of the material in it had been published before, and in its consolidated form it could scarcely be less than what Lockhart calls it—"a formidable monument of mediocrity." The public taste had changed since 1780 and 1782, when praise from any source could be lavished on the *Monody on Major André* and the "poetical novel," *Louisa.* "Poor Miss Seward," as Scott remorsefully calls her, had her own idea of herself, and little suspected that she was to be forgotten. She was fond of saying that she dared to trust her reputation to Posterity.

Miss Seward's *Letters* came out two years after her death—*Letters of Anna Seward: Written Between the Years 1784 and 1807,* in Six Volumes, Edinburgh: Printed by George Ramsey & Company for Archibald Constable and Company, Edinburgh; and Longman, Hurst, Rees, Orme, and Brown, William Miller, and John Murray, London, 1811.

The frontispiece of the first volume is an engraving by A. Cardon, "from the original picture" of Anna Seward, "painted in 1762 by Kettle, in the possession of Thomas White, Esq., Lichfield."

A letter from Southey[9] to Walter Savage Landor, written at Keswick, June 5, 1811, throws some light on

9. *Letters of Robert Southey,* ed. J. W. Warter.

the publication of the *Letters*. Southey says angrily that Miss Seward was "ill-used" by Constable. The publication of the letters all at once, instead of at intervals of two years was an evidence of greed on the part of Constable, "who had no other thought than how to make the most immediate profit by the bequest, in utter contempt of the conditions which accompanied it."

Miss Seward's reason for wishing some time to elapse before the appearance of her later letters was, Southey says, the belief that certain persons of whom she wrote would have passed away before her comments on them were revealed. "That strange part of her own history relative to Col. T. and his wife were never meant to be made public while they lived."

Southey thought Constable unfair in deleting passages at will from Miss Seward's manuscripts. "By not printing the whole which she designed for publication," he said, "he has given some of her hastiest and most violent expressions, which pass now for her settled judgment, because the letters in which they were qualified or retracted do not appear." Southey wrote with the indignation of one to whom manuscripts and literary remains were sacred. There was probably a good deal of truth in what he said. Constable should not have accepted the bequest unless he could live up to its conditions.

The letters attracted a good deal of attention.[10] Like

10. For the attitude of the public toward Miss Seward's *Letters,* and toward her confessed affection for Mr. Saville, see *Letters from and to Charles Kirkpatrick Sharpe, Esq.,* ed. Alexander Allardyce, I, 476, 488, 503, 506.

Mrs. Asquith's revelations, they were expected to contain a vast amount of personal gossip, not to say scandal. In the journals and correspondence of the period the observant reader will note numerous references to Miss Seward's *Letters,* many of them spiteful, some of them sympathetic, and most of them censorious of the affectations of style.

A characteristic comment of the period in which the *Letters* appeared is given in *The Diary of a Lady in Waiting,* by Lady Charlotte Bury: "I think them very entertaining, though the style is too labored and affected. . . . She is a clever woman, and they contain much reflection and criticism; there is more in them than the generality of published letters, but not one atom of simplicity or nature."[11]

George Hardinge wrote: "I hope you are mistaken when you say that Scott is the *real* Editor of the Letters. I cannot but admire many passages of genius and of eloquence, too; of *heart* there is not one, and she *had not one to express.*"[12]

As another example of the hard things said of Miss Seward after her death and after the publication of her *Letters,* we may take the correspondence[13] between Bishop Percy (of Dromore, Ireland) and Mrs. Jane West, author of a considerable number of works, now forgotten. The Bishop's remarks are in the third person, probably written by an amanuensis. He expresses

11. P. 125.
12. Nichols' *Illustrations,* III, 824. Letter to Sneyd Davis.
13. Nichols' *Illustrations,* VIII, 427–432.

pleasure in noting the pleasant things which Miss
Seward says concerning Mrs. West and Mr. Christopher
Smith; "but he wishes he could have extended his approbation to all the other parts of this voluminous publication, in which he is concerned to observe such a
display of vanity, egotism, and, it grieves him to add,
malignity, as is scarce compensated for by the better
parts of her epistles."

He goes on to enumerate the reasons why he bends
his episcopal frown upon the letters: "her abuse of Mr.
Pitt"; "her illiberal treatment of Dr. Johnson"; "her
improper attachment to Saville"; "her (ah! here's the
rub!) disrespect for parsons and the hierarchy"; "her
cruel censure" of various literary works which she disliked.[14]

It is true that Miss Seward assailed Pitt on more than
one occasion, and railed unceasingly at the war policy
of the Government. Many other people did the same.
The Bishop, like other human persons, found it hard
not to think ill of anyone so fundamentally wrong as
to disagree with him in politics. Anyone who failed to
support the policies of Mr. Pitt must be "malignant."
This attitude of the Bishop explains the unnecessary
violence with which the *Letters* were attacked, and the
hateful things which were said about their author. Opposition to her political views was easily transformed
into personal and literary condemnation, and even
slander.

14. For example, Hayley's *Triumph of Music,* which she justly says
is inferior to his other work.

Her "illiberal treatment" of the memory of Dr. Johnson is elsewhere referred to. Miss Seward was far too persistent and vehement, even though there may have been some truth in what she said.

Her "improper attachment to Saville" was another count against her in the Bishop's opinion. That her attachment was romantic, sentimental, and obstinate we may grant, but it was hardly improper in any other sense than unconventional and unwise.

Her "disrespect for parsons and for the hierarchy" was, we may make a shrewd guess, the sin which the Bishop found hardest to forgive. Miss Seward bluntly said[15] that ". . . when we see that man in the pulpit whom we are in the habit of meeting at the festal board and at the card table, perhaps seen join in the dance, and over whose frailties, in common with our own, no holy curtain has been drawn," we are not likely to feel for him any superlative degree of reverence. There are not a few who will assent to what Miss Seward has said, and who will see nothing strikingly "malignant" in her remarks. Those who have lived, as she did, in close touch with ecclesiastical dignitaries, have usually found the hierarchy subject to the same infirmities as the rest of the human race. The Prelate of Dromore was, apparently, one of those unwilling to admit that a Bishop can be a man of like passions with others.

As to Miss Seward's censure of other people's writings, she was frank enough to say what she thought, in letters sent directly to the authors themselves,[16] dur-

15. *Letters,* V, 292.   16. See her letter to Mrs. Piozzi, p. 153.

ing her lifetime. There was nothing covert or sly about her comments. If she could not praise, she criticized adversely. We may not agree with her judgments; but Mr. Hayley and others found in her *Letters* only what they had seen a hundred times in the reviews.

It is not the intention of this book to set up a defense of Miss Seward; but one wishes to see justice done. It seems clear that the strictures of the Bishop were typical in their kind and their injustice. The *Letters* are bad enough, in spots, and they show an individuality of too warm and sentimental a nature for a restrained and classic expression; but they need not be condemned as malignant because of the author's political views, her love affairs, or her critical judgment.

Mrs. West was more lenient. Replying to the Bishop on August 22, 1811, she said:[17]

. . . Indeed I think so ill of this lady's principles, and in some points of her moral conduct, too, that I allow she richly deserves even the severe punishment of your anathema. As to her prose style, I know not what to call it; I agree with you it is not English: and as to her abuse of Johnson, granting that he was the malevolent creature she asserts (which I never thought, and fully take your testimony to the contrary), still in her vindictive enmity she out-Herods Herod. Yet the sweetness and sublimity of the most part of her poetry; her wit and taste, not always pure indeed, but always original and ingenious; the ardour with which she supports the cause of genius; her perfect freedom from envy—witness her zeal for Mr. Scott, Southey, Jephson, etc.—her acute sensibility, and elegant manners, entitle her I think to as high a place as the Ninon de l'Enclos, or Madame Deffand, of France. Suffer me then, my dear Lord, to beg that your critical ban may be confined to Anna Seward, awkwardly tricked out in the Jacobin scratch [wig] and small-clothes of Catharine Macaulay and Mary Woolstonecroft; but let candour, pity and

17. Nichols' *Illustrations,* VIII, 427 *et seq.*

taste admire the British Sappho, "her loose locks waving in the wind," hanging up her votive harp in the temple of Apollo. There was a Phaon, I know; and after his death Sappho settled 100 l. a year on his widow, and amply provided for his daughter. Her fortune was very handsome, and in her latter years she lived at Lichfield in an elegant hospitable way, much admired by strangers, patronizing genius, and quarreling with all who contradicted her.

The malicious comments on Miss Seward after her death can scarcely be explained merely on the ground that in the previous age she had been the recipient of more eulogies than she deserved. Neither can it be accounted for by the fact (which may be cheerfully granted) that her letters, though the matter was often good, were composed in a curiously pompous style. The slurs which were directed at her in death as well as in life were without doubt partly inspired by the fact that she was a woman usurping the prerogatives of men. Then, too, her political opinions and the untempered way in which she had expressed them had drawn upon her the fire of the opposite party; and condemnation of her works and her personality was almost a virtue, coming from a despiser of her doctrine. Discrimination between literary and political sins was not keener in those days than at present.

IN 1863, appeared in two volumes the *Journals and Correspondence of Thomas Sedgewick Whalley, D.D., of Mendip Lodge, Somerset,* edited by the Rev. Hill Wickham, and published by Richard Bentley. This collection of letters includes seventy-eight by Miss Seward, most of them much less restrained than those in the published volumes of the poetess's *Letters*. Mr. Wickham remarks that he has omitted all of Miss Seward's letters which have previously appeared in print. He notes also that the printed letters vary in some points from those in autograph. He says that he has not included "one half of the remainder of her letters" to Dr. Whalley. Whether he destroyed the letters which he failed to publish, the present writer does not know.

The Bishop of Ely, as noted above,[18] possesses a volume of Miss Seward's autograph letters, and a volume of letters to Miss Seward from the Rev. Mr. Whalley. The Johnson Museum at Lichfield owns five autograph letters of the Swan.

The Whalley *Correspondence* revived for a moment the fading interest in the Lichfield poet. Thomas Sedgewick (or Sedgwick: both forms are given in Wickham's volumes) Whalley was born in 1746 and died in 1828. His nephew's *Memoir* in the first volume of the *Journals and Correspondence* shows him to have been a gentle, high-minded literary man of refined and extravagant tastes, which were gratified by means of his three wives' inherited money. Fanny Burney described him as "handsome, but affected; delicate and sentimentally pathetic." This description may be too severe; but no doubt his sentimentalism was exactly the quality which attracted Miss Seward, and which encouraged her to pour out her soul to him in long effusive letters over a period of nearly thirty years. Any student of eighteenth-century literature who is interested

18. See p. 269.

in Miss Seward should by all means read these letters
to Dr. Whalley.

To one who has read attentively every word of her
published letters and all of her poems, Miss Seward
appears to have been a woman of high mental endowments, wide but undisciplined reading, sensitive feelings, unbridled enthusiasms, and great sincerity and
honesty. One wonders why she did not do better than
she did. Her intelligence and ability were greater than
her achievement. The taste of the age, parental domina-
tion, bad training in her early youth (when she was
daily under the influence of Dr. Darwin), lack of organized and symmetrical education, false ideas of what
was becoming to a lady, and too much flattery within
a limited circle, may be said to account for the failure
of Miss Seward to win the high rank in literature to
which her native talents might have entitled her.

She must have been a picturesque creature—a delightful friend and a stimulating companion. Her devia-
tions from strict accuracy may be attributed, not to any
contempt for truth, or to any real desire to deceive; but
to the poetic temperament, which sees things in exaggerated outline, and cannot be held down to commonplace facts. They were the outcome of an overemo-
tional nature and the entire absence of mental discipline
in her education. Her true impulses were undoubtedly
honorable and honest.

That there was benevolence enough and to spare in
her large nature we have plenty of evidence. Hannah
More devoted herself to the propagation of Sunday

schools; Fanny Burney labored for the benefit of the French refugees (being rewarded by the hand of one of them); Helen Maria Williams risked her life in the endeavor to serve the French cause. Miss Seward seems to have conducted her philanthropies in a less spectacular manner. We are told, however, that she was liberal in her gifts of money to the deserving; and we have seen that she gave a good deal of time and energy to "patronising genius." Her patronage of Newton,[19] the Derbyshire Minstrel, took the form of hospitable entertainment, social introductions, and solid cash advances. Her kindness was bestowed not only upon human beings, but upon animals as well. Her dog Sappho was a petted companion. She cherished her cat, Felina Po,[20] and taught her to live in harmony with a dove, a robin, and a lark. No one not a lover of animals could have brought about this amicable relationship. It is worth noting that Miss Seward wrote a poem on *The Future Life of Brutes,* in which a sensitive appreciation is shown for the patience and fidelity of dumb animals,[21] and a rare enough indignation at the sight of their defenselessness, their long-suffering, and their shameful end in slaughter or neglect.

Miss Seward ought to have lived in an age when women were not afraid to go forth from the home, and use their powers in wage-earning and in social service.

19. *Letters,* IV, 134.

20. For lack of space, we have omitted the correspondence of her cat with Dr. Darwin's, given in her *Memoirs of Dr. Darwin.*

21. Miss Seward classed together "gamesters, sots, fops, and fox-hunters."

Several things she could have done extremely well. She could have taught English literature successfully, or she could have been a preceptress of a girls' school.[22] She could have edited a magazine, or written for a woman's journal, or given public readings. She would have been an ardent ally of the Society for the Prevention of Cruelty to Animals, and could have been a speaker and agitator for various causes of the same sort. Possibly, without her limp and her extra allowance of material weight, she might have been an admirable actress.

She suffered from thwarted affections and from repressed energies. Her sensitiveness to criticism made her self-conscious and unwilling to show her work before an unappreciative world; and yet her urge to write, and her good opinion of her talents, forced her to publish what she feared might be contemned. Though she lived the easy life of the lady, without responsibilities or compulsory exertion, one feels that she was not really happy; and that she would have been better for some task or profession which provided the stimulus of a regular occupation, and which called out her powers and made use of her excellent abilities.

Most of the modern comments on her have been too mocking, too much tinged with satire. No person's life as it appears to himself is a subject for sneers. The life of a brilliant and highly organized woman can never be rightly considered an object of ridicule. Anna Seward may not have been a poet of permanent value; but she

22. How intelligent were her ideas on education is shown in a letter to Mrs. Childers. See her *Letters*, V, 7–9.

was worthy of respect for the place which she made for herself among the recognized writers of the eighteenth century, and for her vigorous individuality, which brought her the friendship of eminent people, and preserved her from oblivion, even to the present day.

APPENDICES

APPENDIX A

FOR conjectures as to the lineage of the Rev. John Hunter, see Aleyn Lyell Reade's *Johnsonian Gleanings,* Part I, pages 18-19; also Part III, page 110.

APPENDIX B

IN connection with the story of the encounter between Mrs. Knowles and Dr. Samuel Johnson, referred to on page 121, it may be interesting to call attention to a pamphlet published in 1799, "for J. and A. Arch, Gracechurch St." [London], entitled *A Dialogue between Dr. Johnson & Mrs. Knowles.* This pamphlet is a reprint of a report given by Mrs. Knowles and published in the *Gentleman's Magazine* for June, 1791. There is a prefatory letter to Mr. Urban, signed *A Child of Candour.* The dialogue is couched in terms which strongly suggest Miss Seward, and contains phrases precisely similar to those used in Miss Seward's letter to Mrs. Mompessan, dated December 31, 1785.

APPENDIX C

BELOW is given (in part) the letter to which Bishop Percy refers in his letter to Mrs. Jane West, quoted on page 76. It is from Robert Anderson, M.D., of Glasgow, and is dated June 22, 1811. See Nichols' *Illustrations,* VII, 215, 216.

. . . Miss Seward's Works, especially her Letters, touch on persons and times interesting to your Lordship. They are written, almost throughout, with a disgusting affectation of verbal ornament, and are everywhere tinctured with personal, political, and poetical prejudices. Her illiberal treatment of Darwin and Hayley, the first objects of her idolatry, admits of no excuse. Sir Brooke Boothby re-assured me yesterday, that Darwin, to his certain knowledge, himself wrote the first fifty lines in the Botanic Garden, from a short copy of verses on his garden at Lichfield, but Miss S. sent them to the Gentleman's Magazine with her name, and re-claimed them when he printed the Botanic Garden. Sir Brooke also assures me, from his own knowledge, that Darwin either originated, or wrote over almost anew, the greatest part of the Elegy on Captain Cook. The internal evidence is a strong proof of this account of the composition. Hayley is still living, and must have his feelings hurt by the malignant disclosure of his family differences, upon which it is not safe for a stranger to look, as they involve delicate circumstances which are only known to the parties themselves. Between the poetess and Scott and Southey, her latest idols, the commerce of flattery is extravagant, chiefly on her side. With a few exceptions, the praise of her contemporaries is sparing and invidious. . . . My friend Park and I do not escape her censure for holding an opposite opinion [regarding Miss Bannerman's poems]; but mine she reckons of no value, after calling "the defunct Leonidas" a fine epic poem, which is not accurately true.

It is to be noted in the last sentence that Anderson

wrote with personal pique, because of Miss Seward's remarks concerning him.

Nichols adds a note to that part of Anderson's letter which refers to *The Botanic Garden*. He says:

The Verses are in the Gentleman's Magazine for May 1783, p. 428; sent by a correspondent who signs M.C.S., and there said to be written by Miss Seward; but it does not appear the Verses were sent to the Magazine by Miss Seward herself.

APPENDIX D

SOMETHING more may be said regarding John Saville. Perhaps the earliest reference to him which can be found in Miss Seward's letters is in the "Literary Correspondence" (*Poetical Works,* I, cvii) dated February, 1764:

The ingenious Mr. S——, whose fine voice and perfect expression do so much justice to the vocal music of Handel, was on my side in warmly defending the claims of that great master to an equal degree of excellence in the delicate and pathetic, as in the spiritual and sublime compositions. It was acknowledged that we came off victorious in that controversy.

Saville would have been about twenty-eight years old at this time. He must have married early; for his daughter Elizabeth (Mrs. Smith) was eighty-two when she died in 1839. She must have been born about 1757, when her father was no more than twenty-one. Figuring from Miss Seward's unreliable data, we may conjecture that he was separated from his wife between 1770 and 1774. He seems to have lived for many years quite alone (except for a hired housekeeper), in his tiny house in the Vicars' Close. Miss Seward says that he lived there twenty-eight years, and removed from it in 1802. In the Vicars' Close were a group of extremely small sixteenth-century houses (still standing), then belonging to the College of Vicars. The four priest-vicars, nine vicars-choral (three for each voice), and the organist were privileged to live in these houses. Presumably the men who occupied them would be celibates, since the houses were scarcely large enough to accommodate families of any size. Miss Seward, as noted, purchased a house for Saville a year-and-a-half before he died. She says in a letter to Mr. Whalley, dated August 16, 1803:

Dear Soul, it was never in his power to save money. The maintenance of Mrs. Smith and her children [there were a girl, Honora, and a boy, Saville] came upon him when his best days were passed; and within the last eleven years his nervous disorders prevented all professional emoluments without the pale of this church. But for my assistance, therefore, they must have felt the deprivations of penury. . . . Mrs. Smith was never habitually kind, or grateful for my friendship to her and her children . . . neither herself, her mother, nor Honora, shall know the want of competent subsistence, such as they have been used to, while it is in my power to supply them. They shall live rent-free in the pleasant mansion which I purchased for my lost friend two years back . . . and they shall have from me a hundred a year, and fifty Mrs. Smith has of her own. Her eldest daughter is married, and her son is in business with his uncle, though dependent upon him.

Again we see Miss Seward's freedom from jealousy demonstrated in her generosity toward her friend's dependents.

Saville was not buried in the Cathedral proper, but just outside, where his slab may still be seen, sunk in the grass. In his grave were in due time deposited the remains of his wife, Mrs. Mary Saville (died March 24, 1817, aged 82); and his daughter, Mrs. Elizabeth Smith (died June 4, 1839, aged 82). The will of Miss Seward left the provision that she was to be buried in the vault with her father, if the Dean and Chapter were willing to have the grave opened; but if not, she was to be laid in the grave with Saville. The Dean and Chapter saw to it that she was not buried in the tomb of her beloved Giovanni. For information as to the exact spot of her burial, we have a letter from Canon Bailye of the Cathedral to Richard Polwhele, dated April 2, 1809 (See Polwhele's *Traditions and Recollections,* II, 628):

I have now to relate an event which I know will give you uneasiness, I mean the death of our friend Miss Seward; she died last Saturday, and was privately buried in the choir of our Cathedral this morning. . . . She has died as few poets do, rich; but at present I have received no accurate account of the distribution of her property.

APPENDIX E

NOTES AND CORRECTIONS

PAGE 16, line 14. Perhaps this is a bit fanciful. The author is well aware that great uncertainty exists regarding the number of Johnson's visits to Lichfield between 1737 and 1767.

Page 17. In his *Johnsonian Gleanings,* Part IV, page 146, Mr. Aleyn Lyell Reade identifies another of Miss Seward's reputed admirers as John Adey of Norfolk. See Miss Seward's *Letters,* III, 161.

Page 24. Miss Seward seems to have passed some weeks of her first visit to London in lodgings. She says in a letter to "Emma" ("Literary Correspondence," in *Poetical Works,* I, cxliv):

In October [1764] my long-existing wish is to be indulged of seeing the great Babylon. It is true that this desire slumbered the instant my Sally sickened, but it has awakened beneath my mother's proposal that Nanette and myself, accompanied by her father and Mrs. A. S—— [Simpson?], should pass a few months in London. We are to have lodgings near your brother's house in —— Square.

On the next page there is a confused reference to Mrs. L——, which may refer to another short visit to be made before the trip to London.

Page 38. After the publication of her *Monody on Major André,* Miss Seward was annoyed by the protests of the André family, who charged her with exaggeration, not to say invention.

Page 59. Ladies' Chapel. So Edgeworth. This was the Lady or Lady's Chapel of the Cathedral.

Page 82. The question naturally arises: How could Edgeworth marry his deceased wife's sister? The only answer is that he did. A letter from the present rector of St. Andrews, Holborn, the Rev. Edwin Bedford, is pertinent to our inquiry:

I can only say that the marriage of R. L. Edgeworth and Elizabeth Sneyd is duly recorded in our Register, . . . and there is nothing to show in margin or footnote that the marriage was illegal. The marriage, too, was by banns, but I can only imagine that they were careless in those days, and took the names of the contracting parties, asking no particulars!

Page 115, lines 9–10. These are Miss Seward's assumptions, not those of the present author.

Page 164. In the will of Charles Simpson (dated August 15, 1820), the picture of Miss Seward, by Romney, is left to his daughter Maria, after his wife's death. After its vicissitudes, the picture is now owned by Mr. John W. Hanes, of Rye, New York, who purchased it from Thomas Agnew & Sons in London.

Page 173. *Stow* is now spelled *Stowe*.

Page 219. Attention is called to the fact that the resemblance of Romney's "Serena Reading" to the beauteous Honora Sneyd was purely accidental. Romney never saw Miss Sneyd.

Page 234. Richard Polwhele, in a letter given in his *Traditions and Recollections* (p. 530), says: "The Doctor bears the loss of his son with all the fortitude of a heathen philosopher."

Page 241. Whalley and Miss Seward both contributed poems to the vase at Bath-Easton, and corresponded at great length; but they do not seem to have met personally until after Lady Miller's death. See *Journals and Correspondence of Thomas Sedgewick Whalley, D.D.,* ed. Hill Wickham, I, 349–351.

Page 268. Miss Seward's will provided that most of her effects should be sold at auction.

Page 279. Mention should be made of the letters from Miss Seward printed in Richard Polwhele's *Traditions and Recollections,* published in 1826.

INDEX